FROM RETRIBUTION TO PUBLIC SAFETY

FROM RETRIBUTION TO PUBLIC SAFETY

Disruptive Innovation of American Criminal Justice

**William R. Kelly,
with Robert Pitman and
William Streusand**

ROWMAN & LITTLEFIELD
Lanham • Boulder • New York • London

Published by Rowman & Littlefield
A wholly owned subsidiary of The Rowman & Littlefield Publishing Group, Inc.
4501 Forbes Boulevard, Suite 200, Lanham, Maryland 20706
www.rowman.com

Unit A, Whitacre Mews, 26-34 Stannary Street, London SE11 4AB

British Library Cataloguing in Publication Information Available

Library of Congress Cataloging-in-Publication Data

Names: Kelly, W. R. (William Robert), 1950– author. | Pitman, Robert, 1942– author. | Streusand,
    William, author.
Title: From retribution to public safety : disruptive innovation of American criminal justice / William
    R. Kelly with Robert Pitman and William Streusand.
Description: Lanham, MD : Rowman & Littlefield, [2017] | Includes bibliographical references and
    index.
Identifiers: LCCN 2016049485 (print) | LCCN 2017005706 (ebook) | ISBN 9781442273887 (cloth :
    alk. paper) | ISBN 9781442273894 (electronic)
Subjects: LCSH: Criminal justice, Administration of—United States. | Recidivism—United States.
Classification: LCC HV9950 .K453 2017 (print) | LCC HV9950 (ebook) | DDC 364.973—dc23
LC record available at https://lccn.loc.gov/2016049485

Printed in the United States of America

CONTENTS

ACKNOWLEDGMENTS

I would like to once again thank my wonderful wife and partner, Emily, whose support and encouragement has allowed me to continue on this journey of criminal justice reform. None of this would be possible without her.

I would also like to thank my collaborators Robert Pitman and Bill Streusand. This book has benefited enormously from their expertise on matters such as mens rea, criminal procedure, prosecution, psychiatric assessment, psychological dysfunction, and treatment. The end result was possible because of our collective appreciation of the shortcomings of criminal justice policy and the existence of evidence-based alternatives that can actually accomplish things like reductions in crime, recidivism, criminal victimization, and cost.

Dr. Lawrence Hauser, MD, is a psychiatrist in Austin who has experience working with the mentally ill in jails. He read the manuscript and provided very insightful suggestions. Thank you, Larry.

In February 2016, I was diagnosed with lymphoma. I have been in remission since August 2016. I was fortunate enough to have the best oncologist in Austin, and I would like to thank Dr. Michael Kasper and the wonderful, dedicated folks in the Texas Oncology infusion room, especially Marilyn, for making a difficult situation so much better. Part of the chemo treatment included megadoses of steroids, which kept me awake for what seemed like days on end. I owe a debt of gratitude to the steroids for facilitating much of the writing of this book.

I would like to thank the Charles Koch Foundation for providing me with funding during the summer of 2016. The organization had no substantive or editorial input in this project.

I thank the University of Texas, especially my colleagues in the sociology department, for support during this effort. Lindsey Nichols, an undergraduate psychology major at UT Austin, provided invaluable research assistance on this project.

Last, but not least, I would like to thank Rowman & Littlefield, especially editor Kathryn Knigge, for making this process enjoyable.

William R. Kelly
October 2016

INTRODUCTION

Since the early 1970s, American criminal justice policy has had a nearly singular focus—the relentless pursuit of punishment. From Congress to state legislatures to local city and county governments, the mission was clear and deliberate.

Punishment is intuitive, proactive, logical, and simple. It resonated, the public got it, and few challenged it. Plus there were plenty of collateral benefits to go around. Entire industries flourished, as governments at all levels couldn't get enough. An entire correctional construction industry was born, along with the correctional management and security industry. Moreover, local communities benefited from prisons that became economic engines, especially in rural areas with limited options.

Then there are the political benefits of being tough on crime. Using fear of crime as the problem and more severe punishment as the solution let many, many elected officials ride in on the white horse to save the day. First was the rhetoric and sound bites. Then came the follow-through in the form of tougher and tougher sentencing and parole laws and the massive expansion of prisons and jails. It was a masterful mix of fear, anxiety, and race coupled with an elegant remedy. We saw it again recently in Donald Trump's presidential campaign when he declared himself the law-and-order candidate. In a May 20, 2016, speech accepting the endorsement of the National Rifle Association, Trump tried to instill fear after the Obama administration released nearly 550 nonviolent drug offenders from federal prison: "Obama is even releasing violent criminals from the jails, including drug dealers, and those with gun crimes. And they're being let go by the thousands."

The problem is that despite all the appeal, logic, and common sense, punishment doesn't work. There were approximately 5.4 million violent crimes and 15.3 million property crimes in the United States in 2014. The majority of these crimes were committed by people who had been through the criminal justice system before. Many of them had been through the system on multiple occasions.

How could we have been so wrong? Why has severe punishment not done the trick? The answer is quite simple: The vast majority of criminal offenders have multiple disorders, deficits, impairments, and conditions that are fundamentally related to their criminal behavior, which punishment does nothing to change. These are not excuses. They are reasons for criminality. How does incarceration fix bipolar disorder or executive dysfunction due to traumatic brain injury? How does a stint in jail solve addiction to drugs or raise one's IQ? Most of us have no idea what growing up in an environment of poverty and violence is like or what impacts it can have on cognitive development, mental health, substance abuse, and engaging in risky behavior. However, there is nothing in tough-on-crime policies that either takes these things into consideration or attempts to address them. We have put nearly all of our eggs in the punishment basket. But the evidence is clear—that is the wrong basket.

The failure of tough-on-crime policies has routinely, but unnecessarily and avoidably, exposed hundreds of thousands of individuals to criminal victimization. Then there is the cost. The United States spends approximately $270 billion per year in direct criminal justice costs.[1] All told, tough-on-crime policies and the war on drugs have drained away roughly $2 trillion of public money. Recent research puts the annual price tag of crime, including direct criminal justice costs as well as a variety of collateral costs, at $1 trillion.[2] The recidivism rate over this period has hovered north of 65 percent. We suggest it is impossible to conclude that this is a reasonable return on investment.

Two issues are the primary focus of this book. One is developing a better approach than simple punishment to actually address these crime-related circumstances, deficits, and disorders in order to change offender behavior and reduce recidivism, victimization, and cost. We propose a massive, unprecedented expansion of diversion of disordered offenders to intervention and treatment. This will involve considerations of criminal risk and the extent and severity of any disorders, deficits, and impairments, as well as managing risk while offenders are diverted to community-based treatment.

It will also involve many offenders being criminally prosecuted and punished—offenders who commit violent crime, habitual offenders, or offenders who are otherwise determined to be inappropriate for diversion. But the end game is to substantially ramp up the diversion and treatment of the majority of offenders, who have significant mental illness, substance abuse, neurocognitive impairments, and intellectual deficits.

The second issue is how to do a better job of determining who should be diverted and who should be criminally prosecuted. If things remain as they are, the default decision for the vast majority is criminal prosecution and punishment. That is because we do not have an effective mechanism or process to sort disordered, and thus divertible, offenders from those who are violent or habitual offenders and need to be separated from society, or those who are chronic offenders or just plain criminals and deserve retribution and punishment. To date, we have treated most offenders as deserving of retribution and punishment. That is an expensive proposition.

American criminal law requires that the government minimally prove two things in order to convict someone of a crime—that an individual committed a criminal act, and that the individual who committed that act is culpable, blameworthy, or criminally responsible. This is referred to as criminal intent, or mens rea ("a guilty mind"). Criminal intent or mens rea should be used to differentiate criminal behavior from otherwise innocent behavior, a procedural mechanism that is a gatekeeper at the front end of the system, determining who should and should not be criminally prosecuted and punished. For a variety of reasons that we discuss later, criminal intent rarely serves this gatekeeping purpose today.

Is someone who is in a psychotic episode and hears voices commanding some criminal act truly responsible for that crime? Is someone who has significantly impaired impulse control, due perhaps to a brain injury or some other trauma, culpable if they are incapable of resisting the act? Sixty percent of inmates in U.S. prisons have had at least one traumatic brain injury. Forty percent have a mental illness. Eighty percent have a substance use disorder. While we may question whether these individuals are truly liable for their crimes, in all likelihood they will be criminally prosecuted and punished. Even if they are responsible for their crimes, is punishment the best outcome in terms of a bigger picture of reducing recidivism, crime, victimization, and cost?

One of the fundamental points of departure we propose is that in many cases involving criminal offenders, we are asking the wrong questions. What we currently do is ask whether the individual committed the criminal act and then presume that they did so with criminal intent. They are therefore blameworthy and held responsible for their behavior, which invariably leads to the reflexive question of how much punishment.

We propose asking a different question: how to best reduce recidivism. This involves shifting the culture of crime and punishment away from blameworthiness and retribution (a harm-based decision) to how to most effectively reduce the likelihood of this individual reoffending (a problem-solving, outcome-based approach). That implies and requires a shift away from retribution and wholesale punishment to a much-expanded focus on crime-related disorders and impairments as well as other well-known factors such as education and employment, which then leads to evidence-based, recidivism-reducing intervention and rehabilitation.

As we consider in the following pages the variety of mental health, substance abuse, and intellectual and neurocognitive disorders, impairments, and deficits that many justice-involved offenders have, we hope it will become clear that we need to rethink how we go about the business of criminal justice, of dealing with people who commit bad acts but do so at least in part because of psychiatric, intellectual, and neurocognitive disorders and impairments. We can ask in such situations whether a particular disordered offender is criminally responsible and culpable, which typically leads to an affirmative answer, followed by conviction and punishment. Or we could ask a different question: What will it take to reduce the likelihood that this individual will reoffend?

Please don't misunderstand. We are not suggesting that we should simply send disordered offenders home. We are not proposing a massive get-out-of-jail-free program. What we know is that criminal prosecution and punishment is not productive in cases like these. We propose an alternative that focuses less on blameworthiness and more on the severity of any disorders, impairments, and deficits, and that shifts attention away from retribution to recidivism reduction.

We suggest that the current state of American criminal justice is largely due to four broad and deliberate sets of policy decisions that have involved all layers of government. One is that the primary response of criminal justice is punishment, and a primary rationale or justification for punishment is retribution. That tough-on-crime, just-deserts, eye-for-an-eye focus, which has defined U.S. criminal justice policy for the past five decades, has led to the revolving door of the justice system, where individuals leave in no better condition—and often in worse condition—than when they entered. It is almost like a perpetual motion machine, running on its own inertia.

Second, local, state, and federal policies regarding things such as homelessness, violence, poverty, and unemployment have direct and often substantial consequences for the public health, both physical and mental. As a leading expert on the determinants of health puts it:

> Consider some of the big issues our country faces: violence, homelessness, unemployment, mass incarceration, food insecurity, poverty, income inequality. Each is a major contributor to the physical and mental problems that are experienced by large segments of the population as a whole. We have yet to successfully address any of them. Multiple research studies have supported the idea that mental illness and mental health inequities are driven by the social determinants of health. . . . These determinants are . . . called the fundamental causes of disease. . . . They are problems that are created by public policies and social norms.[3]

Our unwillingness or inability to effectively mitigate these social and economic conditions has a number of broader consequences, including putting larger numbers of individuals at risk of developing mental health, neurocognitive, and addiction disorders, which in turn increases the number of individuals who end up in the criminal justice system.

The third consideration is our failure to adequately address treatment and management of mental illness, substance abuse, neurocognitive impairments, and intellectual deficits. Essentially every major media outlet, including newspapers, magazines, television news, and online sites and blogs, has run recent stories on fixing the broken mental health system in the United States. Dozens of expert reports from a wide variety of government offices and professional associations, including the Surgeon General, the American Medical Association, the American Psychiatric Association, the National Institutes of Health, and many, many more, have called for substantial reform to the nation's mental health system, both public and private. There appears to be much consensus that it is a system in need of massive reform, and a good bit of consensus regarding what needs to be done to fix it. Much of the problem appears to be getting the appropriate legislative branches of government at the local, state, and federal levels to actually do something about it.

Our inability to effectively address the social determinants of health and to provide public health treatment for the crime-related disorders discussed here would not be of such consequence were it not for the fourth set of policy decisions. Several decades of changes to laws and funding at all levels of government have resulted in the fact that many individuals with significant mental, neurocognitive, intellectual, and addiction disorders and impairments essentially have nowhere else to go but the justice system. That conclusion serves as an indictment of policies that for most practical purposes have made the American criminal justice system, in particular the correctional system, the asylum of last resort. In fact, local jails are the largest psychiatric facilities in many urban areas in the United States.

It is time to quit this holding pattern of American criminal justice policy. It is time to quit pretending that punishment will eventually start impacting recidivism rates. It is time to stop warehousing hundreds of thousands of individuals who are in our prisons and jails at least in part because we have made clear, deliberate decisions to not adequately implement and fund public health, public mental health, and substance abuse treatment capacity.

There has been a good bit of discussion, proposed legislation, and policy initiatives focusing on criminal justice reform. We are on the very front end of this process. What we have seen so far are states initiating quite modest reductions in their prison populations. That is a step in the right direction. However, true criminal justice reform is not just a matter of reducing the prison population by 5 or 10 percent. That may be good fiscal reform, but it certainly is not criminal justice reform. Changes that will significantly reduce recidivism require substantial changes to the criminal justice system as well as other systems such as public health.

We have written this book to (a) make the case that the American criminal justice system is fundamentally flawed, is not significantly reducing crime and recidivism, and is wasting massive amounts of public resources; (b) demonstrate that many offenders have a variety of mental health, substance use–related, neurodevelopmental, neurocognitive, and intellectual deficits and disorders that are fundamentally linked to their criminality; (c) make clear that one of the primary reasons criminal offenders are not successful in the criminal justice system is because punishment does nothing to alleviate offenders' primary crime-related disorders and deficits; (d) develop policies, procedures, criteria, and clinical protocols for diverting those who are not criminally prosecuted to community-based settings where their risk of criminality can be managed and their disorders and deficits effectively treated; and (e) provide strategic changes to public health systems that will result in appropriately scaled and effective treatment.

WHO WE ARE

The lead author is William R. Kelly, PhD, a professor of sociology at the University of Texas at Austin. He has studied, taught, researched, and written about criminology, criminal justice, and criminal justice reform for thirty-five years. His recent books include *Criminal Justice at the Crossroads: Transforming Crime and Punishment* (2015) and *The Future of Crime and Punishment: Smart Policies for Reducing Crime and Saving Money* (2016).

Kelly brings to the table scientific evidence as well as decades of conducting evaluation research and policy analysis for a variety of justice agencies at the federal, state, and local levels.

Robert Pitman, JD, M.St. (Oxon), was appointed in 2014 by President Obama and confirmed by the U.S. Senate to serve as a federal district court judge for the Western District of Texas. In 2011, Pitman was appointed by President Obama and confirmed by the Senate to be the U.S. attorney for the Western District of Texas, during which time he was appointed to the U.S. Attorney General's Advisory Committee. Prior to that he served as the interim U.S. attorney for the Western District of Texas, as the deputy U.S. attorney, and as a U.S. magistrate judge in the Western District of Texas.

Judge Pitman brings extensive knowledge, on-the-ground experience, insight, and a profound interest in criminal justice reform.

Dr. William Streusand, MD, received his medical degree from Baylor College of Medicine, and then took an internship in psychiatry and a residency in child and adolescent psychiatry at Baylor. He has board certifications from the American Board of Psychiatry and Neurology in psychiatry, child and adolescent psychiatry, and psychosomatic medicine.

Dr. Streusand has lectured extensively throughout the United States, and he has held a variety of teaching positions and received numerous honors, including chief fellow in child psychiatry at Baylor College of Medicine and Texas Children's Hospital; clinical assistant professor of psychiatry at Baylor College of Medicine; clinical assistant professor, Department of Psychiatry and Behavioral Sciences UTMB; assistant professor of psychiatry, UT-Southwestern at Austin; American College of Psychiatrists; and American Board of Psychiatry and Neurology.

I

THE GREAT AMERICAN PUNISHMENT EXPERIMENT

One would have to look far and wide to find a greater public policy failure than the American criminal justice system. It is a fiasco of staggering magnitude and broad consequence. Since the early 1970s, U.S. criminal justice policy has fundamentally shortchanged taxpayers, adult and juvenile criminal offenders, criminal victims, the economy, communities, the mentally ill, the substance addicted, the poor, and many more. The toll has been profound, including recidivism rates north of 65 percent, hundreds of thousands of unnecessary and avoidable criminal victimizations, the waste of hundreds of billions of dollars, compromised economic productivity, irreparable shredding of the fabric of poor and minority communities, the creation of a seemingly permanent class of individuals dependent on public services, and the institutionalization of an endless cycle of offend–arrest–convict–punish–repeat. Add in the war on drugs, and one need look no further. We have arrived at the nadir of politics and policy.

American criminal justice policy has been characterized by one thing: tough punishment. The result has been a nearly relentless mission to punish more and more criminal offenders more and more severely. The hallmark of tough on crime is incarceration. The United States leads the world in the use of prisons and jails. Whether measured by the sheer number of prison and jail inmates, or the population-adjusted incarceration rate, the United States is well ahead of all other countries. Today, the United States incarcerates approximately 2.3 million individuals in state and federal prisons and jails, juvenile correctional facilities, and other detention centers. That number is essentially the entire population of Houston, the nation's fourth-largest city. Perhaps the most dramatic statistic is that since 1975, state prison populations increased by 400 percent and federal prison populations increased by 600 percent. Over this period of time, prison capacity increased by over 430 percent. These increases in the capacity and use of incarceration are unprecedented in U.S. history—and in the history of any other nation.

The United States incarcerates nearly 700 per 100,000 individuals. The incarceration rates for our Western European allies pale by comparison: Denmark (68), France (100), the United Kingdom (148), Germany (78), Italy (86), and Spain (140). The incarceration rates for some nations that we probably consider rather draconian or punitive are Cuba (510), the Russian Federation (442), Iran (287), China (118), Rwanda (434), North Korea (600 estimated), and the nations of the former Soviet Union (ranging between 180 and 580).[1]

We also lead the world in the use of correctional control, meaning either prison or jail for incarceration and probation and parole for community supervision. The United States has over seven million individuals under a form of correctional control. Over the past four decades, the number of people under correctional control increased by 375 percent.

It seems to be common knowledge or conventional wisdom that criminals commit crimes because they make bad decisions. At least that is how we often hear policymakers describe the etiology of crime. That logic has driven justice policy for decades. So what is better for getting people to think more clearly and make better decisions than punishment or the threat of punishment?

The concept of punishment is intuitive, logical, proactive, and, on the surface, seemingly hard to debate. Unfortunately, the premise that we can punish our way out of a crime problem is fundamentally flawed. Consider the following: Today, approximately 40 percent of individuals in the criminal justice system have at least one diagnosable mental illness. Roughly half of those with one diagnosis have at least one co-occurring disorder. That is 2–2.5 times the incidence in the general population. Roughly 80 percent have some form of a substance use disorder, including dependence, abuse, or addiction. This is eight times the incidence in the general population. The prevalence of intellectual deficiencies among offenders in the justice system is well above that in the general population.[2]

Nearly 60 percent of U.S. prison inmates have at least one traumatic brain injury, implicating a variety of neurocognitive dysfunctions and impairments. The clear majority of offenders in the criminal justice system come from poverty and disadvantage, which is associated with a variety of physical and psychic assaults, such as exposure to lead paint and other environmental toxins with a clear link to neurodevelopmental impairments and disorders, as well as lethality and violence, parental abandonment, and many other traumas.

Why does punishment not change behavior and reduce recidivism? The reason U.S. recidivism rates are over 65 percent is that punishment changes none of the underlying factors that contribute to criminality. Prison does nothing to address mental illness and, in all likelihood, aggravates existing conditions. Abstinence due to incarceration is not substance abuse treatment. Punishment does nothing to mitigate the effects of trauma on cognitive dysfunction. Correctional control does not fix a traumatic brain injury, nor does it add IQ points.

All incarceration does is keep someone off the street for a while. And even then, locking up the criminal does not necessarily lock up the crime. Criminal offending is often like a labor market. Assume a drug dealer gets arrested, convicted, and incarcerated. That in turn results in a job opening, which in all likelihood someone else will fill. The offender is in prison, but the crime is still on the street. That is one reason why the crime-reducing impact of the expansion of incarceration is quite minimal. Approximately 10–15 percent of the crime decline in recent decades is due to U.S. incarceration policies.

Despite what we might like to think, despite our personal experiences, there really is little about punishment that changes criminal behavior, especially when we consider that many criminal offenders present with an array of disorders, deficits, and impairments.

The bottom line is this: There is little in U.S. criminal justice policy that addresses recidivism reduction. Our approach to public safety ignores the complexity of criminal behavior in favor of a very simplistic, catchy, tough "lock 'em up and throw away the key," "do the crime, do the time" policy. That thinking has guided justice policy at all levels of government, spanning the fifty states, the federal system, and the administration of justice in the 3,100-plus counties in the United States. "Tough on crime" has been our brand, and it remains alive and well.

A number of factors have played key roles in the transformation of U.S. criminal justice policy over the past five decades. We next briefly discuss the components of tough on crime, and then turn our attention to the hows and whys of the unique American crime experiment.

THE POLITICS OF CRIME CONTROL

U.S. crime control policy took a dramatic turn in the late 1960s and early 1970s, a turn that has persisted to this day. Under the influence of unprecedentedly high crime rates in the 1960s and 1970s, massive racial disorders that swept the nation between 1965 and 1970, and sometimes violent campus protests over the Vietnam War, the Nixon presidential campaign of 1967 declared crime and disorder as a high priority for the Republican Party. It was not a hard sell. The evidence was routinely reported in the media—crime rates at an all-time high; massive race riots in all major cities in the United States, resulting in tens of billions of dollars in property damage, hundreds killed, thousands injured and arrested; and angry encounters between students and police as campus protests took on Vietnam.

The crime and disorder theme developed by the national Republican Party and the Nixon campaign was compelling. So was the solution of getting tough on crime. Nixon was clear that the way to enhance law and order was with punishment, not liberal strategies like a war on poverty.

The Republican Party's ownership of tough on crime provided political leverage throughout the electoral landscape for nearly twenty-five years. Ronald Reagan certainly made use of tough on crime and is credited with moving the crime control agenda forward in many important ways, including overseeing the implementation of the federal sentencing guidelines (the federal sentencing scheme that resulted in much more severe punishment for many more individuals convicted of federal crimes). The Reagan administration also provided substantial financial support for expansion of state prison capacity and also provided important incentives to states for implementing mandatory sentencing.

Perhaps one of the boldest examples of the politicization of crime and criminal justice is the so-called Willie Horton ad that was used by the

George H. W. Bush presidential campaign in 1987 against Michael Duka-kis, the governor of Massachusetts. Willie Horton was a black man who had committed bad crimes and had served time in the Massachusetts prisons. As his sentence neared completion, he was released on a week-end furlough per Massachusetts state law. Unfortunately, while on the furlough he committed assault, armed robbery, and rape. The Bush cam-paign masterfully used Willie Horton as the poster boy for being soft on crime. But it went beyond just soft on crime, because it made race and fear central elements.

The message was clear: tough on crime sells. Rarely did a Republican candidate lose an election because he or she was too tough on crime. However, a Democratic candidate portrayed as soft on crime or even a Republican positioned as just not tough enough was at substantial risk of political defeat.

The politics of crime control took an interesting turn in 1991 when Bill Clinton and Al Gore campaigned as the "new Democrats." One of the things that was new about Clinton/Gore was the fact that they no longer were willing to let the Republican Party have sole ownership of tough on crime. In a highly symbolic detour during the campaign, with ample media in tow, candidate Clinton returned to Arkansas, where he had been governor, to witness the execution of an inmate who had been sentenced to death. Thus began the sharing of tough on crime across the two major political parties. For Clinton, it went far beyond symbolism with the 1994 Crime Bill, which is arguably the single toughest piece of federal anti-crime legislation in U.S. history. It was Clinton's initiative and went a long way in establishing the punitive bona fides of the Democratic Party.

September 11, 2001, had broad implications for crime control policy. While terrorism is not what we think of when discussing typical predato-ry crimes like robbery, burglary, and assault, the attacks on the World Trade Center towers and the Pentagon heightened fear and insecurity. That fear and insecurity quickly led to linking terrorism and typical pred-atory street crimes. President George W. Bush explicitly tied drug control policy and terrorism by claiming during a Super Bowl ad in 2002 that drug trafficking in the United States funds terrorism: "Terrorists use drug profits to fund their cells to commit acts of murder." Blurring the lines between crime and terrorism and enhancing the strategy of tough was the result, but now that meant tough on crime and tough on terrorism.

Understanding the politics of tough on crime goes a long way in helping us understand why a policy shift in response to real and significant threats to public safety (the historically high crime rates in the 1970s and 1980s, the urban race riots during the 1960s, and Vietnam War protests) has persisted well beyond when those threats dissipated. Crime rates increased in the United States between 1960 and 1981, then declined over the next five years, increased again, and began a precipitous drop in 1991. If tough on crime was a solution to the problem of high crime, then why did the solution persist well after crime dropped to levels not seen since the mid-1960s? The answer is the political inertia that kept crime control policies on the trajectory of ever-increasing punishment.

SENTENCING REFORM

Prior to the tough-on-crime initiative, sentencing in the United States was characterized by what is called indeterminate sentencing, whereby judges have wide discretion in determining the sentence. Indeterminate sentencing provided a sentence that fit not only the crime but also the offender. Sentencing reformers articulated two problems with indeterminate sentencing. When judges have such wide latitude with sentencing, elements of bias or discrimination can enter into the process, resulting in sentencing disparity. The other perceived problem is that when judges have broad discretion, they tend to be too lenient.

Both of these problems were mitigated by the same solution—minimizing the role of the judge. Sentencing reform shifted the process away from indeterminate to determinate sentencing. Determinate sentencing limited judicial discretion by essentially prescribing sentences in statutes. Common types of determinate sentences have been mandatory sentences such as mandatory minimums and habitual offender sentences (so-called three strikes laws). Whether in the form of mandatory sentences or simply fixed or predetermined sentences, the advantage from the perspective of crime control was that it ensured more severe punishment for more offenders. That, in turn, ensured that the new incarceration capacity that had been created over the past forty years would be filled.

THE ROLE OF DRUGS

We return to the Nixon administration in order to understand the role of drugs in the bigger picture of U.S. crime control policies. In 1971, Nixon declared illicit drugs "public enemy number one in the United States" and thus launched the war on drugs. The war on drugs has persisted for decades, with the vast majority of the resources in that effort devoted to supply control. After forty-five years and $1 trillion, it is reasonable to ask to what end.

The evidence we have today indicates that by any standard the war on drugs has been a failure. One is hard pressed to find many experts in drug policy, judges, or even prosecutors who will candidly admit that this effort has been successful. The United States has a nearly insatiable appetite for illicit drugs. That demand for illicit drugs is significantly the result of the failure of U.S. drug control policy to take demand reduction (i.e., drug treatment) seriously. U.S. drug policy has relentlessly continued to define the drug problem as a criminal matter, rather than the public health problem that most experts agree it is.

Our unrelenting demand for illicit drugs provides the Mexican cartels and their distribution networks with the financial incentives to meet that demand by whatever means are necessary. That is one of the reasons supply control efforts have failed miserably. The amount of money involved is so staggering that it motivates suppliers to devote the resources, technology, and creativity to get the job done.

Setting aside the drug control debate for a moment, the key question is what role all this has played in the bigger picture of criminal justice policy. If nothing else, defining the drug problem as a matter for the criminal justice system rather than the public health system has resulted in substantial numbers of criminal offenders cycling in and out of the justice system over the past several decades. Those drug offenders have played a significant role in the overall size of the prison and correctional control populations, contributing hundreds of thousands of offenders to the ever-expanding state and federal prison systems.

THE ASYLUMS OF LAST RESORT

On June 8, 2015, the *Atlantic* published a story with the headline "America's Largest Mental Hospital Is a Jail," referring to the Cook County (Chicago) jail. A few years earlier, in 2008, National Public Radio reported that the Los Angeles County jail was the nation's largest mental institution. Add in the Rikers Island jail in New York City, and we get the headline "Why Are the Three Largest Mental Health Care Providers Jails?"[3]

The unfortunate reality is that U.S. prisons and jails have been inundated with mentally ill individuals. This is in part the result of decisions made decades ago regarding public mental health treatment. Over the past fifty years, psychiatric hospitals have been shuttered in favor of local community-based mental health treatment centers—a reasonable concept, but poorly implemented. Local community-based treatment facilities lack the resources and capacity needed to address the demands of public mental health treatment. For that reason, the justice system has, by default, become the repository for hundreds of thousands of mentally ill individuals who in essence have nowhere else to go.

Understanding the bigger picture of the American punishment experiment requires that we appreciate the convergence of a variety of circumstances, influences, interests, and anxieties that led us down a remarkable path. The events and circumstances of the 1960s and 1970s spelled a departure from business as usual for the criminal justice system, and the logical choice was to get tough on crime and disorder. Illicit drug use, primarily in inner city minority neighborhoods and college campuses, led to the prosecution of an ill-fated fifty-year war that has haplessly tried to control the supply of drugs. Something as simple as tracking the street-level prices of drugs confirms that supply has remained robust despite the best efforts of thousands of federal agents as well as local police and prosecutors. The arrest, prosecution, conviction, and punishment of offenders for dealing, manufacture, and possession of drugs provided a steady flow of inmates into state and federal prisons. Sentencing reform, which may have had its origins in concerns with equity and fairness, was nevertheless an absolutely essential tool for getting as many individuals under correction control as possible and for ramping up the severity of the punishment. If the American punishment experiment is largely a matter of numbers, then plea bargaining has also served us well, dramatically expediting the conviction and punishment of 95 percent of criminal offenders.

CRIMINAL INTENT

In order for the government to lawfully prosecute, convict, and punish someone, two things must be proven: the criminal act, or what is known as actus reus, and criminal intent, or mens rea. The logic of mens rea is embedded in the Latin phrase well ingrained in English Common Law of the past three centuries—*actus facit reum nisi mens sit rea* (the act does not make one guilty unless the mind is guilty). Many terms are used to reference mens rea, including guilty mind, evil mind, vicious will, conscious will, and moral blameworthiness. Regardless of the particulars, the point is that in order to hold someone liable for a crime, and thus to punish them, in most circumstances there must be a volitional, intentional state of mind. The criminal must be culpable or morally blameworthy for the government to extract revenge.

The primary importance of criminal intent is as a gatekeeper at the front end of the criminal justice process. It should be used to sort those who are truly guilty from those who may have committed a criminal act, but did so without the necessary intent. As will hopefully become clear shortly, whether the question of mens rea, or criminal intent, is even considered in criminal prosecution and conviction is highly problematic. The reality of contemporary American criminal procedure appears to relegate criminal intent at best to a presumption. When the goal is the maximization of punishment for as many criminal offenders as possible, deliberate, routine consideration of intent can be considered a roadblock. We suggest that the state of criminal intent procedure is quite consistent with the goals and objectives of tough, retributive U.S. crime control policies of recent decades and has greatly expedited the prosecution, conviction, and punishment of hundreds of thousands of offenders.

INTERNATIONAL COMPARISONS

We can learn much from the policies and practices of our European allies. In February 2013, participants in the European-American Prison Project toured German and Dutch prisons. The goal was to show the visitors how German and Dutch prisons were structured and operated by seeing them firsthand, as well as speaking with corrections officials, elected officials, policymakers, and inmates.

One of the most striking differences between U.S. and European correctional policy is the use of prisons—the incarceration rates in Germany and the Netherlands are about 10 percent of those in the United States. Recidivism is also dramatically lower (between half and two-thirds of U.S. recidivism).[4] Much of the lower recidivism is attributable to the philosophy of punishment and how German and Dutch prisons are run.

The U.S. correctional system is embedded in punishment and retribution. By contrast, Dutch and German systems are designed for rehabilitation and resocialization. The Vera Institute of Justice, which cosponsored the tour, notes that this approach to corrections is codified in German and Dutch law.

> According to Germany's Prison Act, the sole aim of incarceration is to enable prisoners to lead a life of social responsibility free of crime upon release, requiring that prison life be as similar as possible to life in the community (sometimes referred to as "the principle of normalization") and organized in such a way as to facilitate reintegration into society. The German Federal Constitutional Court stated that the protection of the public is not an "aim" of confinement in and of itself, but a "self evident" task of any system of confinement—a task that is resolved best by an offender's successful re-integration into society. Similarly, the core aim of the Netherlands 1998 Penitentiary Principles Act is the re-socialization of prisoners in which incarceration is carried out with as few restrictions as possible through the principle of association (both within prison and between prisoners and the community), and not separation.[5]

These policies not only inform how prisons are operated but also result in the vast majority of German and Dutch offenders being diverted to noncustodial settings. Prison is a last resort that is used infrequently. That is evident from the incarceration rates referenced above.

When incarceration is used, prison sentences are considerably shorter than in the United States, and the conditions of confinement stand in stark contrast to ours. They are not meant to be punitive, instead focusing on helping inmates lead productive, crime-free, and independent lives when they are released. They are given a fair amount of autonomy, including cooking their own meals, dressing in their own clothes, and participating in remunerated work and education. Interactions between staff and inmates rely mainly on incentives and rewards, rather than punishment, and the clinical evidence certainly supports the functional superiority of rewards over punishment. Moreover, prison staff members receive extensive training not only in security but also in social work, psychology, conflict management, and communication, among others.

Perhaps the most important difference between U.S. and German and Dutch correctional policy is the culture of the latter two. The entire correctional process is focused on outcomes. One U.S. observer put it succinctly: "If you treat inmates like humans, they will act like humans."

In both Germany and the Netherlands, prosecutors have broad discretion for diverting offenders away from prosecution and incarceration. Given the extraordinarily low incarceration rates, it is obvious they exercise that discretion frequently.

Another substantial difference between the United States and Germany and the Netherlands is the availability and use of drug and mental health treatment. In both Germany and the Netherlands, there is extensive availability of detoxification, substitution therapy (e.g., methadone), and inpatient and outpatient substance abuse treatment.[6] In Germany, mentally ill offenders are diverted to psychiatric hospitals, not prison. The Dutch system has what are called Forensic Psychiatric Care Institutions, which are within the authority of the Justice Ministry. The Dutch employ teams of experts that include psychiatrists, psychologists, social workers, judges, lawyers, and behavioral therapists to determine whether an offender's disorder is connected to any alleged criminal conduct, and if the individual has any mitigated criminal responsibility.[7]

It is clear that much can be learned from how other countries go about the business of criminal justice. Consideration of the criminal justice practices, policies, philosophies, and cultures of our European neighbors may very well help us to develop more effective strategies for reducing crime, recidivism, victimization, and cost.

A PATH FORWARD

This is a book about criminal justice reform. Our goal in the pages that follow is to develop a strategy for the dramatic expansion of diversion of many of the offenders who enter the justice system with a variety of disorders, impairments, deficits, and circumstances related to their criminal offending and involvement in the justice system. This will entail the development of a process for sorting offenders at the front end of the justice system, with the goal being the identification of offenders with acceptable risk levels and the presence of sufficiently serious mental illness, substance abuse, neurocognitive and neurodevelopmental disorders, and intellectual deficits, among others. The point is to (1) divert disordered offenders to treatment and supervision/risk management in order to mitigate and/or manage the problems that are associated with their involvement in the justice system, in turn reducing recidivism; and (2) criminally prosecute those who are too risky for diversion, who do not have significant disorders, impairments, or deficits, or who, because of the seriousness of their offense, their criminal history, or otherwise by determination of the prosecutor, are not suitable for diversion.

The criminal justice system has for decades served as a repository for mentally ill and addicted individuals, many of whom have neurocognitive problems and intellectual deficiencies. It is also the case that most of these individuals leave the justice system no better, and often worse, than when they entered. Allowing the justice system to serve as the default warehouse for such individuals is clearly not smart, effective, or fiscally prudent. In fact, all indications are that using the justice system to manage large numbers of individuals with psychiatric, addiction, and cognitive disorders is an ill-informed policy that compromises public safety, places us all at risk of unnecessary, avoidable criminal victimization, accelerates the revolving door of the justice system, and wastes tremendous amounts of money. That is a horrible return on investment.

The strategy going forward is in some respects quite simple—for those criminal offenders who need them, provide the psychiatric, neurocognitive, behavioral, and addiction interventions using the evidence-based practices from medicine, psychiatry, psychology, neuroscience, and addiction science. If we are serious about changing behavior and reducing recidivism, then we should be applying the best science has to offer to change behavior and reduce crime and recidivism. In turn, we can reduce criminal victimization, enhance the productivity of a significant segment of the U.S. population, reduce their dependence on public assistance, and save money.

The point is not to let off or pamper individuals who commit a crime because they have a substance addiction problem or a mental illness. The goal here is to build the necessary legal, procedural, and clinical mechanisms, protocols, and resources needed to *effectively* sort, divert, and treat the underlying behavioral problems related to criminality. Our goal is to strike a balance between clinical intervention and recidivism risk by providing evidence-based clinical treatments for effective behavioral intervention while managing the risk of reoffending among those who have been diverted.

These initiatives will also require changing how we think about crime and punishment, responsibility, culpability, retribution, rehabilitation, criminal prosecution and conviction, and costs and benefits. Perhaps most important, this will require a serious consideration of the purpose of American criminal justice. It will be necessary to redefine success, which will mean changing the culture of the administration of criminal justice to think more broadly and more pragmatically about how to best achieve success in day-to-day decision making. Success, as we see it, includes recidivism reduction and public safety as well as reducing criminal victimization and saving money.

What we propose in these pages is aggressive. We will provide a road map based on what the evidence indicates is the prudent, effective, and cost-efficient path forward. It is our goal to develop appropriate, effective diversion strategies for addressing the psychiatric disorders, intellectual deficiencies, neurodevelopmental and neurocognitive deficits, and substance abuse problems that characterize the majority of criminal offenders in the U.S. justice system. This will include developing clinical protocols, diagnostic strategies, and treatment interventions of appropriate scale that are qualitatively and quantitatively different from anything the U.S. criminal justice system has experienced.

2

FOUR MAJOR THREATS TO RECIDIVISM REDUCTION

Intellectual Deficiencies, Drug Addiction, Neurodevelopmental Problems, and Mental Illness

In this chapter, we discuss in detail four significant threats to recidivism reduction: mental illness, substance abuse, neurodevelopmental and neurocognitive deficits and impairments, and intellectual disability. There are many other threats to recidivism reduction, but these are the four that have been largely swept under the rug of justice policy, that collectively affect the vast majority of criminal offenders, and that require much more sophisticated, evidence-based interventions to remedy.

The failure to adequately address these problems in the public domain has rendered the justice system the default repository for many of these disordered and impaired individuals. It has become obvious to us that this is an unsustainable and intolerable situation that compromises public safety, places us all at a heightened but avoidable risk of being victims of crime, and wastes billions of dollars every year.

We discuss each of these four issues separately in this chapter, beginning with intellectual disability.

INTELLECTUAL DEFICIENCIES

Aaron Hart was born and raised in Paris, a town of 25,000 in far northeast Texas. In 2008, Aaron was mowing a neighbor's yard in order to earn extra money. At some point, the neighbor saw Aaron with his pants down, fondling the genitals of the neighbor's six-year-old grandson. Local police arrested Aaron, read him his Miranda warnings, and booked him into jail. He was charged with five felony counts of sexual assault and indecency with a child. Aaron confessed to all counts during police interrogation, without counsel present. He was convicted and sentenced to three thirty-year terms and two five-year terms in prison. The judge could have imposed a concurrent sentence but decided to require that Aaron serve them consecutively. That resulted in a one hundred-year sentence. Aaron had no prior criminal history and no history of violence.

What Aaron does have is an IQ of 47. He was diagnosed with mental retardation as a child, has the intellectual ability of a kindergartner, and has a severe speech impediment. He was placed in special education classes in school. He never learned to read or write. Aaron's appellate attorney David Pearson said, "The original case was tried no differently at all than if Aaron was just a kid with normal intellectual functioning. There was no regard whatsoever to his limitations."[1]

The case of Aaron Hart involved a bad crime. But it also highlights a number of problems with the arrest, prosecution, conviction, and punishment of individuals with intellectual disabilities.

The fifth edition (2013) of the *Diagnostic and Statistical Manual of Mental Disorders* (DSM-5)[2] revised the diagnosis of intellectual disability from how it was detailed in the DSM-4. One important difference is changing the label from mental retardation to intellectual disability, although the term *mental retardation* is still commonly used in the law today. The more important substantive change is specifying how intellectual disability impacts an individuals' day-to-day functioning.

According to the DSM-5, an intellectual disability (ID) is an impairment of an individual's general mental abilities that significantly impacts adaptive functioning. The DSM-5 utilizes a multidimensional framework of adaptive functioning, which consists of three domains that determine how well one deals or copes with everyday tasks and activities. These three domains of adaptive functioning are conceptual/academic, social, and practical.

The conceptual/academic domain includes skills such as reading, writing, language, reasoning, math or quantitative skills, and knowledge. The social domain includes things such as empathy, communication skills, social judgment, and the ability to make and maintain relationships. The practical domain consists of self-management including personal care, job responsibilities, financial management, and day-to-day school and work activities.

The DSM-5 moves away from the previously heavy reliance on IQ and emphasizes impairment to adaptive functioning. Both clinical assessment and standardized intelligence testing are used for diagnosis and determining the severity or extent of impairment. As such, diagnosis and severity are more a function of abilities. IQ is a consideration (IQ of 70 or below) but not the defining criterion. There is no longer a strict age criterion (it had been required that onset begin prior to age eighteen), just the requirement that symptoms begin during an individual's developmental period.

The American Association on Intellectual and Developmental Disabilities estimates that between 2 and 3 percent of the general population in the United States meet the standard criteria for intellectual disabilities. Prevalence data for individuals with intellectual disabilities in the U.S. criminal justice system are scarce, and estimates vary considerably. The primary reason the prevalence estimates are so varied is due to the different definitions of intellectual disability that have been used over time.

The bottom line is that individuals with ID are substantially overrepresented in the criminal justice system. The evidence shows that approximately one-quarter of prison inmates scored below 80 on IQ tests. Slightly more than 9 percent of the general population score 80 and below. Just under 10 percent of the inmate population have an IQ above 110, compared to 25 percent of the general population. [3]

The best estimates place prevalence in the justice system between 4 and 14 percent. [4] This means that on any given day, there are between three hundred thousand and one million criminal offenders in the U.S. criminal justice system who have intellectual disabilities.

A good bit of research has focused on the connection between involvement in the criminal justice system and intellectual disabilities. The results of this research indicate first that individuals with moderate to severe ID are not commonly justice-involved. More typically, it is individuals with mild to borderline ID. Moreover, the results show that the characteristics and risk factors among the justice-involved ID population are essentially no different than those without ID in the justice system. In addition, studies show that the types of crimes committed by individuals with ID do not differ significantly from those without ID. What may drive the overrepresentation of ID offenders is a higher risk of detection due to compromised adaptive functioning.

Offenders with ID tend to share a number of characteristics that probably are implicated in their risk of detection, arrest, conviction, and punishment. These include naïveté, acquiescence, cognitive rigidity, slow information processing, poor decision making, poor planning for the future, difficulty learning from experiences and understanding the reactions of others, poor impulse control, and poor logical reasoning.

> Certain characteristics are more common to members of this population, including: poor memory (does not attend to details and poor recall), significantly reduced intelligence, poor ability to use abstract thought (very rigid and concrete in their thought patterns), problems with concentration or focusing (easily distractible), poor transference and generalization skills (unable to make logical connections), impulsive behaviors (difficulty controlling repetitive and inappropriate behaviors), poor planning and coping skills (unable to see cause/effect, easily frustrated), poor judgment skills (unable to recognize dangerous situations), and a tendency to acquiesce (in order to please significant others and those in authority).[5]

Research has borne out particular vulnerabilities of individuals with ID as they are processed through the justice system. First, there are Fifth Amendment concerns associated with custodial interrogation. The Miranda warnings were developed by the U.S. Supreme Court as a way to level the playing field for criminal suspects by reminding them of their rights. The court held that the Miranda warnings may be waived (implying a suspect will talk with police) if that waiver is voluntary, knowing, and intelligent. Research conducted on comprehension of the Miranda warnings of individuals with ID consistently shows that they have substantial difficulty understanding what the five elements of the Miranda warnings mean (50 percent of ID subjects were unable to correctly paraphrase any of the elements).[6]

Studies also show that individuals with ID are more likely to be influenced by suggestions made by police in an interrogation and fail to understand basic legal concepts like guilty and not guilty. To be clear, a key goal of a police interrogation is to obtain a confession. Law enforcement typically utilizes a variety of tactics that are designed to facilitate a confession. These tactics are often effective with suspects without ID. Add in ID, and we are looking at individuals who may not understand their rights, who are more likely influenced by suggestion and pressure, and who tend to have a strong need to please others, especially those in authority.

There are also Sixth Amendment issues regarding assistance of counsel. Depending on the severity of the impairment, defendants with ID may or may not be able to meaningfully participate in their own defense. It has also been suggested that ID defendants may present a demeanor that implies a lack of remorse.

While some protections are afforded defendants with ID, for the most part, criminal arrest, prosecution, and conviction do not occur on a level playing field.

> Thus, because of their susceptibility to falsely confessing, their impaired ability to assist counsel, the frequency with which their demeanor will be misinterpreted . . . persons with mental retardation face a heightened risk of wrongful conviction.[7]

Atkins v. Virginia

On August 16, 1996, Daryl Atkins and William Jones abducted Eric Nesbitt, robbed him of the money he had with him, and drove him to an ATM machine, where he was forced to withdraw more money. They then took him to a remote location and shot him eight times. Nesbitt died.

Both Jones and Atkins testified at Atkins's trial. Jones testified that Atkins shot Nesbitt and Atkins testified that Jones shot him. The record indicates that Jones's testimony was more coherent and articulate and persuaded the jury. Atkins was convicted.

At the penalty phase, the defense presented one expert psychologist who concluded that Atkins was mildly mentally retarded. This was based on interviews with people who knew Atkins, reviews of school records, and a standardized IQ test that indicated Atkins had an IQ of 59.

Atkins was sentenced to death by the jury, based in part on the prosecutor's expert psychologist, who testified that Atkins was not mentally retarded, but rather of average intelligence.

The case was petitioned to the U.S. Supreme Court and granted certiorari. A joint amici brief was filed by the 155,000 member American Psychological Association, the 40,000-member American Psychiatric Association, and the 2,500-member American Academy of Psychiatry and the Law (AAPL). We begin with the conclusions of the amici brief and then turn to the court's landmark decision.

The brief is quite clear that mental retardation (MR) is a significant impairment to intellectual and adaptive functioning. As such, individuals with MR are

> substantially less capable of both abstract reasoning and practical or adaptive functioning than non-retarded adults. These very real and serious impairments are reflected in diminished capacities to understand basic facts, foresee the moral consequences of actions, learn from one's mistakes, and grasp the feelings, thoughts, and reactions of other people.[8]

The brief then declares that because of their disability, mentally retarded individuals are not able to achieve the very high level of culpability or blameworthiness that they must have to be punished by death. It concludes by detailing how determinations of mental retardation should be made (by comprehensive professional assessment) and then stating that a categorical prohibition of execution of individuals diagnosed with mental retardation is warranted.

The Supreme Court decided in 2002 in *Atkins* to categorically exclude the death penalty for mentally retarded defendants. The decision involved the diminished culpability or moral blameworthiness of mentally retarded individuals, the limitations of their intellectual and adaptive functioning, and the purposes of punishment. The court acknowledged that mental retardation involves not only below-average intellectual functioning but also significant limitation on day-to-day activities. While mentally retarded defendants may know the difference between right and wrong, their impairments result in

> diminished capacities to understand and process information, to communicate, to abstract from mistakes and learn from experience, to en-

gage in logical reasoning, to control impulses, and to understand the reactions of others. There is no evidence that they are more likely to engage in criminal conduct than others, but there is abundant evidence that they often act on impulse rather than pursuant to a premeditated plan, and that in group settings they are followers rather than leaders. Their deficiencies do not warrant an exemption from criminal sanctions, but they do diminish their personal culpability.[9]

The court's decision was also based on the link between the diminished capacity of defendants with an intellectual disability and the potential for error. The risk of error

is enhanced, not only by the possibility of false confessions, but also by the lesser ability of mentally retarded defendants to make a persuasive showing of mitigation in the face of prosecutorial evidence of one or more aggravating factors. Mentally retarded defendants may be less able to give meaningful assistance to their counsel and are typically poor witnesses, and their demeanor may create an unwarranted impression of lack of remorse for their crimes.[10]

While *Atkins* was a very important case in terms of death penalty jurisprudence and culpability, critics have argued that it did not go far enough, since it left it up to the states to determine what mental retardation is. For example, Robert Ladd was executed in Texas in January 2015. Ladd had been diagnosed as mentally retarded at age thirteen when his IQ was determined to be 67. The long-established threshold for ID is an IQ of 70 or below. Prior to his execution, a doctor concluded that Ladd was in fact mentally retarded. In 2012, Texas executed Marvin Wilson, a convicted murderer with an IQ of 61.

Criminal Responsibility Beyond the Death Penalty

The court in *Atkins* acknowledged that as a class, mentally retarded defendants have limited culpability and diminished moral blameworthiness compared to non-mentally retarded defendants. The court fashioned a *relative culpability* argument based on the severity of punishment associated with the death penalty. The court stated that the death penalty is of such consequence that the bar for culpability is quite high. This reasoning makes sense since the issue in *Atkins* was the Eighth Amendment prohibition against cruel and unusual punishment. The basis of the decision is proportionality of punishment—"punishment must be tailored to his responsibility and moral guilt."[11]

It is important to recognize that this same limited culpability and diminished moral blameworthiness exists independent of any anticipated punishment. Thus, we hold that an argument can also be made for *absolute culpability* and *absolute moral blameworthiness*. The impacts of an intellectual disability on an individual's ability or capacity to understand, analyze, and process information, engage in rational reasoning and decision making, plan, control behavior, and exercise sound judgment still remain, regardless of the severity of the punishment.

The court in *Atkins* also raised important questions about deterrence of punishment and retribution for defendants with an intellectual disability.

> [T]here is a serious question as to whether either justification that we have recognized as a basis for the death penalty applies to mentally retarded offenders. *Gregg v. Georgia* identified "retribution and deterrence of capital crimes by prospective offenders" as the social purposes served by the death penalty. Unless the imposition of the death penalty on a mentally retarded person "measurably contributes to one or both of these goals, it is nothing more than the purposeless and needless imposition of pain and suffering."[12]

We suggest that the same question about deterrence hold regardless of the severity of the punishment. A defendant either has the intellectual ability or capacity to be deterred or not. If one is incapable of being deterred because of the cognitive and behavioral consequences of ID, it does not matter whether the punishment is death, prison, or a fine. Again, overwhelming scientific evidence reveals that, as a policy, the severity of punishment does not effectively deter criminal offending among individuals with or without ID.

The court held in *Atkins* that "[w]ith respect to retribution—the interest in seeing that the offender gets his 'just deserts'—the severity of the appropriate punishment necessarily depends on the culpability of the offender." If a criminal defendant is not morally blameworthy because of an intellectual disability, then it seems that the government is on shaky moral ground in imposing just deserts.

The focus of *Atkins* was on punishment. We argue that the questions raised in *Atkins* regarding the abilities and capacities of individuals with intellectual disabilities need to be applied to the question of innocence or guilt.

Procedural Error

One final point involves the concerns that the *Atkins* court had about the risk of procedural errors for individuals with an intellectual disability, including false confessions, limited ability to assist counsel, and misperception of lack of remorse. The concern was due to the special risk of wrongful execution. Regardless of the crime and the punishment, however, those concerns remain. A defendant with an intellectual disability can still make a false confession in a burglary case and/or be of little or no assistance to counsel in a drug case. Yes, a wrongful execution is a horrible outcome, but a wrongful conviction and thus unjustified punishment is also a substantial harm.

Comorbidity

All of the issues and concerns raised by the court in *Atkins* and expanded upon here are dramatically magnified when we consider the likelihood of comorbidity among individuals with an intellectual disability. This is a matter that the court did not address in *Atkins*, but it is real and of substantial consequence.

A variety of analyses have been conducted on studies of the prevalence of psychiatric disorders among children and adults with an intellectual disability. The diagnostic strategies vary across the studies, as do sample size and other factors. For these reasons, there is no single reliable estimate of the prevalence of comorbidity with psychiatric disorders. What we have is a range of prevalence among children of 30–50 percent.[13] Rates for adults range between 25 and 50 percent.[14] Common co-occurring disorders include major depression, ADHD, bipolar disorders, anxiety, autism spectrum disorder, impulse control disorder, and neurocognitive impairments, among others.

SUBSTANCE ABUSE

While substance abuse disorders are classified as a mental disorder in the *Diagnostic and Statistical Manual of Mental Disorders*, we discuss addiction and substance abuse separately here, as well as in the context of our later discussion of mental illness. We believe substance abuse deserves a separate discussion because of the sheer volume of substance abuse disorders among the criminal and juvenile justice populations, and because drug possession and possession of drug paraphernalia are illegal behaviors.

Today, 27 million individuals have used an illicit drug within the past year, and 140 million are alcohol drinkers. There are 21.5 million individuals in the United States who have a substance use disorder, including 14.4 million with an alcohol use disorder, 4.5 million with an illicit drug use disorder, and another 2.6 million with both a drug and an alcohol use disorder.

The United States is exceptional in a number of ways, including drug use. Surveys comparing U.S. drug use with that in other nations show we are a world leader. A recent World Health Organization analysis concluded that we are more likely to try illicit drugs (lifetime use) than anyone else in the world.[15] Marijuana use is the most common, but we also are more likely to try cocaine, amphetamines, and prescription painkillers. In addition, we have higher current drug use rates (past year use) than most other nations of the world. One of the reasons that the Mexican drug cartels are so phenomenally successful is because there is so much demand in the United States for illicit drugs and, in turn, so much money to be made supplying these drugs. For example, a RAND study estimates that Americans spend more than $100 billion annually for just four illicit drugs—marijuana ($41 billion), cocaine ($28 billion), heroin ($27 billion), and methamphetamine ($13 billion).[16]

The criminal justice response to drugs has been exceptional as well. Since 1970, when Richard Nixon declared drugs public enemy number one, the war on drugs has consumed $1 trillion and resulted in forty-five million arrests.[17] At the state and federal level, nearly one-third of all prison admissions are for drug offenses. U.S. drug control policy has largely been focused on trying to limit the supply of drugs by prosecuting drug possession, distribution, and manufacture. State and federal efforts have been aided by punitive mandatory and mandatory minimum drug sentences. Nearly fifty years later, the report card is not impressive—the supply of drugs is robust, and street prices are as low as ever.[18] It is difficult to find any careful observers of U.S. drug policy, including law enforcement officials and judges, who in all seriousness would say this has worked. Moreover, expert panel after expert panel and commission after commission have all concluded that U.S. drug policy has been a failure.[19]

Drug addiction is defined by the American Society of Addiction Medicine as

> a primary, chronic disease of brain reward, motivation, memory and related circuitry. Dysfunction in these circuits leads to characteristic biological, psychological, social and spiritual manifestations. This is reflected in an individual pathologically pursuing reward and/or relief by substance use and other behaviors. Addiction is characterized by inability to consistently abstain, impairment in behavioral control, craving, diminished recognition of significant problems with one's behaviors and interpersonal relationships and a dysfunctional emotional response. Like other chronic diseases, addiction often involves cycles of relapse and remission.[20]

The *Diagnostic and Statistical Manual of Mental Disorders* identifies ten classes of drugs within the diagnosis of a substance use disorder. These include alcohol, caffeine, cannabis, hallucinogens, inhalants, opioids, sedatives and hypnotics, stimulants, tobacco, and other. All of these substances share in common the direct activation of the brain's reward system when taken in excess.

The DSM-5 refers to a substance use disorder as a problematic pattern of using alcohol or other substances that results in impairment in daily life or noticeable distress. The DSM-5 identifies the following criteria for diagnosing a substance use disorder.

Impaired Control

- Taking more of a substance over a longer period of time than planned.
- Expressing a desire to cut down on use and/or reporting multiple unsuccessful attempts to decrease or discontinue use.
- Spending a considerable amount of time obtaining, using, and recovering from the effects of the substance.
- Craving or an intense desire for the substance.

Social Impairment

- Failure to fulfill work, school, or home responsibilities or obligations as a result of continued substance use.
- Continued substance use despite persistent social or interpersonal problems that are caused or aggravated by substance use.
- Significant social, occupational, or recreational activities are limited or discontinued as a result of continued substance use.

Risky Use

- Continued use of a substance in situations when it is physically harmful.
- Continued use despite awareness of persistent physical and/or psychological problems that are due to or aggravated by substance use.

Pharmacological Criteria

- Increasing tolerance that requires increased dosage or a significantly reduced effect of the substance when the usual dosage is consumed.
- Withdrawal symptoms after discontinuation of the substance.

It is clear from the DSM-5 criteria that the diagnosis of a substance abuse disorder is based largely on the impacts that substance use has on day-to-day activities. Of particular importance are the impairments that occur as a result of persistent substance use.

Moral Failing or Brain Disease?

For much of our history, substance abuse has been viewed as a moral failing, a weakness, perhaps a character flaw, or a simple lack of willpower or discipline. After all, the Reagan administration's anti-drug message was "Just Say No."

The belief or perception that drug or alcohol addiction or dependence is mainly a matter of not drinking or not taking drugs seems to have informed U.S. drug control policy for the past half century. Just as it is inaccurate to claim that crime is mainly a matter of making poor decisions, drug and alcohol abuse is more than a lack of willpower.

As our efforts at punishment have failed to reduce recidivism, it is equally naïve to try to punish addiction out of someone with a substance use disorder. Nothing about punishment changes the neurological, psychological, and physiological elements of substance abuse. If only it were that simple!

The scientific community has, with minor exceptions, resoundingly rejected the folk psychology view of substance abuse as a moral failing, in favor of the evidence-informed conclusion that it is a disease of the brain, a chronic, relapsing disorder characterized by compulsive drug taking in the face of substantial negative consequences. Addiction is the most severe stage of substance abuse, marked by the transition from impulsive substance abuse (dependence) to compulsive substance use. A defining characteristic of both dependence and addiction is a loss of control over limiting or ending substance use.

The basis for the disease model of substance abuse is found in neuroscientific research on how and to what extent ingestion of drugs or alcohol impacts the brain and brain function. Addictive drugs work through the reward regions of the brain by releasing dopamine, the neurotransmitter associated with pleasure and reward. Those areas of the brain impacted by the release of dopamine include the limbic regions (the nucleus accumbens, amygdala, and the hippocampus) and the prefrontal cortex, those areas that regulate reinforcement learning, cognition, executive functioning (self-control, awareness, decision making), and inhibition of impulses. As Harvard's Steven Hyman describes it:

> Normally dopamine serves as a "learning signal" in the brain. Dopamine is released when a reward is new, better than expected, or unpredicted in a particular circumstance. When the world is exactly as expected, there is nothing new to learn; no new circumstances to connect either to desire or to action—and no increase in dopamine release. Because addictive drugs increase synaptic dopamine by direct pharmacologic action, they short-circuit the normal controls over dopamine release that compare the current circumstance with prior experience. Thus, unlike natural rewards, addictive drugs always signal "better than expected." Neural circuits "overlearn" on an excessive and grossly distorted dopamine signal. Cues that predict drug availability such as persons, places, or certain bodily sensations gain profound incentive

salience and the ability to motivate drug seeking. Because of the excessive dopamine signal in the prefrontal cortex, drugs become over-
valued compared with all other goals.[21]

Dopamine release reinforces continued drug/alcohol use, and at the
same time, addictive drugs are able to circumvent the brain's natural
satiation, continuing to increase dopamine levels and further reinforcing
ingestion of drugs. This lack of satiation is one of the reasons why addictive drugs lead to compulsive behaviors compared to other pleasurable
activities that have natural rewards.

However, the effects go beyond the dopamine-based prioritization and
reinforcement of drug use. *Drug use changes the functioning of the brain
in substantial ways.* Continued drug use among those who become addicted results in adaptive changes to neuro pathways and circuits in the
brain that lead to continued drug seeking and use, an effect that is over
and above the reinforcement effects of dopamine. An example of a neuroadaptive change is synaptic plasticity, a molecular and cellular process
that changes the strength of neural connections in the brain. In turn, these
adaptations at the molecular level become entrenched in the brain's reward system, strengthening the neural connections that appear to be associated with the maintenance of key addictive behaviors such as craving,
drug seeking, and compulsive drug use.

The consequences of neuroadaptive changes can be profound among
addicts.

> [D]rug-induced neuroadaptations alter homeostatic set points and thus
> the ability of the brain to function "normally," reducing the ability to
> process the adverse consequences of drug taking. Neuroadaptations
> also play a role in the lack of flexibility in the control over addictive
> behaviours which results in a window of opportunity before drug-
> related behaviours switch from goal-directed actions that are still sen-
> sitive to devaluation to habitual-based responses. This corresponds to a
> neuroadaptive shift in the brain regions mediating these responses.
> Consequently neuroadaptations are believed to underlie the switch
> from voluntary controlled drug use to habitual, compulsive drug use
> and the maintenance of drug-seeking behaviours. They appear stable
> and persistent and are linked to the high incidence of relapse following
> a period of abstinence.[22]

A key question is the extent to which drug addicts are able to exercise voluntary control over drug use. A wide variety of experts have offered nearly universal consensus that a defining characteristic of addiction—compulsive drug seeking and drug use—means at a minimum a diminished voluntary control over drug use even when confronted by significantly negative consequences.[23] Nora Volkow, the director of the National Institute on Drug Abuse at the National Institutes of Health, has since 2003 defined drug addiction as a disorder of disrupted self-control. The rationale is the impact of the use of drugs on the prefrontal cortex and impaired executive functioning. She concludes in a 2016 *New England Journal of Medicine* article:

> Thus, altered signaling in prefrontal regulatory circuits, paired with changes in the circuitry involved in reward and emotional response, creates an imbalance that is crucial to both the gradual development of compulsive behavior in the addicted disease state and the associated inability to voluntarily reduce drug-taking behavior, despite the potentially catastrophic consequences.[24]

The science is clear that addiction and dependence are much more complex than simply a matter of choice, moral strength, or willpower. The impact of drug ingestion on the reward system of the brain has profound consequences for repeated drug use. Moreover, when we appreciate that drug use can also alter the structure of the brain through plasticity and neuroadaptations, repeated drug use and relapse are much better understood, as are the requirements for successful interventions.

As we learn more about the impacts that chronic drug and alcohol dependence and addiction have on the structure and function of the brain, the definition of addiction—as a chronic brain disorder characterized by relapse—makes sense. The stories we hear about alcoholics drinking while on their deathbeds with terminal cirrhosis of the liver, or methamphetamine addicts continuing to use meth when their teeth have fallen out and they weigh a fraction of what is considered healthy, can be reconciled when we understand the science of addiction. It also makes sense in the case of the homeless heroin addict who would rather use heroin than deal with unemployment, homelessness, and physical health, or the professional married father of three who has a cocaine habit that he is keeping a secret from his family, friends, and employer.

Why would people risk everything for drugs or alcohol? And when they do quit, why do they often repeatedly relapse? Why does it often seem to take multiple attempts at treatment to get an addict on a sustained path to sobriety? The answers to these questions can largely be found in how drug and alcohol abuse, dependence, and addiction fundamentally change the brain in ways that often make it extraordinarily difficult to quit. When we understand the role the brain plays in substance abuse disorders, it should not be surprising that punishing a substance user as we have done relentlessly for the past fifty years is futile. There is nothing about punishment that alters executive dysfunction or that rewires the brain. The evidence of this futility of punishment for our drug problem is the phenomenally high relapse and recidivism rates of drug offenders (not dealers but drug possession cases) who have been released from prison, or are on probation and have their supervision revoked, and then return to prison for a supervision violation.

Treatment of substance use disorders is not a public health priority. A telling comparison may help put treatment of substance abuse disorders in perspective. In 2010, $28 billion was spent on substance abuse treatment for the forty million individuals with addiction disorders. In the same year, the United States spent $44 billion treating diabetes (affecting twenty-six million individuals), $87 billion on cancer (affecting nineteen million), and $107 billion on heart conditions (affecting twenty-seven million individuals).

Comorbidity

As challenging as drug addiction and drug dependence are, the picture becomes much more complex when we add comorbidity. The National Comorbidity Study of a nationally representative sample discovered that 40–65 percent of individuals with any lifetime substance abuse disorder also reported a lifetime mental health disorder.[25] A sample of individuals seeking treatment for addiction revealed that nearly 80 percent had a lifetime history of a psychiatric disorder. Two-thirds of those had a current mental health disorder at the time of treatment intake.[26]

The Epidemiologic Catchment Area study[27] found that among individuals with an alcohol disorder, nearly 40 percent have a comorbid mental disorder. More than half of those with a drug disorder have a comorbid mental disorder. Mood disorders and anxiety disorders are common among substance abusing individuals. The bottom line is that substance use disorders and mental health disorders tend to co-occur.

Implications of Addiction for Behavior

Addiction, the most severe stage of substance abuse, is described as leading to enduring changes to the brain's reward circuits and control centers. Moreover, "addiction-related behavior is seen as largely stimulus driven and subject to minimal conscious control."[28] Experts estimate that between 50 and 80 percent of substance addicts exhibit some form of executive dysfunction.[29] Executive functions include the following cognitive faculties: attention, working memory, behavioral/cognitive flexibility, inhibition, valuing future events, planning, regulation of arousal and emotional reactions, and higher-order cognitive skills.[30] The research findings regarding impairments of each of these eight cognitive abilities due to substance abuse and addiction is compelling. For example:

- Impairment to sustained attention is found in alcohol-dependent individuals, methadone-maintained opioid addicts, former opioid addicts, methamphetamine addicts, and cannabis users.
- Impairment to behavior-inhibition controls (preventing an action before it starts, stopping an ongoing behavior) is common among addicted individuals; this includes chronic and dependent cocaine users, alcohol-dependent individuals, and dependent methamphetamine users.
- Valuing future events involves prioritizing future considerations and the influence of that choice on current decision making (it is also referred to as being future oriented as opposed to present oriented); individuals who are addicted to or abuse alcohol, cocaine, methamphetamine, and heroin have a higher likelihood of being present versus future oriented.
- Cognitive flexibility refers to the ability to modify behavior in light of environmental situations or cues; cognitive inflexibility was found more commonly among heavy cannabis users, chronic cocaine users, and chronic amphetamine users, compared to controls.
- Working memory is the ability to retain information for future use and the ability to edit or curate that information so it can be prioritized or removed; working memory has been found to be deficient

among cannabis users, methamphetamine users, amphetamine users, opioid users, cocaine users, and alcoholics.

- Planning involves knowing and organizing the steps that are required to achieve a particular goal or outcome; the ability to plan
has been found to be deficient among heroin users and amphetamine users.

- Arousal and emotional regulation refers to the ability to self-regu-
late emotions or affective states (this also includes the ability to
self-motivate to achieve goals); emotional regulation is often impaired among addicted individuals including poly-substance abusers, heavy drinkers, cannabis users, cocaine users, opioid users,
methamphetamine users, and amphetamine users.

- Higher-order cognitive skills refer to decision making in more complex situations requiring consideration of others' perspectives as
well as one's own; these skills involve reading cues correctly and
accurately interpreting others' intentions, thoughts, and behaviors
(they also include self-awareness of one's abilities, skills, and
weaknesses). Deficits in higher-order cognitive skills have been
found among alcoholics, methamphetamine addicts, cocaine-depen-
dent individuals, and cannabis users.[31]

Reviews of the research on substance use, abuse, dependence, and
addiction all lead to the same general conclusion:

> It is evident from studies reviewed in this article that most drugs of
> abuse may induce adverse effects on brain structures associated with
> cognitive functions. In most cases, these effects seem to impact brain
> circuits linked to important aspects of cognition, such as memory and
> learning, attention, risk taking, motivation, mood and wanting.[32]

Several researchers have addressed the ability of individuals with substance addiction and dependence disorders to exercise free will. For example, research from the late 1990s indicates that the impact on the
prefrontal cortex and the subsequent impairments to executive functioning result in a loss of so-called self-directed or self-motivated behavior in
favor of more automatic, sensory-driven behavior. That characterizes
drug use and seeking as well as other aspects of the substance abusing or
addicted individual.[33]

Moreover, the research is clear that the areas of the brain and the neural processes that are related to addiction are largely the same that impact cognitive functioning such as learning, reasoned decision making, and memory. In effect, the impairments and processes that support or sustain addiction also are implicated in a variety of cognitive impairments and deficits.[34]

Antoine Bechara and his colleagues have developed an approach for understanding the effects of addiction on the brain, and in turn how addiction, dependence, and abuse can impact day-to-day decision making, self-control, willpower, and behavior. They argue that addiction or drug abuse contributes to and is a result of an imbalance between the more impulsive, present-focused amygdala-dependent system for signaling *immediate* pain and pleasure and the more reflective, prefrontal cortex system for signaling *future* prospects for pain and pleasure. Drug-induced hyperactivity in the impulsive amygdala-dependent system and dysfunction of the reflexive system leads to impaired self-control. Bechara and his colleagues summarize what the evidence indicates about the impact of substances on brain functioning and behavior.

> Although the act of using substances can be resisted under extreme conditions (e.g., a gun to the head), in most cases there is no gun to the head. The research discussed provides evidence that the loss of willpower in individuals with substance dependence is likely the result of their experiencing the world differently. Addiction is a condition in which the person becomes unable to choose according to long-term outcomes. However, this inability can result from a dysfunction of one or more of several mechanisms of cognitive and behavioral control within the reflective system, or hyperactivity of the impulsive system. The breakdown of one or more of these cognitive and emotional mechanisms constitute one of the principal mechanisms responsible for the switch from a controlled to uncontrolled and compulsive behavior.[35]

What appears from the outside to be irrational or poor decision making on the part of the substance abuser is often better understood as uncontrollable, compulsive behavior driven or facilitated by imbalances in as well as physical changes to the brain. The impairment of self-control and decision making impacts not only substance-related behaviors but also a variety of other behaviors, such as criminal activity. The leading neuroscientists on the matter conclude:

Our research has shown that substance dependence is associated with impairment of the neural processes subserving decision making and that this impairment is global (i.e., it applies to many decisions, not only decisions about whether to engage in substance use). Therefore, well over half of people who are arrested and held in jails may be operating with an ability to decide and exercise willpower that is lower than that of the average person. [36]

Supreme Court Cases Involving Addiction and Substance Abuse

Some cases involving the U.S. Supreme Court are moving in the direction of declaring addiction a disease. *Robinson v California* (1962) is the first major U.S. Supreme Court case to do so, striking down a California law that criminalized being addicted to narcotics. In turn, the court held that it is unconstitutional to punish someone for having a disease. Justice Potter Stewart wrote in the majority opinion that "one day in prison for the 'crime' of having a common cold" would be cruel and unusual. [37]

In 1968, the U.S. Supreme Court held in *Powell v. Texas* that it is constitutional to punish someone for being intoxicated in public. The county court that handled Powell's appeal acknowledged that the appellant was a chronic alcoholic and that (1) chronic alcoholism is a disease that destroys the alcoholic's will to resist drinking; (2) a chronic alcoholic does not appear in public under his own volition, but under a compulsion related to his disease; and (3) the appellant is a chronic alcoholic who is afflicted by the disease of chronic alcoholism. However, the appellate court held that under the law, alcoholism is not a defense to the charge. The U.S. Supreme Court, in upholding the lower court's appellate finding, held that, among other things, Powell was not convicted for being a chronic alcoholic but for being intoxicated in a public place; as such, this decision is distinguished from the *Robinson* decision.

Several state court cases (*State v. Margo*, Supreme Court of New Jersey; *Salas v. State*, District Court of Appeal of Florida, Third District; *State v. Brown*, Arizona Supreme Court) all held that being under the influence of drugs is not the same as addiction as in *Robinson*. In all three cases, defendants were convicted of being under the influence, and on appeal they attempted to argue that the *Robinson* decision held. In all three cases, the appellate courts rejected the addiction argument, simply distinguishing between using drugs and being addicted.

We have routinely punished drug and alcohol addiction, despite what the scientific community has told us about addiction. This has been accomplished through the prolific use of plea negotiation. It has also been accomplished by courts upholding laws like those discussed above, which argue that drug possession and use are different from drug addiction. However, it is unclear how often defendants attempt to prove addiction when the vast majority of felony defendants cannot afford their own attorney, let alone hire expert witnesses who can assess whether a defendant is in fact addicted. In such situations, the benefits and advantages of the government far outweigh those of the defendant.

NEUROBIOLOGICAL IMPLICATIONS

To be clear, placing neurodevelopmental and neurocognitive disorders in a separate category is in a way a forced fit, in that many brain-related disorders are on a broader continuum ranging from neurological or neurodevelopmental disorders at one end to more commonly considered psychiatric disorders at the other. We believe that a separate discussion of neurodevelopmental and neurocognitive impairments is warranted since neurobiology has a unique perspective on behavior that is useful in our discussion of crime and recidivism. We also believe that the exponential growth in research on neuro impairments and criminal behavior is further justification for a separate section.

The Brain, Genetics, and the Environment

In fairly general terms, we come into the world with genetic predispositions that are then shaped, nuanced, or conditioned by our experiences in the environment. I describe it this way:

> Our interactions, experiences, observations, thoughts, and feelings are registered in our brains through new connections among brain cells. These neural connections, some of which are established early in development through the influence of genes and other inputs, which are established on an ongoing basis through interaction with the environ-

ment, determine how we think, perceive, feel, interpret, and react to the social and physical environment. The neural connections shape our thoughts, emotions, and feelings, our self-identity and our personality. And they are experience dependent, shaped by the environment in interaction with genetic influences.[38]

Neurobiology focuses on the cells (neurons) in the brain and how they communicate through substances known as neurotransmitters. The communication pathways that are established in the brain and the neural networks that result are constantly being established and reinforced or eliminated based on the frequency and intensity of experiences. The old adage applies: "Those that fire together wire together." Well-worn pathways tend to persist.

In effect, our behavior as well as our thoughts, beliefs, and attitudes are acquired or shaped by the ongoing interaction of genetic tendencies and experiences in the environment. Those experiences influence gene expression, rendering the old nature versus nurture dichotomy obsolete. In every sense, it is nature *and* nurture.

Two key systems in the brain help us understand the basics of behavior. The behavior-activating system (BAS) and behavior-inhibiting system (BIS) are part of the limbic system of the brain, which then extend into the prefrontal cortex. The behavior-activating system is largely influenced by the neurotransmitter dopamine, and thus the pleasure areas of the brain. The release of dopamine associated with a particular action tells us what we just did is pleasurable, in turn providing reinforcement for that behavior. The BAS is the accelerator in the brain, motivating pleasure seeking and the pursuit of rewarding stimuli. If the BAS is the accelerator, the behavior-inhibiting system is the brake. The BIS is associated with the neurotransmitter serotonin and is sensitive to punishment, thus the regulatory function of the BIS.

Dopamine and serotonin are very powerful influences or regulators of behavior, and when in proper balance help us successfully navigate the social environment. However,

> [i]f the BAS/BIS is out of balance, whereby the BAS dominates (excess dopamine and insufficient serotonin), that imbalance can result in sensation seeking behavior, impulsiveness, low self-control, low empathy, behavior driven by reward and relatively insensitive to punishment or consequences. The outcomes can include addictive behavior,

anti-social behavior and criminal behavior. Serotonin and dopamine are powerful regulators of behavioral and cognitive functions, thus any aspect of reduced or enhanced serotonergic or dopaminergic functioning results in emotional, behavioral and cognitive dysregulation.[39]

The prefrontal cortex (PFC) is the part of the brain that is responsible for a variety of activities known as executive functions. As the name implies, executive functions are higher-order cognitive processes such as planning, synthesizing, analyzing, problem solving, reasoning, working memory, making moral judgments, regulating emotions and behavior, controlling impulses, interpreting the actions of others, inhibiting impulsive behavior, and processing and communicating information, among others. It is also involved in making judgments as well as correctly identifying the emotional states of others (i.e., empathy). The PFC does all this within cognitive, emotional, and social contexts. Proper functioning of the PFC requires appropriate levels of dopamine; thus imbalances in the dopamine/serotonin mix have significant implications for the PFC.

The PFC and Executive Dysfunction

It is quite clear today, after several decades of research, that antisocial behavior is associated with brain impairments, especially impairments to the prefrontal cortex.[40] As Adrian Raine, one of the most widely respected and cited neuroscientists puts it, "[T]he best replicated brain imaging abnormality found to date across a wide variety of antisocial groups, across structure and function and across different imaging methodologies is the PFC."[41]

While the data should be taken with some caution due to varying definitions, prevalence estimates show a rather dramatic presence of brain dysfunction among criminal offender populations. Estimates range from as high as 90 percent among homicide offenders, 60 percent among chronically aggressive adults, 67 percent of death row inmates, 50 percent and higher among sex offenders, and 75 percent among juvenile offenders.[42] More recent research reported in *Scientific American* reveals that 60 percent of adults in U.S. prisons have had at least one traumatic brain injury, compared to 8.5 percent of the non-incarcerated population.[43]

The evidence increasingly implicates brain impairments in antisocial behavior, and the evidence is particularly strong for impairments to the PFC. For example:

> Neurological patients suffering damage to the ventral prefrontal cortex exhibit psychopathic-like, disinhibited behavior, autonomic and emotional blunting, and bad decision-making. Magnetic resonance imaging (MRI) research has shown that those with antisocial personality disorder have an 11 percent reduction in prefrontal gray matter. . . . Structural prefrontal impairments are paralleled by functional prefrontal impairments (i.e., reduced brain functioning) in a wide range of antisocial populations. Murderers have been found to show reduced glucose metabolism in the prefrontal cortex. This impairment also specifically characterizes impulsively violent offenders, suggesting that the prefrontal cortex acts as an "emergency brake" on runaway emotions generated by limbic structures. Brain imaging studies are supported by findings from neuropsychological, neurological, and psychophysiological studies, indicating robustness of findings.[44]

There is growing consensus that damage to the PFC found among antisocial individuals is characterized by emotional deficits (lack of empathy), inappropriate and incorrect moral reasoning, poor decision making, poor planning and organization, and poor problem solving. A rather comprehensive assessment (meta-analysis) of thirty-nine studies involving more than 4,500 participants provided convincing evidence that individuals involved in criminal behavior performed significantly less well on neuropsychological tests of aspects of executive functions such as decision making, planning, judgment, and self-monitoring.[45]

The PFC and Impulse Control

PFC dysfunction is also related to impulsive behavior, due largely to damage to the neural circuit that connects the amygdala to the frontal lobes, a circuit that is responsible for impulse control, among other things. As Redding puts it:

> Analogizing to classic Freudian terms, one could conceptualize the frontal lobes as serving the functions of the Ego, which keeps in check the primitive drives and emotions of the Id. Normally, the frontal lobes act as a circuit breaker for the reactive emotional responses generated by the amygdala. But the circuit breaker may fail when the frontal

lobes are damaged. Frontally damaged individuals may be unable to inhibit quick response reactions generated by the amygdala or to judge the consequences of an aggressive response.[46]

While much of the research to date is correlational rather than causal, it is clear that damage to the brain, which results in significant impairment of the PFC, is strongly related to impulsive antisocial behavior, aggression, and violence. For example, research demonstrates that homicide perpetrators have reduced glucose metabolism in the PFC, thus predisposing them to lower self-control and increased impulsive behavior. Other research shows that decreased activity in the PFC can reflect dysfunction in the behavioral regulation function of the PFC among murderers, compromising their ability to foresee the consequences of their behavior as well as reducing their ability to control their behavior.[47]

Neurotransmitter systems are also implicated in antisocial and violent behavior. Low levels of serotonin are associated with aggressive, impulsive behavior.

Brain imaging studies consistently show that reduced functioning of the frontal lobe is associated with antisocial behavior and violence. Dysfunction of the dorsolateral PFC is linked to impulsivity and impaired behavior control. Individuals with damage to the anterior cingulate are more likely to be aggressive and uninhibited and have impaired emotional processing and self-control.

The PFC and Moral Reasoning

Neuroscience has made impressive progress in isolating the PFC as the part of the brain responsible for moral judgment and reasoning, particularly the orbitofrontal cortex and the ventromedial prefrontal cortex (vmPFC).[48] Damage to these regions may impair moral reasoning and the ability to know right from wrong. Impaired moral reasoning increases the likelihood of engaging in rule-breaking and immoral behavior, potentially leading to antisocial behavior.

While this area of research is less developed than, for example, the link between PFC impairment and executive dysfunction and PFC dysfunction and impulse control, the research is clearly suggestive of potentially significant implications of PFC damage or impairment and compromised moral decision making or judgment.

The PFC and Psychopathy

Psychopathy is a disorder characterized by antisocial behavior and emotional dysfunction such as shallow affect (weak emotions) and lack of empathy, remorse, and guilt. A distinguishing feature of psychopathy is the presence of both reactive and instrumental aggression. Reactive aggression is typically emotional, impulsive aggression aimed at some perceived threat or risk. It is distinct from instrumental aggression in that it is engaged without any potential goal. Instrumental aggression is goal-oriented and does not require an emotional state such as anger.

Psychopathy plays a very prominent role in criminality. It is estimated that approximately 1 percent of the noninstitutionalized males over age eighteen are psychopaths. However, 16 percent of individuals in prison and jail or on probation or parole are psychopaths.[49]

Cognitive neuroscience has established that dysfunction in two key components of the brain, the amygdala and the vmPFC, is clearly implicated in psychopathy. The amygdala is involved in stimulus-reinforcement learning. Stimulus-reinforcement learning is essential for socialization—for learning proper behavior, social norms, the law, and so forth. Absent the ability to learn in this manner, individuals with impaired amygdala functioning often learn antisocial strategies to achieve goals. Impairment of stimulus-reinforcement learning is characteristic of psychopaths and drives much of the syndrome.[50] Psychopaths fail to respond in typical ways to reinforcement or punishment, and they have diminished capacity for empathy-based learning. The dysfunction of the amygdala sheds considerable light on the characteristic behaviors of psychopaths.

Dysfunction of the vmPFC among psychopaths leads to impaired decision making, increased antisocial behavior, increased frustration in attempting to achieve goals, and, in turn, an increased probability of reactive aggression.

In light of what cognitive neuroscience tells us about dysfunction of the amygdala and the vmPFC among psychopaths, it should be obvious that punishing psychopaths for criminal behavior and expecting their behavior to change as a result is futile. However, that is precisely what we continue to do as we watch the revolving door spin. Recent research from Britain confirms that distinctive neural dysfunctions among violent offenders with antisocial personality disorder and psychopathy can severely impair the ability to learn from punishment.[51]

While research on neurocognitive impairment, executive dysfunction, and criminality is still emerging, there currently is some quite compelling evidence. A 2011 meta-analysis, based on 126 studies, found a clear, robust relationship between executive dysfunction and antisocial behavior.[52] A more recent study found that particular executive dysfunctions are implicated in crime.[53] The most common executive dysfunctions among prison inmates compared to controls include impaired impulse control (the inability to suppress harmful impulses), impaired set shifting (impaired ability to change perspectives, such as changing from dysfunctional behavior to pro-social behavior, or to develop new responses to situations), and impaired working memory (difficulty working toward goals). The authors conclude that

> executive dysfunction in regular prisoners has important implications
> for future reoffending. . . . Out of various treatment strategies, e.g.,
> sanctions and supervision, rehabilitation treatment and cognitive be-
> havior interventions, cognitive behavior interventions focusing on im-
> proving specific cognitive skills (e.g., inhibition) were found to be the
> most effective in decreasing recidivism.[54]

Origins of PFC Dysfunction

Prevalence estimates establish a clear overrepresentation of individuals with a traumatic brain injury (TBI) among criminal offenders. For example, more than half of samples of domestic violence perpetrators had a TBI; more than 80 percent of individuals entering the Australian prison system self-reported a TBI.[55] A longitudinal study in Sweden of more than 200,000 individuals revealed that there was a three-fold increase in violent crime after a TBI.[56]

Research has made considerable progress in elucidating the link between traumatic brain injury and criminality. One involves elevations in norepinephrine in TBI patients. Norepinephrine has been correlated with aggression and impulsive behavior. Another link involves increases in dopamine levels in TBI patients, resulting in aggression and agitation. Moreover, TBI has been associated with reduced levels of serotonin, which again leads to heightened impulsivity and aggression.[57] These changes to neurotransmitter levels, as well as damage to brain white matter, increase the likelihood of significant post-TBI disturbances in PFC-mediated cognition, emotion, and behavior.[58]

TBI is also implicated in executive dysfunction. TBI has been linked to attention deficits, impulse control, memory deficits, and difficulty controlling anger.[59] The evidence implicates injury to the dorsolateral prefrontal subcortical circuit (DLPFC), the part of the PFC that subserves executive functioning. The DLPFC facilitates autonomous, self-directed behavior, as well as normatively appropriate, flexible, and adaptive responses to the challenges and contingencies of day-to-day life. Injury to the DLPFC compromises problem solving and increases the likelihood of engaging in behavior that is environmentally bound (i.e., behavior that is the same regardless of the context or situation). The result of injury to the DLPFC is an impaired ability to engage appropriate adaptive responses to difficult or stressful situations, in turn increasing the likelihood of inappropriate reactions like aggression.

In short, TBI is associated with an increased probability of aggression and violence, and TBI with PFC dysfunction reduces the ability to control or inhibit that violent behavior.

Poverty is associated with a variety of measures of well-being including physical health, school performance, cognitive ability, and behavioral outcomes. For example, children living in poverty are 1.3 times more likely to have learning disabilities and experience developmental delays.[60] Moreover, children living in poverty are more likely to experience emotional and behavioral problems.

There is a good bit of evidence showing a relationship between poverty and executive dysfunction. In particular, poverty appears to have more of a negative effect on working memory and cognitive control, as well as language.[61] Recent research shows a significant relationship between poverty and the structural development of the brain. In particular, measures of socioeconomic status were significantly related to overall brain size, particularly in areas that affect executive functioning, memory, and language.[62]

Exposure to lead has been shown to impact a variety of developmental domains, leading the Centers for Disease Control to declare many years ago that no level of lead exposure is considered safe. Additional research has established that measurable behavioral outcomes are associated with lead exposure.[63] In particular, lead exposure was associated with heightened levels of violent, nonviolent, and total crime.

Poverty is also associated with problematic parenting skills, abuse, and neglect. Research has established a clear link between these types of emotional deprivation and the development of traits of psychopathy or sociopathy.

> Abuse and neglect, combined with prenatal insults to normal brain development, both of which are more common in lower-SES environments, lead to early predisposition to antisocial behavior which, with the right genetic profile, may reach psychopathic/sociopathic proportions. . . . Thus, this study, along with many others that have looked at the neurobiological consequences of abuse and neglect, shows that children who suffer early socioemotional deprivation can indeed develop a number of the neurobiological abnormalities seen in psychopathy.[64]

A broader inventory of negative experiences is contained in the Adverse Childhood Experiences (ACEs) database. The ACEs database consists of emotional abuse, physical abuse, sexual abuse, and household dysfunction including substance abuse, mental illness, domestic violence, parental separation or divorce, and incarceration of a member of the household. Among other findings is that criminal offenders are much more likely than non-criminal controls to have been exposed to substantially more adverse childhood experiences.[65] The offender group reported four times as many adverse experiences as the control group.[66] The authors interpret their findings based on the abundant research literature on factors affecting neurodevelopment and structural and functional impairments to the brain. That is, they rely on neurobiological dysfunction as the mediating factor in their finding of a positive relationship between frequency of adverse childhood experiences and criminality.

MENTAL ILLNESS AND CRIME

The *Washington Post* headline of June 7, 2016, declared "Mental Health Crisis Ensnares Inmates, Judges, Jailers and Hospitals." The story unfortunately was not news. It just detailed the problems associated with dealing with seriously mentally ill (SMI) individuals in the justice system in a couple of counties in Maryland. There is nothing unique about these counties or the state of Maryland. In essentially every jurisdiction in the United States, local criminal justice officials have been charged with managing a public health crisis of exponential proportions. As the *Post* story indicates, in a survey of twenty-five states, more than 1,950 SMI inmates are in local jails awaiting transfer to psychiatric hospitals. The executive director of the nonprofit Treatment Advocacy Center based in Virginia is quoted as saying, "If you design a system to treat these people as ineffectively and expensively as possible, you'd use jails the way we do."

The problem of relying on local jails and courts to manage the mental health crisis is not getting better. Rather, the front door to the jail is simply being opened more widely. The *Post* article notes that between 2011 and 2015, the number of inmates booked into Maryland's Montgomery County jail in need of mental health intervention increased by over 113 percent, from 1,011 to 2,137. A profound lack of resources, including inadequate inpatient psychiatric hospital beds as well as often nonexistent outpatient treatment, have turned jails into makeshift holding facilities and judges into case managers. This is not what the criminal justice system was designed to do, it does not have the resources to do it, and it is not something that it does well. However, the extraordinary prevalence of the mentally ill in the U.S. criminal justice system is one of the primary reasons that recidivism rates are so high today. It is also one of the primary reasons that the administration of criminal justice is so breathtakingly expensive. We now turn to a discussion of mental illness in general and the mentally ill in the U.S. criminal justice system.

Adult Mental Illness and Criminality

The replication of the National Comorbidity Survey[67] updated prevalence and severity statistics for mental illness in the United States among individuals eighteen years of age and older. The estimates were based on diagnoses in the *Diagnostic and Statistical Manual of Mental Disorders*, fourth edition. The data, published in 2005, revealed that the twelve-month prevalence in the general population of any mental health disorder was 26 percent. This represents nearly fifty-eight million individuals in the United States, or the combined populations of Texas, New York, and Ohio.

The most common specific diagnoses were anxiety disorders (18 percent), mood disorders (10 percent), impulse control disorders (9 percent), and substance abuse disorders (4 percent). Nearly 15 percent of those with a disorder had only one; about 6 percent had two diagnoses, and

6 percent had three or more. Among those with any disorder, nearly a quarter were classified as serious, 37 percent as moderate, and 40 percent as mild. Severity was strongly related to comorbidity—10 percent with one diagnosis, 25 percent with two, and 50 percent with three or more were classified as serious. Another view of this information reveals that about 5 percent of the entire adult population in the United States suffers from a serious mental illness. The results also confirm the relationship between socioeconomic disadvantage and mental illness.

Substance use disorders are very common among individuals with another mental illness diagnosis. Among individuals with a past year substance abuse disorder, nearly 40 percent had an additional mental health diagnosis. Among those without a substance abuse disorder, only 16 percent had a mental illness diagnosis.[68] Substance abuse disorders are especially common among individuals with a severe mental illness disorder, including bipolar disorder, schizoaffective disorder, and schizophrenia.[69]

Data from the National Alliance on Mental Illness indicate that 60 percent of adults with a mental illness received no treatment services in the past year.[70] The bottom line is that the majority were either untreated or poorly treated. Access to treatment is largely a function of socioeconomic status.[71] To aggravate that situation, nearly 570,000 mentally ill individuals in the United States are uninsured. Under the provisions of the Affordable Care Act (Obamacare), those uninsured individuals could have received mental health treatment if the states they were living in had decided to expand Medicaid—states like Texas, Louisiana, Kansas, Utah, Mississippi, Florida, Alabama, Georgia, and the Carolinas. The vast majority of the states that elected not to extend Medicaid to the poorest in their states were led by Republican-controlled legislatures and Republican governors. On top of that, states reduced their spending on public mental health treatment by $4.35 billion between 2009 and 2012. The National Alliance on Mental Illness has concluded that

> significant cuts to general fund appropriations for state mental health agencies have translated to severe shortages of services, including housing, community-based treatment and access to psychiatric medications. Increasingly, emergency rooms, homeless shelters and jails are struggling with the effects of people falling through the cracks . . . due to lack of needed mental health services and supports.[72]

Many of those individuals who lack access to mental health treatment end up in the criminal justice system. To be clear, this flooding of U.S. prisons and jails with mentally ill individuals is partly the result of very deliberate, conscious decisions by state legislatures and Congress to dramatically roll back funding and capacity for public mental health treatment.

The most commonly cited source (a 2006 Bureau of Justice Statistics report) for the presence of mentally ill individuals in U.S. prisons and jails indicates that about 45 percent of federal prison inmates, 56 percent of state prison inmates, and nearly two-thirds of local jail inmates have a mental health problem.[73] These statistics represent approximately 1.26 million individuals in state and federal prisons and local jails—705,600 in state prisons, 78,800 in federal prisons, and 480,000 in local jails. To add some perspective, the state prison figure of 705,600 mentally ill inmates represents the entire prison populations of Texas, California, Florida, New York, Arizona, Georgia, Illinois, Ohio, and Pennsylvania.

Common disorders include anxiety, antisocial personality disorder, PTSD, major depressive disorder, and bipolar disorder. Substance abuse disorders are very common among inmate populations.[74]

Estimates are varied regarding how many prison and jail inmates with a mental health problem have a serious mental illness. Serious mental illness is usually defined in terms of diagnoses of major depression, bipolar disorder, and schizophrenia. The "best guesses" put it between 10 and 25 percent.[75]

By way of comparison, the prevalence estimates of mentally ill prison and jail inmates are six to twelve times that of community-based, non-justice-involved individuals. Without question, the mentally ill are substantially overrepresented in the inmate population.

The same Bureau of Justice Statistics study also looked at the co-occurrence of a mental health problem and substance abuse. Three-quarters of state prison inmates with a mental health problem also had a substance abuse problem. Of those without a mental health problem, 56 percent had a substance abuse disorder. A very similar pattern is found in local jails—much higher comorbidity of mental illness with substance abuse.

Studies of mental illness among probation and parole populations are few and far between. Estimates put the prevalence of mental illness among community supervision populations between 25 and 45 percent.[76]

While research on treatment of mentally ill prison and jail inmates is sparse, the consensus is that the majority do not receive any treatment while incarcerated. For those who do, very little information is available regarding the quality and extent of that care. Two surveys conducted by the U.S. Department of Justice in 2002 and 2004 indicate that less than half of prison and jail inmates with a mental health problem had ever received any treatment for that problem. Fewer still reported that they had received any treatment while incarcerated. [77]

An important question is: What is the link between mental illness and crime? There obviously is a profound connection between the two, but how do we understand the link between the justice system and the mentally disordered offender, other than the fact that there are few other places for mentally ill individuals to go?

The answer, which is supported by evidence from dozens of scientific research studies investigating a variety of mental illnesses as well as a number of different crimes, may be surprising. Despite what one may think due to the presence of so many mentally ill individuals in the criminal justice system, it does not appear that criminal involvement is routinely directly linked to mental illness. In fact, only about 10 percent of crimes committed by mentally ill individuals are directly related to the symptoms of their disorder.

The research evidence is clear—it is not mental illness itself that is predictive of violent or nonviolent crime. For example, one major study estimated that only 4–13 percent of crimes were mostly or completely due directly to the symptoms of a mental illness. [78] The extent to which crimes were directly a result of symptoms varies by disorder: 3, 4 and 10 percent of crimes, respectively, were directly related to the symptoms of depression, schizophrenia, and bipolar disorder. Even individual offenders were inconsistent in terms of their crimes being directly related to their mental illness. This makes sense, given that there is no plausible model that explains why criminal offending should be a direct result of mental illness. [79]

Rather than criminal offending being largely a result of the symptoms of a serious mental illness, it is the co-occurrence or comorbidity of mental illness and substance abuse disorders that is responsible for much of the criminal justice involvement of the mentally ill. This pattern of crime being a function of the comorbidity with substance use disorders has been consistently found for bipolar disorder and violent crime, [80] schizophrenia and violent crime,[81] and major depression and violent crime.[82] The relationship between mental illness, substance abuse, and criminality also holds across a variety of other psychiatric diagnoses in addition to the three primary serious mental illnesses.[83] This combination of mental illness and substance abuse accounts for roughly seven out of ten violent acts committed by mentally disordered individuals.[84]

Earlier, we discussed the role of trauma in neurocognitive impairments. A separate line of research on trauma, civilian post-traumatic stress disorder, and criminality is reporting strong links with criminal justice involvement. The prevalence of PTSD in the general population is estimated to range between 9 and 12 percent. However, the evidence indicates a pronounced concentration of PTSD in inner-city, poor, minority neighborhoods.[85] Studies of urban minority individuals living in poverty show rates of PTSD and trauma-related disorders four times that of the general population.[86] Comorbidity of PTSD with substance use disorders is also common. Moreover, recent studies show a very strong relationship between PTSD and arrest, commission of a violent crime, and incarceration in jail or prison, controlling for factors such as income, employment, gender, race, and substance abuse.[87]

The mentally ill in the justice system are not a homogeneous group. Some enter the justice system after being arrested for low-level misdemeanor public-order crimes that are often related to the symptoms of their disorders. Still others enter because of common risk factors like poverty, homelessness, and family instability, factors that often are exacerbated by mental illness. Moreover, the common presence of substance abuse disorders among those with serious mental illness, estimated at 50–75 percent,[88] as well as less serious mental disorders, provides a direct avenue into the criminal justice system on drug possession charges. Moreover, the research indicates that the risk of recidivism is clearly linked to mental illness and substance abuse. That combination of mental illness and substance abuse, along with generally inadequate or nonexistent drug and mental health treatment in the justice system, contribute to the nearly endless cycle of arrest–conviction–incarceration–release–repeat. Individuals with mental illness not only recidivate more frequently than controls without mental illness but also reoffend more quickly after release.[89] As one of the leading experts on mental illness and crime states:

[T]he current war on drugs and the high rate of comorbidity between drug use and psychiatric disorders accounts partially for the large numbers of PSMI [persons with serious mental illness] in our nation's jails and prisons. Fragmented drug and mental health treatment systems fail to provide fully integrated care for persons with such co-occurring disorders, compounding their problems in both areas of concern and elevating the risk for arrest and incarceration. PSMI share many of the same socioeconomic and other characteristics as criminally involved people (young, unemployed, poor, uneducated, substance using) and live in the same criminogenic neighborhoods where the presence of police and the likelihood of arrest are high (especially for drug crimes), presenting an expansive gateway for PSMI to enter the criminal justice system.[90]

The research shows that the appropriate interventions in situations like we have described here are more complex than many assume. Because of the very common comorbidity of mental illness with substance use disorders, failure to address the substance use disorder will do little to reduce recidivism. Moreover, the presence of many of the more common crime-related risk factors among mentally ill offenders, such as a history of violent behavior, parental arrest record, homelessness, unemployment, and poverty,[91] also requires that attention be paid to these matters as well as the mental illness.

CONCLUSIONS

Many criminal offenders enter the criminal and juvenile justice systems with a variety of significant disorders, impairments, and deficits. Many are psychiatric and substance abuse disorders, some are neurodevelopmental or neurocognitive impairments, others involve diminished intellectual abilities, and many are situational such as poverty, unemployment, homelessness, poor education, the typical problems associated with having a criminal record, and gang affiliation, among others. Moreover, trauma and its mental health, substance abuse, and neurodevelopmental consequences have significant implications for criminality.

While it may be convenient, and to some degree comforting, to rely on the conventional wisdom that crime is mainly a matter of making bad decisions, which in turn justifies our reliance on punishment as a way to convince offenders to make better decisions, the reality is that many criminal offenders present with multiple, complex crime-related disorders, impairments, and problems. All of these contribute in various and important ways to crime and recidivism.

The unfortunate reality is that the criminal justice system is not where individuals with such disorders and impairments can get much help. That is not the business of the justice system, which is reflected in the remarkably inadequate funding of correctional treatment and the culture of punishment that pervades American corrections.

The good news is that we are in a much better position today to grasp the scope and complexity of factors that contribute to criminality and recidivism. The other good news is that much can be done to reduce crime and recidivism by focusing on screening, assessing, and appropriately addressing these crime-related problems, disorders, and deficits utilizing evidence-based interventions. We will spend considerable time discussing where the evidence indicates our efforts and funding should be focused to effectively change behavior, reduce crime and recidivism, and save money. All this is placed squarely within the context of broader efforts at criminal and juvenile justice reform.

What is clear to us is that the types of disorders we are describing here cannot be effectively addressed with any real success by the justice system. It is not designed and resourced to do that. The justice system does one thing well—punishment. Unfortunately, punishment does little to mitigate these crime-related disorders and deficits. What we propose is diversion from traditional criminal adjudication, conviction, and punishment to community-based intervention and rehabilitation. That minimizes the recidivism-enhancing effects of justice system involvement and mitigates these disorders and impairments.

3

THE SPECIAL CASE OF
THE JUVENILE BRAIN

NEURODEVELOPMENTAL AND
NEUROCOGNITIVE ISSUES

The rate at which sixteen- to eighteen-year-olds are involved in motor vehicle accidents is three to seven times that of drivers twenty-five to sixty-five years old. The rate at which eighteen- to twenty-five-year-olds are diagnosed with a substance use disorder is three times that of individuals twenty-six and older.[1] The top three causes of death among adults are heart disease, cancer, and stroke. The top three for adolescents are accidents, homicide, and suicide.[2] The morbidity and mortality rates for adolescents are 200 percent higher compared to children. As a leading child and adolescent psychiatrist states:

> This doubling in rates of death and disability from the period of early school age into late adolescence and early adulthood is not the result of cancer, heart disease or mysterious infection. Rather, the major sources of death and disability in adolescents are related to *difficulties in the control of behavior and emotion.*

Figure 3.1 is what is referred to as the age-crime curve. It shows the typical age distribution of involvement in crime, reflecting the fact that individuals between the ages of twelve and nineteen are involved in crime at rates two to five times that of adults. Once youth reach age twenty, the rate of crime involvement drops dramatically.

Figure 3.1 confirms what the Surgeon General's report on youth violence shows—between 30 and 40 percent of boys and between 16 and 32 percent of girls commit a serious violent crime by age seventeen.[3] These prevalence statistics for youth are ten to twenty times that for adults. By age twenty, 80 percent of youth involved in violent crime cease offending. For a variety of reasons, there are circumstances and conditions unique to youth that tend to make them prone to crime.

What these statistics on motor vehicle accidents, morbidity and mortality, substance abuse disorders, and crime reflect is that adolescents are dramatically more likely to engage in risky behavior compared to children and adults. An obvious question is why, and for answers we turn to neuroscience.

Neurodevelopment

The natural course of the development of the brain provides a compelling explanation for the heightened risk-taking behaviors seen among adolescents. In effect, the behavior of adolescents is governed in large part by a developmental sequence that begins around puberty and initially involves the development of the limbic system of the brain, specifically the amygdala (which is associated with aggressive and impulsive behavior) and the

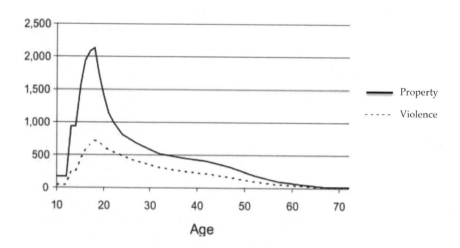

Figure 3.1. The Age-Crime Curve (data from 2008 UCR arrest data and current population data from U.S. census; available at https://www2.fbi.gov/ucr/cius2008/)

nucleus accumbens (the dopamine-rich area of the brain associated with reward processing). The limbic system, which is referred to as the motivational system of the brain, is implicated in matters such as the recognition of socially relevant stimuli, social judgments, assessing others' intentions, social reasoning, and other dimensions of the processing of social information, reward seeking, and emotions.

This developmental sequence involves changes in the dopaminergic system of the brain as well.[4] Roughly around the onset of puberty, adolescents experience a dramatic increase in dopaminergic activity in the motivational systems of the brain. At the same time, adolescents have relatively lower levels of serotonin, which is the neurotransmitter responsible for inhibitory control.

These changes to the brain that begin around puberty drive dopamine-reinforced impulsive, reflexive, risky, sensation-seeking behavior as a consequence of increases in reward salience and sensitivity. Reward sensitivity is understood as increased motivation to obtain reward and an increased arousal as a consequence of reward. It also involves a heightened sensitivity to emotional stimuli, which in turn causes adolescents to act impulsively, in part by prioritizing short-term rewards or gains over long-term rewards. In effect, it biases adolescents to being present oriented rather than future oriented. Moreover, the evidence indicates that engaging in risky behavior is more likely in the presence of peers.

The neuroscience of brain development dispels myths that the risky behavior of adolescents is a function of ignorance, irrationality, or perceptions of invulnerability. Rather, it is a reflection of how the typical adolescent brain develops, evaluates rewards, responds to rewards, interprets social situations, makes judgments, and interprets the actions of others, among other functions.

This development of the limbic system and associated changes to the dopaminergic system typically occur before the full development of the prefrontal cortex (PFC), which is the system responsible for self-regulation, cognitive control, and behavior control. It is this disjuncture or imbalance between the development of the limbic system and the PFC that is largely responsible for the risky behaviors typical of adolescents. In essence, adolescents are subject to brain changes that drive impulsive, reflexive, risky behavior (the accelerator) without the full development of the part of the brain that is associated with emotional and behavioral regulation (the brakes).

The decline in impulsive, emotionally reactive, risky behavior, including criminal behavior, is understood neurobiologically in terms of the development of the self-regulatory capacity of the PFC. The PFC involves a number of important cognitive abilities, such as executive functioning. It also integrates information across various parts of the brain, which supports control over more impulsive behaviors, planning of voluntary goal-focused behavior, more accurate risk assessment, and the proper evaluation of rewards and punishments. In essence, the developed PFC facilitates decision making, making moral judgments, assessing and evaluating future consequences of actions, working memory, and response inhibition.

There are three important ways in which the adolescent PFC is immature and thus unable to effectively control behavior. First, as the PFC develops, there is a reduction in gray matter associated with what is called synaptic pruning, a process whereby unused neuronal connections are eliminated. This pruning enhances the ability of complex information processing and executive functioning. Pruning and maturation of the gray matter of the brain takes place through adolescence and into adulthood, and it is largely a function of an individual's experience.

Pruning is used as an indicator of brain maturation. The developmental timing of pruning of the PFC means that the PFC is one of the last areas to fully mature. As concluded in a joint amici curiae brief prepared by the American Medical Association and the American Academy of Child and Adolescent Psychiatry:

> This means that one of the last areas of the brain to reach full maturity, as measured by pruning, is the region most closely associated with risk assessment, impulse control, emotional regulation, decision-making and planning—in other words, the ability to reliably and voluntarily control behavior.[5]

The second important process that reflects the maturity of the brain is referred to as myelination, or the insulation of neuronal connections with a fatty white matter called myelin. This insulation of the connections makes communication among parts of the brain faster, more efficient, and more reliable. The process of myelination is ongoing through adolescence and into adulthood.

The third process involves what is called top-down connectivity, or the ability of the executive regions of the PFC to exercise control over the response regions of the brain. Top-down connectivity is part of the developmental process of the brain and continues through adolescence into adulthood. The underdevelopment of top-down connectivity in adolescents further helps our understanding of risky, impulsive, reflexive behaviors.[6] The joint brief by the experts from the American Medical Association and the American Academy of Child and Adolescent Psychiatry sums it up nicely:

> [A]dolescent behavior is characterized by a hyperactive reward-driven system (involving the nucleus accumbens and increased dopamine), a limited harm-avoidant system (involving the amygdala), and an immature cognitive control system (involving the prefrontal cortex and decreased serotonin). As a result, adolescent behavior is more likely to be impulsive and motivated by the possibility of reward, with less self-regulation and effective risk assessment. In other words, the adolescent brain is biologically biased to engage in exploring new environments and experiences, which can involve taking risks.[7]

Neurocognitive Impairments

It was in the late 1990s that the issue of trauma began to gain traction in terms of effects on behavior, cognition, mental health, and brain development. In response, a federal initiative of trauma-informed care was launched. In this section, we focus on the impacts of trauma and maltreatment on the development of the child and the adolescent brain. We also will take a look at the variety and prevalence of adverse childhood experiences, an analysis that links neurobiology and epidemiology.

Just as positive experiences promote healthy brain development, negative experiences such as maltreatment by a caregiver, growing up in an environment of poverty and violence, exposure to environmental toxins such as lead paint or lead in drinking water, and physical injury can lead to significant impairments to brain development and cognitive functioning.

Toxic stress is the term that applies to extreme stress that is associated with frequent, extended activation of the stress management system. The evidence clearly shows that chronic toxic stress can lead to a number of neurodevelopmental and neurocognitive impairments. Severe chronic abuse of children and adolescents can lead the brain to overdevelop neural connections associated with fear, anxiety, and impulsive responses and underproduce those connections related to behavioral control, reasoning, and planning. These changes can lead to an overly sensitive stress response system that is activated for excessively long periods of time. As a result, children and adolescents are more likely to respond impulsively to situations perceived as threatening when in fact they are not.

The stress response system involves the hormonal system known as the hypothalamic-pituitary-adrenal (HPA) system. Under normal stress circumstances, the HPA system releases a series of hormones that assist the body in dealing with stressors, including the mobilization of energy. Long-term or sustained activation of the HPA stress response system can lead to chronic hyperarousal or hypervigilance, a dissociative response, or decreased responsiveness. The effects of toxic stress on the HPA system can be aggravated by the presence of overt physical or sexual abuse or mitigated by the presence of a secure attachment relationship. Behavioral and cognitive implications include significant and substantial impairments to mood regulation and cognitive function such as memory, learning, regulation of the stress response, and failure of response inhibition.[8]

In short, the research supports the conclusion that childhood maltreatment is related to disruption and dysfunction of the HPA axis. In turn, dysfunction of the HPA can lead to emotional and cognitive dysfunction.

Child maltreatment has been linked to a number of behavioral outcomes such as criminality, emotional dysregulation, mood disorders, anxiety disorders, use of threatening behavior, physical abuse against dating partners, substance use, and other high-risk behaviors.[9] Child maltreatment is associated with poor performance on assessments designed to measure cognitive functioning. Childhood maltreatment and neglect have been linked to functional brain development including a variety of cognitive impairments affecting short-term verbal memory, executive functioning, impulse control, attention, academic performance and learning, and memory. Other impairments affect abstract reasoning, the speed of information processing, mental flexibility, and inhibition.

Chronic stress and child maltreatment have also been implicated in a variety of structural impacts on the brain. One of the more consistent findings is reduced size of the corpus callosum. This part of the brain is involved in inter-regional communication involving processes such as arousal, emotion, and higher cognition. These structural impacts have been provisionally linked to cognitive and emotional impairments found among maltreated children.[10]

There is some evidence pointing to a reduction in the size of the hippocampus, that part of the brain responsible for learning and memory. The prefrontal cortex (executive functioning, impulse control, and emotion regulation) can also be negatively affected by childhood maltreatment, resulting in a reduction in the size of the PFC.[11] In turn, an underdeveloped PFC can lead to problems with controlling impulsive behaviors, as well as an increased likelihood of engaging in risky behavior.

Parental neglect is a form of maltreatment that can have profound and widespread consequences for both the structure and the functioning of the child and adolescent brain. Research has found significant structural abnormalities in various areas of the brain among children who have experienced neglect. These include abnormalities in the hippocampus, the amygdala, the frontal lobe, and the limbic system. Functional impacts include impaired executive functioning, attention, information-processing speed, social skills, language, and memory.[12]

A rather pointed conclusion is that maltreated children often "develop brains that focus on survival, at the expense of the more advanced thinking that happens in the brain's cortex."[13]

We now turn to the broader question of the effects of poverty on behavioral risk, the structure and function of the brain, and neurocognitive impairment.

Today 21 percent, or 15.4 million, children under eighteen years of age live in poverty. Over 31 million children under eighteen years of age live in low-income households. The effects of poverty on behavior are well established—children and adolescents (as well as adults) have poorer cognitive abilities and academic performance, as well as a higher risk of engaging in antisocial and violent behavior. Contributing factors include nutrition, parental care and attachment, stress, exposure to environmental toxins, and lack of cognitive stimulation.[14] Research has demonstrated that a variety of neurocognitive systems are implicated in the behavioral and intellectual outcomes associated with poverty, especially memory, executive function and cognitive control, stress regulation, and language development.[15]

The question that has been a recent focus of neurobiological research is the impact of poverty on brain structure and function. Poverty is associated with a variety of negative experiences including family turmoil, marital instability, violence, lack of social support, lack of proper parental attachment, reduced cognitive stimulation, and fewer learning resources.

The results indicate significant and substantial negative effects of poverty and factors related to it on the hippocampus, the amygdala, and the prefrontal cortex. For example, imaging research utilizing appropriate controls has confirmed significant reduction of the size of the hippocampus and amygdala in children who have been raised in poverty.[16] These findings are important because the hippocampus and amygdala are involved in stress regulation and the processing of emotion. Earlier, we discussed the negative consequences of dysfunction of the stress response system and processing of emotions.[17] A leading expert states the impact of poverty on neurocognitive functioning as follows:

> The stress response is one pathway by which SES status affects neurophysiology and cognitive function of low-income youth. Stress activates several neuropeptide-secreting systems, primarily the hypothalamic-pituitary-adrenal (HPA) axis' "fight or flight" response. In the short term, the HPA axis mobilizes energy resources to deal with the stressor by producing corticosteroids, such as cortisol. Over time, however, chronic stress leads to the overproduction of cortisol, which can lead to hippocampal cell death.[18]

One of the more consistent research findings regarding structural abnormalities of the brain is a reduced hippocampus volume among children living in poverty.[19] The largest study to date, involving one thousand children aged three to twenty years, assessed the relationship between parental education and hippocampal volume. The research revealed significant differences in the surface area of the children's cerebral cortex as a function of educational attainment. Low levels of parental education were associated with smaller surface areas of the cerebral cortex, especially in areas that are responsible for language, reading, and self-regulation.[20]

Poverty also has substantial consequences for executive functioning, primarily through the prefrontal cortex. Research has established that poverty and its common correlates such as lack of cognitive stimulation, inattention from parents and caregivers, and stress have significant negative impacts on the functioning of the PFC, very similar to the functioning of the PFC among individuals with lateral PFC lesions.[21] The evidence indicates that exposure to poverty results in reductions in attention, working memory, and inhibitory control in infancy, adolescence, and adulthood.[22] Additional studies have documented impaired executive functioning and cognitive control among children and adolescents raised in poverty.[23] Behavioral outcomes associated with PFC impairment include impulsive decision making, problems with selective attention, and deficits in cognition, reading, and language.

There is also evidence of structural and developmental delays for the brains of children growing up in poverty. Studies confirm that the development of the PFC is delayed significantly in children who live in households with low socioeconomic status.[24]

A study published in 2013 found that low socioeconomic status (SES) is associated with lower volumes of frontal lobe gray matter in toddlers and children up to four years of age.[25] The differences in frontal lobe development between the low SES subjects and controls widened with age, a product of continued exposure to the cumulative, negative effects of poverty. Prior research has established impaired executive functioning among low SES children and adolescents. The 2013 study provides a compelling structural, developmental explanation for impaired planning, decision making, and impulse control, in turn linking these deficits with behavioral problems.

A prospective study followed individuals from birth to age twenty-five to determine the long-term effects of poverty on brain structure.[26] The results indicated that early exposure to poverty resulted in a lower volume of the orbitofrontal cortex (OFC), a part of the frontal cortex involved with cognitive processing, decision making, and adaptive learning (i.e., learning from reward and punishment). The reduced volume of the OFC persisted into young adulthood for those who had early exposure to poverty.

The Adverse Childhood Experiences (ACEs) research, a collaboration between Kaiser Permanente and the Centers for Disease Control, is a study that consists of data on a number of negative or toxic experiences that occur in childhood and are the basis for epidemiological research investigating a variety of behavioral outcomes. A 2012 review of research[27] on the effects of adverse childhood experiences on neurodevelopment and functioning of the frontal lobe concluded that the most consistent findings among children who had adverse psychosocial experiences was a reduction in the size of the frontal lobe. This deficit in the volume of the PFC is accompanied by impaired executive functioning and behavioral problems. The research also shows that deficits in the volume of the PFC persist into adulthood. Both children and adults who had adverse childhood experiences had structural abnormalities (reduced volume of the PFC) and functional impairments (impaired executive functioning and impulse control). These abnormalities are likely linked to behavioral problems such as substance abuse, antisocial behavior, impulsivity, and conduct problems.

An important study analyzing the relationship between the number of adverse childhood experiences and behavioral outcomes found some very compelling results. The number of adverse childhood experiences was strongly related to the prevalence of mental health disorders (affective disorders, panic attacks, depression, anxiety, and hallucinations), substance abuse (smoking, alcoholism, illicit drug use, and intravenous drug use), risky sexual behavior, impaired memory, stress, impaired ability to control anger, and risk of engaging in intimate partner violence. The researchers also found that the number of adverse childhood experiences was related to the number of comorbid or co-occurring outcomes. These epidemiological findings are consistent with neurobiological research on the impacts of trauma, stress, neglect, and poverty on brain development, structure, and function.[28]

The point of this discussion of the neurodevelopmental and neurocognitive impacts of poverty and adverse childhood experiences is to determine the extent to which these functional impairments and structural deficits of the brain can help us identify and understand important precursors to crime. While the evidence is continually advancing, the research does allow us to draw a very important conclusion—growing up in poverty, with its collateral disadvantages, and being subject to adverse childhood experiences (which include poverty but other experiences as well) place individuals at significant risk of engaging in crime.

This is not an excuse for criminal offending, but it is an important set of factors to consider. As I concluded in a recent book:

> [M]any chronic, persistent, habitual offenders have neurocognitive and psychosocial impairments, including spatial and verbal impairments, impairments of memory and non-memory cognitive function, intellectual impairments, executive dysfunction, etc. . . . longer-term habitual offenders . . . have pronounced and profound neurocognitive and psychosocial impairments that distinguish them from others. Brain scans comparing antisocial individuals with controls reveal significant reductions in the frontal lobe of the brain (between 9% and 18% reduction), that part of the brain responsible for executive functioning. Com-

parisons of the brains of psychopaths with controls showed deforma-
tions in the amygdala and up to an 18% reduction in the volume of the
amygdala, which is a part of the limbic system responsible for memory
and emotional regulation . . . neuroimaging studies of aggressive, violent and antisocial individuals . . . show consistent patterns of brain
dysfunction and criminal activity, involving the prefrontal lobe . . . and
the neural circuitry regulating emotion in aggressive and violent behavior . . . there is a significant neurological basis of aggression and/or
violent behavior over and above contributions from the psychosocial
environment.[29]

The point is that exposure to poverty and adverse childhood experiences should serve as primary risk factors. It raises the important question
of whether individuals with significant neurodevelopmental deficits and
neurocognitive impairments should be held to the same standards of responsibility as offenders without these deficits and impairments.

The U.S. Supreme Court has provided a partial answer to this question
in a series of cases involving juvenile offenders and the death penalty and
life without parole sentences. We turn to these decisions now.

THE U.S. SUPREME COURT HAS DETERMINED THAT THE ADOLESCENT BRAIN IS DIFFERENT

If there is any doubt that juveniles can be the "low-hanging fruit" in the
criminal justice system, consider what happened to Davontae Sanford. In
2007, at the age of fifteen, Sanford confessed to killing four people when
he was fourteen years of age. He pled guilty to second-degree murder and
was sentenced to prison. It turns out that the murders were committed by
a professional hit man who later confessed to the crimes. Sanford spent
seven years in prison. He was released on June 8, 2016, and the charges
were dismissed.

We do not know the extent to which intellectual or cognitive problems
contributed to Sanford's false confession. Regardless, the point is that
juvenile offenders are different from adults in important ways. The U.S.
Supreme Court has recognized this and provided some limited protections for juveniles.

In a series of cases, beginning in 2005 with *Roper v. Simmons*, the
U.S. Supreme Court has recognized differences between juveniles and

adults in terms of culpability or responsibility due to developmental, structural, and functional impairments in the adolescent brain. *Roper* is the first case that made such distinctions based on neuroscientific evidence.

In 1993, Christopher Simmons, at the age of seventeen, developed a plan to murder a woman named Shirley Crook. The plan involved burglarizing her house, abducting her, and then throwing her off a bridge. Simmons and a friend carried out the plan, and Ms. Crook was murdered by drowning. Simmons was arrested the next day and confessed to the crime after waiving his right to counsel.

The result of *Roper* was to render the death penalty unconstitutional for offenders who committed a capital offense while juveniles. The majority opinion held:

> Three general differences between juveniles under 18 and adults demonstrate that juvenile offenders cannot with reliability be classified among the worst offenders. First, as any parent knows and as the scientific and sociological studies respondent and his amici cite tend to confirm, a lack of maturity and an underdeveloped sense of responsibility are found in youth more often than in adults and are more understandable among the young. These qualities often result in impetuous and ill-considered actions and decisions. Even the normal 16-year-old customarily lacks the maturity of an adult. It has been noted that adolescents are overrepresented statistically in virtually every category of reckless behavior. In recognition of the comparative immaturity and irresponsibility of juveniles, almost every State prohibits those under 18 years of age from voting, serving on juries, or marrying without parental consent.
>
> The second area of difference is that juveniles are more vulnerable or susceptible to negative influences and outside pressures, including peer pressure. Youth is more than a chronological fact. It is a time and condition of life when a person may be most susceptible to influence and to psychological damage. This is explained in part by the prevailing circumstance that juveniles have less control, or less experience with control, over their own environment. As legal minors, juveniles lack the freedom that adults have to extricate themselves from a criminogenic setting.
>
> The third broad difference is that the character of a juvenile is not as well formed as that of an adult. The personality traits of juveniles are more transitory, less fixed. The susceptibility of juveniles to imma-

ture and irresponsible behavior means their irresponsible conduct is not as morally reprehensible as that of an adult. Their own vulnerability and comparative lack of control over their immediate surroundings mean juveniles have a greater claim than adults to be forgiven for failing to escape negative influences in their whole environment. The reality that juveniles still struggle to define their identity means it is less supportable to conclude that even a heinous crime committed by a juvenile is evidence of irretrievably depraved character. From a moral standpoint it would be misguided to equate the failings of a minor with those of an adult, for a greater possibility exists that a minor's character deficiencies will be reformed. Indeed, the relevance of youth as a mitigating factor derives from the fact that the signature qualities of youth are transient; as individuals mature, the impetuousness and recklessness that may dominate in younger years can subside. For most teens, risky or antisocial behaviors are fleeting; they cease with maturity as individual identity becomes settled. Only a relatively small proportion of adolescents who experiment in risky or illegal activities develop entrenched patterns of problem behavior that persist into adulthood. [30]

In *Roper*, we see the court rely on scientific evidence regarding the emotional and cognitive underdevelopment of juveniles as a way of defining anyone who commits a capital crime under age eighteen as categorically less responsible or culpable. The court took a shortcut in that the class of less responsible or culpable juveniles is defined by age rather than by any case-by-case assessment of emotional maturity or neurocognitive development.

Graham v Florida, decided in 2010, based the decision to outlaw life without parole for juvenile offenders largely on neuroscientific evidence. At age sixteen, Terrance Graham attempted to rob a restaurant with three other school-age kids. No money was taken, but the store manager was injured from being hit on the head with a metal bar by one of Graham's accomplices. Graham was arrested and tried as an adult for the first-degree felony charges of armed burglary with assault and battery. Graham pled guilty, and the court withheld adjudication and placed him on twelve months' probation. Graham was rearrested six months later on a new home invasion robbery charge with two other twenty-year-old accomplices. Graham's probation officer filed a motion to revoke probation based on the violations of supervision. The court held a sentencing hearing, and Graham was sentenced to life on the prior armed burglary and fifteen years for the attempted robbery. The sentence was effectively a life without parole sentence since Florida had abolished parole.

The majority opinion included some background information about Graham and his upbringing, including the facts that his parents were addicted to crack cocaine and actively used crack as Graham was growing up. Graham was diagnosed with attention deficit-hyperactivity disorder in elementary school and began drinking alcohol at age nine and smoking marijuana at age thirteen.

The U.S. Supreme Court relied on the findings in *Roper* as well as an influential amici curiae brief by the American Medical Association that argued that the adolescent brain is not fully developed, especially areas of the brain that influence behavioral control: "[D]evelopments in psychology and brain science continue to show fundamental differences between juvenile and adult minds. For example, parts of the brain involved in behavior control continue to mature through late adolescence."[31] For that reason, the court held that life without parole is unconstitutional.

Two additional cases decided together in 2012 (*Miller v. Alabama*; *Jackson v. Hobb*) reinforced the Supreme Court's position on adolescent brain development and responsibility. *Jackson v. Hobb* involved Kuntrell Jackson, a fourteen-year-old male who participated in an armed robbery of a video store. One of the codefendants had a sawed-off shotgun that he used to threaten and then kill the clerk of the video store. Under Arkansas law, the prosecutor has the discretion to charge juveniles as adults under certain conditions, in turn making adult punishment available upon conviction. Jackson was charged as an adult with capital felony murder and aggravated robbery. He was convicted and sentenced to mandatory life without parole. The Arkansas Supreme Court affirmed his conviction and sentence. The majority decision relied heavily on the findings in *Roper* and *Graham* regarding the neurodevelopment of juveniles. The U.S. Supreme Court extended the role of neuroscience in these cases by arguing that the underdevelopment of the adolescent brain impairs higher-order executive functioning such as impulse control, risk avoidance, and planning. The result was the finding that life without parole for juvenile homicide offenders was unconstitutional. The majority held:

> Mandatory life without parole for a juvenile precludes consideration of his chronological age and its hallmark features—among them, immaturity, impetuosity, and failure to appreciate risks and consequences. It prevents taking into account the family and home environment that

surrounds him—and from which he cannot usually extricate himself—
no matter how brutal or dysfunctional.[32]

In 2016, in *Montgomery v. Louisiana*, the U.S. Supreme Court made it
clear that the prohibitions against life without parole for crimes committed by juveniles are retroactive. The court held that life without parole
sentences imposed before *Miller* were unconstitutional. The only exception the court carved out was in situations in which the offender demonstrated "irreparable corruption."

We view these decisions as clear acknowledgment by the Supreme
Court that neurodevelopmental and neurocognitive impairments are important considerations in assessing the culpability or responsibility of
juvenile offenders. At the same time, neuroscience has clearly demonstrated that neurodevelopmental impairments and deficits can and do extend well beyond adolescence, as do their consequences. Here is what we
know.

Experts from the American Academy of Pediatrics and the Centers for
Disease Control,[33] among others, have concluded that the effects of
abuse, stress, and adverse childhood experiences can and do have lasting
effects.

> The organization and functional capacity of the human brain depends
> upon an extraordinary set and sequence of developmental and environ-
> mental experiences that influence the expression of the genome. Un-
> fortunately, this elegant sequence is vulnerable to extreme, repetitive,
> or abnormal patterns of stress during critical or circumscribed periods
> of childhood brain development that can impair, often permanently,
> the activity of major neuroregulatory systems with profound and last-
> ing neurobehavioral consequences. Now, converging evidence from
> neurobiology and epidemiology suggests that early life stress such as
> abuse and related adverse experiences cause enduring brain dysfunc-
> tion.[34]

Subsequent research established that the array of enduring negative
outcomes of adverse childhood experiences includes physical and mental
health disorders, substance abuse, risky behavior, criminality, and aggressive behavior.[35] The researchers concluded that the mediating factors that
account for or explain the relationship between adverse experiences and
crime are neurobiologic dysregulation and attachment pathology.

Neurocognitive impairments are also important predictors of which youth who have been involved in criminal activity will desist engaging in crime (called adolescent limited offenders) versus those who persist into adulthood (called life course persistent, or LCP). A very important 2005 study revealed that the life course persistent offenders were differentiated from adolescent limited offenders in the extent of neurocognitive impairments. The authors conclude that

> the current findings indicate that neurocognitive perspectives are especially applicable to LCP offenders, that both spatial and memory impairments are salient, that neurocognitive impairments cannot be easily explained by psychiatric or psychosocial confounds, and that instead, they may stem from very early environmental or genetic influences.[36]

Additional research by Moffitt and her colleagues further confirms the role of neurodevelopmental impairments (especially executive dysfunction and low self-control) and adverse family experiences in adolescence in accounting for persistent criminality in adulthood.[37] Differences in self-control between individuals are present in early childhood and can predict multiple indicators of health, wealth, and crime across three decades of life in both genders. Furthermore, it was possible to disentangle the effects of children's self-control from effects of variation in the children's intelligence, social class, and home lives of their families, thereby singling out self-control as a clear target for intervention policy.[38]

While the evidence is clear that neurodevelopmental problems and neurocognitive impairments that originate in childhood and adolescence can and do persist past age eighteen, the U.S. Supreme Court has essentially had a hands-off policy regarding implications for adults. A search of U.S. Supreme Court cases regarding neurodevelopmental and neurocognitive impairments in adults resulted in two cases that only tangentially deal with neurological issues in adults. In *Gall v. U.S.*, 552 U.S. 38 (2007), the Supreme Court found that it was not unreasonable for the district court to consider studies at sentencing (cited in *Roper*) that conclude that brain development may not become complete until the age of twenty-five. In *Abdul-Kabir v. Quarterman*, 550 U.S. 233 (2007), the petitioner argued that the trial judge's jury instructions did not allow the jury that sentenced him to death to consider relevant mitigating factors, including past neurological damage. The Supreme Court determined that the instructions prevented jurors from considering relevant mitigating evidence, including the testimony regarding neurological damage.

The absence of a clear class identifier such as age may have deterred the Supreme Court from extending the logic of *Roper*, *Graham*, and other relevant cases to adults who are involved in crime. There is no quick and easy way to demarcate crime-involved adults with a history of neurodevelopmental problems or neurocognitive impairments that persist into adulthood other than on a case-by-case basis. However, such challenges should not drive the law. The evidence is really quite clear—an important subset of juvenile offenders with neurocognitive problems graduate to adult crime. Their impairments accompany them. If the courts are willing to carve out exceptions for juveniles, it is difficult to understand why the same logic should not apply to neuro-impaired adults. It is time for the law to catch up with science.

JUVENILE MENTAL ILLNESS AND SUBSTANCE USE DISORDERS

Today, approximately one in five youth ages eighteen and under has a diagnosable mental illness. Nearly 50 percent of youth ages thirteen to eighteen have a lifetime prevalence of a mental health disorder. Anxiety disorders are the most frequent, followed by behavior disorders, mood disorders, and substance abuse disorders. One in ten currently has a mental disorder that is severe enough to significantly impair day-to-day functioning at school, at home, or in the community. One in five has had (at any point in their lifetime) a serious mental illness. Roughly 8 percent of youth have a substance abuse disorder, and about 10 percent are illicit drug users.[39]

Comorbidity is common, especially a mental health diagnosis in conjunction with a substance abuse disorder. Estimates of co-occurring mental health and substance abuse disorders vary a bit but are generally around 70 percent. One source, Youth.gov, puts it between 60 and 75 percent. The National Center for Children in Poverty indicates that 70 percent of youth in treatment for a substance abuse disorder also have a mental health disorder.[40]

Important risk factors for juvenile mental illness involve a variety of individual and environmental factors. Individual characteristics include gender, age, ethnicity, physical health, alcohol and drug use, and cognitive psychological functioning, among others. Environmental factors include trauma such as exposure to toxins, stress, poor parenting and family functioning, parents' psychiatric history, living in poverty, and being in foster care. Nearly 60 percent of youth with a mental disorder come from households at or below the federal poverty level.

The majority of youth with a mental health disorder (50–75 percent and more) do not receive any treatment services.[41] For those who have received treatment services, the average time between onset of symptoms (which for over 90 percent of individuals with mental health disorders occurs in childhood or adolescence) and accessing treatment is ten years.

National data estimate that approximately two million youth between the ages of twelve and seventeen are in need of substance abuse treatment. Less than 10 percent of those youth will receive any substance abuse treatment. Still fewer receive treatment in a facility specializing in substance abuse treatment.[42]

The consequences of mental health disorders among youth are widespread and often substantial. They struggle to succeed in school and, as a result, are at a much higher risk of suspension and expulsion, missed school days, and dropping out. Those in the child welfare system are less likely to be placed in permanent homes.

Access to mental health services varies by state—the best case state has 51 percent unmet mental health treatment need; the worst case state has 81 percent unmet need.[43] The American Academy of Child and Adolescent Psychiatry has documented that approximately fifteen million children and adolescents are in need of the special expertise of child and adolescent psychiatrists. However, there are only 8,300 practicing child and adolescent psychiatrists in the United States. The numbers obviously are not manageable. On top of too few practicing psychiatrists, there is the cost issue. A clear link exists between insurance coverage and mental health treatment. Individuals with insurance (private pay, Medicaid, or State Children's Health Insurance Programs) are well over twice as likely to access mental health treatment compared to those without insurance.[44]

Access to care is only one aspect of adequate mental health care. Quality of care regarding mental health and substance abuse treatment of youth is often unknown. There are no ongoing national-level efforts to collect quality of care metrics. The research that does exist raises serious questions about quality of care. For example, one study that used the

American Psychiatric Association recommendations for treating major depression found that only 34 percent of adolescents had received adequate treatment. Another study using the American Academy of Child and Adolescent Psychiatry guidelines for treating children and adolescents with depressive disorders found that only 28–34 percent of those treated met the guidelines.

Researchers at the National Center for Children in Poverty have noted:

> Even among those children and youth who are able to access mental health services, quality of care is often deficient. There is an insufficient number of providers, and many of them do not use effective, evidence-based, or empirically supported practices. The service delivery system lacks key elements of supportive infrastructure which results in poor provider capacity and competency.[45]

JUVENILE MENTAL ILLNESS, SUBSTANCE USE DISORDERS, AND CRIMINALITY

In 2003 and 2004, the lead author of this book was a principal in a prevalence study of mental illness in the juvenile justice system.[46] He headed the data collection in Texas, which included conducting interviews and reviewing medical and psychiatric records for juveniles in secure detention (prison and jail) and in halfway houses for those released from detention. There were several remarkable things about this experience, but three that are persistent include (1) what horrific childhoods many of these youth had experienced; (2) how extensive the psychiatric histories were for these juveniles; and (3) how lost these kids seemed. Sparing details, the things that many of these kids went through growing up, experiences documented in their records, are almost incomprehensible. For some, it was a result of growing up in poverty, but much of it was associated with profoundly dysfunctional families of origin, with experiences including abandonment, sexual abuse, physical abuse, and constant exposure to drugs and alcohol, among many, many others. Moreover, as a result of many of these experiences as well as inherited predispositions, these kids, many of whom were even too young to legally drive, had multiple and often serious psychiatric disorders. Some of their files were in multiple binders consisting of hundreds and hundreds of pages.

As I mentioned, many of the juveniles whom I interviewed and observed just seemed lost. One girl I interviewed was barely fifteen years old and, without being asked, told me about the long-term sexual abuse perpetrated by her extended family beginning when she was eight, her early onset drug use, and the fact that she became a prostitute at age eleven. All of this was documented in her history, so she was not making it up. These facts are horrific. However, the thing that stuck with me is the fact that as she was telling me her story, her eyes were empty—like no one was there. It seemed she had given up—at age fifteen.

Every year, approximately two million youth (under age eighteen) are arrested, and the vast majority of those arrests are for nonviolent felonies and misdemeanors. Nearly six hundred thousand are subsequently placed in juvenile detention centers and seventy thousand end up in correctional facilities (prison).

What is particularly striking about juvenile offenders is the prevalence of mental illness. Study after study has confirmed that youth with mental illness are substantially overrepresented in the juvenile justice system. Approximately 20 percent of the general adolescent population has a mental health disorder; roughly 70 percent of youth in the juvenile justice system have at least one mental illness including substance abuse.[47] Conduct disorders are common (nearly 50 percent of justice-involved youth), as are substance abuse disorders (also nearly 50 percent of those youth in the justice system). Moreover, between 20 and 30 percent of juvenile offenders have a mental health disorder that is serious enough to require immediate, substantial treatment. The corresponding statistic for the non-offending youth population is 10 percent.[48]

Comorbidity is quite prevalent among juvenile offenders with a mental health problem. Estimates vary across studies, but what they all confirm is that comorbidity is quite common. One of the more comprehensive studies reported that nearly 80 percent of justice-involved youth who met the criteria for one mental health diagnosis also met the criteria for two or more diagnoses.[49] The majority of those with one diagnosis also met the criteria for a substance abuse disorder (over 60 percent).

A review of more than one thousand articles, books, and reports by the Columbia University National Center on Addiction and Substance Abuse led to a number of very important conclusions.[50] First, they found that substance abuse was fundamentally related to the vast majority of crimes committed by juvenile offenders (nearly 80 percent). That involvement of substance abuse encompassed being under the influence of drugs or alcohol when committing a crime, testing positive for drugs, and/or being arrested for a drug or alcohol charge. Compared to juveniles who have never been arrested, those who have are more than twice as likely to have used alcohol, more than three and a half times more likely to have used marijuana, three times more likely to have used prescription drugs for nonmedical purposes, and nine times more likely to have used cocaine.

As is the case with adult offenders, mental illness—excluding substance abuse disorders—does not appear to have much of an effect on juvenile criminality once other risk factors are considered. Rather, the occurrence of substance abuse disorders alone, the co-occurrence of a mental health disorder and a substance abuse disorder, or the co-occurrence of mental health disorders and other common risk factors substantially increased the likelihood of criminal involvement.[51]

Trauma plays a very prominent role in juvenile mental health, comorbidity, and criminality. One recent study of youth in the Cook County (Chicago) Juvenile Temporary Detention Center found that the vast majority (more than 90 percent) had experienced at least one trauma; 84 percent had experienced more than one, and 57 percent had experienced six or more traumas.[52]

The Adverse Childhood Experiences (ACEs) data have recently been used to investigate the impact of ACEs on juvenile mental health and criminality. In short, juvenile offenders were much more likely to have had ACE exposure and to have had multiple ACE exposures.

Adverse childhood experiences have consistently been implicated among juveniles in the initial involvement in crime as well as recidivism. The risk of recidivism is linked to the number as well as the type of trauma. In terms of sheer numbers, youth with the lowest recidivism risk reported the lowest number of ACEs; those with the highest risk reported the highest number of ACEs. The most predictive ACEs in terms of recidivism include physical neglect, family violence, household substance abuse, and having a household member incarcerated.[53]

Further research clarifies at least part of the effect of ACEs on criminality, which is the impact on mental health. A 2007 study demonstrated that ACEs are strongly related to juvenile mental health—specifically, depressive symptoms, antisocial behavior, and drug use.[54]

The 2013 Cook County Juvenile Detention study found prevalence of post-traumatic stress disorder (PTSD) among juvenile offenders that is three and a half times the prevalence in community samples. PTSD is also strongly related to comorbidity, especially substance abuse disorders, which are the most common comorbid disorder for those with PTSD.

Exposure to childhood trauma, especially witnessing violence, having been threatened with a weapon, and being in a situation where they thought they or someone close to them would be injured or killed, has implications for the development of mental health disorders, including PTSD. In turn, there is a strong relationship between PTSD and the presence of other psychiatric disorders, especially substance abuse, which is clearly implicated in juvenile offending.

Research also shows that while the prevalence of psychiatric disorders declines with age, a substantial proportion of youth who have been in the juvenile justice system still have significant disorders well after they have left juvenile detention:

> Many psychiatric disorders are likely to persist as these juveniles become young adults. Risk factors for psychiatric disorders are common among delinquent youth: maltreatment, dysfunctional families, family substance abuse and brain injury. Because delinquent youth have few protective factors to offset these risks, many are vulnerable to continued psychiatric morbidity as they age.[55]

Sixteen years ago, the surgeon general of the United States concluded that because of the failure to appropriately diagnose mental illness and inadequate or nonexistent mental health treatment for children and youth, the justice system has become the default repository for many mentally ill youth:

> The nation is facing a public crisis in mental healthcare for infants, children and adolescents. Many children have mental health problems that interfere with normal development and functioning. . . . Unmet need for services remains as high now as it was 20 years ago. . . . Concerns about inappropriate diagnosis—that is, either over- or under-diagnosis—of children's mental health problems and about the availability of evidence-based (i.e., scientifically-proven) treatments and services for children and their families have sparked a national dialogue around these issues. There is broad evidence that the nation lacks a unified infrastructure to help these children, many of whom are falling through the cracks. Too often, children who are not identified as having mental health problems and who do not receive services end

up in jail. Children and families are suffering because of missed opportunities for prevention and early identification, fragmented treatment
services, and low priorities for resources. [56]

This was not really news in 2000 when the surgeon general's report
was issued, and little has changed since. Recent estimates show that only
about 15 percent of youth with serious mental disorders receive any treatment while detained in the juvenile justice system. [57] Today, the failures
of community mental health treatment have resulted in mentally ill youth
flooding the juvenile justice system, a system ill equipped to address the
mental health, substance abuse, and neurodevelopmental and intellectual
impairments of those who enter. [58] Major problems with mental and behavioral health service delivery in the juvenile justice system include lack
of adequate funding, failure to use validated screening and assessment
instruments, lack of properly trained staff, extraordinarily high caseloads,
inadequate number and variety of programs, lack of evidence-based interventions, lack of a comprehensive continuum of behavioral health services, absence of appropriate ongoing or continuing care, and limitations
of Medicaid coverage for behavioral health for individuals in correctional
facilities (although the Affordable Care Act does provide opportunities to
remedy some of those limitations). Additional barriers include detained
youths' perceptions that they do not need help or that any mental health
or substance abuse problems they may have will remedy themselves.
Many also deny that they have a mental health problem.

CONCLUSIONS

There are many common sources of child and adolescent disorder, including poor parenting, poverty, exposure to environmental toxins, and a
variety of traumatic experiences, among others. These constitute major
risk factors for criminality. Unfortunately, the juvenile justice system
does little to mitigate these disorders and, therefore, does little to mitigate
the risk they pose for criminal offending. That failure, which unfortunately characterizes how we go about the business of crime control, contributes considerably to the pipeline between the juvenile justice and adult
justice systems.

It is beyond ambitious to think that we could prevent juvenile crime by removing the negative influences that cause or are related to disorder. That simply seems too much to ask. However, utilizing evidence-based interventions to address mental health, substance use, and neurodevelopmental disorders is with our reach and can go a long way in reducing recidivism.

4

THE PATH FORWARD

Changing Behavioral Health

The inability of the criminal justice system to adequately and effectively address the primary mental health, substance abuse, and neurocognitive disorders of the majority of offenders goes a long way in accounting for the unacceptably high recidivism rate of offenders who have been through the justice system. Moreover, the inadequacy of public and private treatment for mental health, substance abuse, and neurocognitive disorders helps us understand the stark reality of why so many disordered individuals end up in the criminal justice system. Much of what may look like a massive crime problem resulting in the world's largest prison system is, to a significant extent, a failed public health system leading to the world's largest prison system.

In this chapter, we first discuss the state of correctional rehabilitation. We then turn to the status of public and private treatment of mental illness, substance abuse, comorbid mental illness and substance abuse, and neurocognitive deficits and impairments. We also discuss changes to the mental health and substance abuse treatment systems. What we propose is comprehensive change, assuming the goal is to improve public health and reduce the revolving door of disordered individuals continuously entering and exiting the justice system.

CHAPTER 4

THE TREATMENT AND REHABILITATION OF CRIMINAL OFFENDERS IS IN NEED OF DISRUPTIVE INNOVATION[1]

"When physicians and pharmaceutical companies induce us to use faulty treatments and drugs, we are appalled and call out the lawyers. Our outrage with correctional malpractice should be no less pronounced."[2]

—Francis Cullen, one of the preeminent
criminologists in the United States

We know that mentally ill individuals are substantially overrepresented in the U.S. criminal justice system. While many mental health and substance use disorders emerge in childhood and adolescence and therefore predate incarceration, there is evidence that incarceration itself has substantial mental health consequences. First, the experience of incarceration aggravates many existing psychiatric disorders, and lack of adequate treatment contributes heavily to negative consequences in both the short term and the long term. Second, incarceration is directly linked to subsequent mental health disorders, especially mood disorders and bipolar disorder.[3]

Incarceration does, however, have a persistent relationship with mood disorders, and for this class of disorders, the relationships are quite strong. . . . Mood disorders are strongly related to disability and play an important role in explaining the additional difficulties former inmates experience after release. Indeed, our results suggest that disability differences between former inmates and others could be greatly reduced by addressing psychiatric disorders.[4]

For a variety of reasons, including the failure to provide adequate public health resources for treating and managing mental illness, substance abuse, intellectual deficiencies, and neurocognitive deficits, the U.S. criminal justice system has by default become the repository for many individuals with these disorders and impairments. As a result, the justice system has been handed some of the most clinically complex and challenging cases. The ironic twist is that the task that the justice system is designed, resourced, and told to do—to punish more offenders more severely—is precisely what makes the situation worse.

The courts have established that incarcerated offenders have a constitutional right to mental health care (*Estelle v. Gamble, Bowring v. God-*

win, Inmates of Allegheny County Jail v. Pierce). The U.S. Supreme Court established in 1976 in *Estelle v. Gamble* (429 U.S. 97 (1976)) that an inmate's Eighth Amendment right against cruel and unusual punishment is violated if prison officials exhibit deliberate indifference to that inmate's medical needs, including mental health needs—indifference that results in the unnecessary and wanton infliction of pain. *Estelle v. Gamble* has been the basis for many deliberate indifference Eighth Amendment findings by the courts. In the *Bowring* case (551 F. 2nd 44 (4th Cir. 1977)), Bowring was denied parole because of mental health problems. He maintained that the state must provide him with appropriate mental health treatment so that he may ultimately be granted parole. The state's denial of mental health treatment, he argued, was a violation of his Eighth Amendment protection against cruel and unusual punishment. The federal appellate court concurred that Bowring and any other inmates have a right to proper diagnosis and treatment when there is evidence of the presence of a recognized mental illness. The *Inmates of Allegheny County Jail* case involved allegations that psychiatric care was constitutionally inadequate due to insufficient staffing and the use of restraints in lieu of treatment. This case is significant because it addressed psychiatric care in a jail. Jails are used for a variety of purposes including pre-trial detention, incarceration for individuals convicted of misdemeanors, and convicted offenders awaiting sentencing. The federal appeals court found psychiatric care insufficient in the jail and ordered the trial court to require appropriate remedies.

The two most influential U.S. Supreme Court cases with regard to mental health care are *Ruiz v. Estelle* (503 F. Supp. 1265 (S.D. Tex. 1980)) and *Brown v. Plata* (563 U.S. (2011)). These cases challenged the two largest prison systems in the country, Texas in 1980 with *Ruiz* and California in 2011 with *Brown*.

In *Ruiz*, the U.S. District Court for the Southern District of Texas, decided by Judge William Wayne Justice, found that the Texas prison system provided "rudimentary" psychiatric care at best, devoted few resources to mental health care, and had few (if any) professional treatment personnel working in the units. Essentially the only treatment, when provided at all, was the administration of psychotropic medication. Segregation of mentally ill inmates was also common. The state had no systematic procedures for assessing the mental health of inmates, and it made no effort to develop treatment plans for any inmates determined to be mentally ill. For these and a few other reasons, the court held that "TDC's mental health care program falls short of minimal adequacy in terms of each of these components and is, therefore, in violation of the eighth amendment."[5]

The more recent U.S. Supreme Court decision *Brown v. Plata* found the California prison system in violation of inmates' Eighth Amendment rights because of inadequate mental health care:

> For years the medical and mental health care provided by California's prisons has fallen short of minimum constitutional requirements and has failed to meet prisoners' basic health needs. Needless suffering and death have been the well-documented result . . . specifically the severe and unlawful mistreatment of prisoners through grossly inadequate provision of medical and mental health care. Prisoners in California with serious mental illness do not receive minimal, adequate care . . . inmates awaiting care may be held for months in administrative segregation, where they endure harsh and isolated conditions and receive only limited mental health services. Wait times for mental health care range as high as 12 months.[6]

The bio-psycho-social status of incarcerated mentally ill offenders reveals a complex array of psychiatric, social, medical, and socioeconomic disadvantages and disorders that severely compromise such inmates' likelihood of a successful outcome after release.[7] Incarcerated mentally ill inmates have a substantially higher likelihood of having had prior incarcerations, one or multiple medical problems, being unemployed before and after incarceration, having a comorbid substance abuse disorder, having neurocognitive problems, being homeless before and after incarceration, and having one or more incarcerated family members.

The President's New Freedom Commission on Mental Health, Subcommittee on Criminal Justice, declared in 2003 that mental health treatment in the criminal justice system was far short of adequate:

> The people with serious mental illnesses who come in contact with the criminal justice system are typically poor and uninsured, are disproportionately members of minority groups, and often are homeless and have co-occurring substance abuse and mental disorders. They cycle in and out of homeless shelters, hospitals, and jails, occasionally receiving mental health, substance abuse services, but most likely receiving

no services at all. The majority of these individuals has committed misdemeanor crimes and do not belong in the criminal justice system.[8]

It is unfortunate that what the subcommittee found was nothing new. It is also unfortunate that not much has changed since then in terms of criminal justice, mental illness, and substance abuse treatment, except that many, many more disordered individuals have cycled in and out of the justice system.

Importantly, a 2006 Justice Department study and a 2003 Human Rights Watch study both confirmed what experts and some courts have observed for many years—only a minority of mentally ill inmates in state and federal prisons and local jails receive any treatment for a mental health disorder. About one-third of mentally ill state prison inmates, one-quarter of federal inmates, and 17 percent of jail inmates received *any* treatment.[9] The Human Rights Watch report concluded that mental health services were "woefully deficient," and that seriously mentally ill inmates were neglected.

The Vera Institute of Justice 2013 investigation of mental illness treatment in the U.S. justice system concluded:

> Despite these high rates [of prevalence of mental illness in the justice system], between 83 and 89 percent of people with mental illness in jails and prisons do not receive care. Moreover, mental health treatment in correctional settings is generally inadequate. People with serious psychiatric needs are more likely to be violently victimized and more likely to be housed in segregation while in prison and stay for longer periods [compared to those without mental illness].[10]

The results of evaluations of those who do receive some mental health treatment while in prison or jail indicate that we do not know much about the effectiveness of such efforts.[11] What is being done in terms of custodial mental health treatment is so under-evaluated that one leading expert concluded in 2007[12] that we do not have sufficient proof to label any of them evidence-based. "Thus, clinicians treating OMI [offenders with mental illness] do so without sufficient efficacy or effectiveness data on which to base their practices."[13]

What is known is that there is tremendous variation in what passes for mental health treatment in prisons and jails. Another issue that is pretty clear is the failure to adequately prepare for and provide assistance prior

to and after release. Such assistance includes things like case management, as well as access to community-based treatment, medication, housing, transportation, employment (when feasible), and necessary entitle-
ments. Some evidence exists of successful clinical and recidivism outcomes when there is proper post-release planning and implementation.

Substance abuse is a very common crime-related disorder among
those incarcerated. In spite of the tremendous need for substance abuse
treatment, and the popularity of drug treatment—such as therapeutic
communities in jails and prisons and drug courts in the justice system—
only a fraction of those in need receive any significant treatment. About
15 percent of state prison inmates and 17 percent of federal prisoners
received any professional substance abuse treatment while incarcerated.

In prison, therapeutic community drug treatment (a common model or
approach for treatment in custody) has been shown to reduce substance
abuse and criminal behavior. The evidence supports the conclusion that
the therapeutic community model can have significant benefits for individuals with severe addiction and significant comorbidities.[14] While effective, both in-custody drug treatment and diversion treatment such as
drug courts fall short. There are many reasons for this, which we will
discuss shortly.

To be clear, we are simply referring to any treatment for prison and
jail inmates, and for offenders on probation and parole release. This says
nothing about the type of treatment; the level, intensity, or dosage of
treatment; the quality of treatment; and any follow-up or continuing care.
Moreover, it is rare that a criminal offender enters the justice system with
just one disorder or crime-related problem. We know that comorbidity of
mental illness and substance abuse is quite common. That combination
clearly ramps up the risk of recidivism and increases the treatment challenges. Failure to address both, or failure to mitigate other important
crime-related risk factors, seriously compromises clinical and recidivism
outcomes.

The Substance Abuse and Mental Health Services Administration
(SAMHSA) paints a rather bleak picture of the assessment and treatment
of justice-involved offenders with co-occurring mental health and substance abuse disorders:

> People with CODs [co-occurring disorders, meaning mental illness
> and substance abuse] present numerous challenges within the justice

system. These individuals can at times exhibit greater impairment in psychosocial skills and are less likely to enter and successfully complete treatment. They are at greater risk for criminal recidivism and relapse. The justice system is generally ill-equipped to address the multiple needs of this population, and few specialized treatment programs exist in jails, prisons, or court and community corrections settings that provide integrated mental health and substance use services. A major concern is that the justice system does not have a built-in mechanism for personnel to identify individuals with these types of behavioral health issues, and there is all too often a failure to effectively screen and assess people with CODs who are in the justice system. The absence of adequate screening for CODs prevents early identification of problems; often undermines successful progress in treatment; and can lead to substance use relapse, recurrence of mental health symptoms, criminal recidivism, and use of expensive community resources such as crisis care and hospital beds. Lack of screening for CODs also prevents comprehensive treatment/case planning, matching justice-involved people to appropriate levels of treatment and supervision, and rapid placement in specialized programs to address CODs. [15]

There is another layer of complexity when we consider the presence of neurocognitive impairments and disorders. We know that a majority of inmates in U.S. prisons and jails have experienced at least one traumatic brain injury. We also know that the circumstances and experiences of many criminal offenders place them at substantial risk of neurocognitive impairments and disorders. [16]

The situation becomes much more complex for individuals with neurocognitive problems combined with co-occurring disorders, especially mental illness and substance abuse. The evidence compiled by SAMHSA shows that individuals with comorbid mental illness and substance abuse disorders, which comprise a significant proportion of the justice population, often have cognitive impairments that affect comprehension, memory, judgment, problem-solving, planning, motivation, understanding the consequences of criminal behavior or violations of conditions of community supervision, responses to stress, and social functioning.

Determining the presence and severity of neurocognitive impairment is critical to the success of rehabilitative efforts since functional impairment affects the ability to engage with and participate in treatment. While we do not have quantitative information on this, it is quite likely that untreated cognitive impairment is an important correlate of treatment failure (in those instances when treatment even occurs) and recidivism.

One of the stark realities is that the vast majority of those in prison and jail will be released, and therein lies the public safety, recidivism concern. The number and variety of crime-related circumstances, disorders, and impairments discussed above, in combination with the failure to provide appropriate treatment for the majority of disordered offenders, paint a pretty bleak picture regarding success after release from prison or jail.

The Size of the Problem

Every year, roughly 350,000 inmates who are mentally ill are released from prisons.[17] Most of these individuals received no mental health treatment while incarcerated. Research shows that the longer mentally ill individuals go without treatment, the more problematic are long-term clinical outcomes. Earlier treatment leads to better outcomes.[18]

Each year, over 500,000 inmates are released from prison with a substance use disorder—addiction, dependence, or abuse. Most of them also received no substance abuse treatment while incarcerated.[19]

Every year, local jurisdictions release about nine million inmates from the nation's jails. Approximately six million of these jail releasees have some type of mental illness; two million have a serious mental illness.[20] Four and a half million inmates released from jail each year have a comorbid mental illness and substance abuse disorder. As noted above, the majority of these mentally ill or comorbid inmates received no intervention or treatment while in jail.[21]

Nearly four million individuals are on probation today. Probation is a post-conviction sentence of diversion from prison (for those convicted of a felony) and jail (for those convicted of a misdemeanor). It is defined as conditional, supervised release in the community. The conditional part means that individuals on probation are required to comply with a variety of conditions that are imposed at sentencing. The supervised part refers to probationers being assigned to a probation officer who is responsible for monitoring and managing their risk of reoffending and violating the conditions of supervision. If a probationer violates conditions or commits a new offense, probation can be revoked, and the individual will then go to prison or jail to serve the sentence of incarceration that was originally imposed.

Between 25 and 35 percent of probationers have a mental illness. About 40 percent have a substance use disorder.[22] The majority receives little or no treatment while on probation or during prior incarceration in jail or prison. Moreover, probationers with mental health and substance abuse issues are more likely than those without such disorders to fail on probation and be sent (revoked) to jail or prison.

We do not have as much data on the prevalence of offenders with neurocognitive impairments and deficits. What we do know is that executive dysfunction is clearly implicated in criminality,[23] resulting in large numbers of adults and juveniles with neurocognitive impairments in the criminal justice system. Research by the Bureau of Justice Statistics, U.S. Department of Justice, shows that prison inmates are four times more likely and jail inmates are six and a half times more likely to report a cognitive disability, compared to the general population.[24] Moreover, the presence of traumatic brain injury among the incarcerated population is at least twice what it is in the general, non-incarcerated population. The evidence suggests that one link between traumatic brain injury and crime is impaired emotional regulation.[25]

The situation regarding juveniles is particularly troubling in light of quite common neurodevelopmental impairments and deficiencies that are a collateral consequence of adolescent development. Research compiled by the Howard League for Penal Reform documents the substantial discrepancies between prevalence of various neurocognitive disorders and intellectual deficiencies among juveniles in criminal justice custody compared to the general population. For example, the prevalence of learning and intellectual disabilities among juveniles in the justice system is ten times that in the general population. Communication disorders are ten to twelve times more prevalent in the justice population, autism spectrum disorder is well over ten times more prevalent, and dyslexia is more than five times more prevalent.[26]

THE PRINCIPLES OF EFFECTIVE CORRECTIONAL INTERVENTION

The principles of effective correctional intervention, which have been developed over the past thirty years, are evidence-based practices that have a demonstrable track record for reducing recidivism. It is important to point out that these are principles and practices that were developed within the constraints of the justice system. They include targeting interventions on high-risk offenders (who to target); addressing crime-related problems, deficits, and disorders (what to target); addressing all primary crime-related problems (multiple needs); utilizing behavioral interventions that focus on current behavioral problems, ensuring that the characteristics of any programming are consistent with the abilities of participants (the responsivity principle); and ensuring that the development and operation of intervention programs are faithful to the evidence-based model (program integrity).

The good news is that proper, faithful implementation of these practices can significantly reduce recidivism by as much as 25–30 percent and sometimes more. For example, well-designed, -operated, and -funded drug courts can reduce recidivism by as much as 35 percent. That, unfortunately, is the exception rather than the rule.

The bad news is that tremendous variation exists across jurisdictions and among criminal justice agencies in terms of adopting these practices. Moreover, even when they are adopted, there is considerable variation in how well they are implemented and funded. Another bit of bad news is that in most instances, successful programs like drug diversion courts, drug treatment programs, and mental health courts are quite limited in terms of capacity. Drug courts, which are the most common type of diversion court, have the capacity to address about 5–10 percent of the need.[27]

More bad news is that, as successful as these principles can be in reducing recidivism, at least for certain segments of the offender population, they are not enough. What is apparent is that correctional treatment for mental illness and substance abuse, the two behavioral disorders for which there has been much intervention effort at all (we know essentially nothing about any correctional attempts to address neurocognitive impairments and intellectual deficiencies, other than educational deficits), has evolved and operated in a silo, set apart from the evidence-based practices utilized for mental health and substance abuse treatment in the free world. Importantly, diversion courts tend to focus on only one problem—substance abuse or mental illness. We know that recidivism is commonly driven not only by these disorders but also by a variety of related risk factors. Failing to address these additional problems needlessly compromises recidivism reduction.

These limitations can in part be understood in terms of the constraints imposed by the primary purposes of the criminal justice system, which are public safety, risk management, and supervision and control, as well as financial limitations on treatment and intervention. One only needs to look at correctional budgets to appreciate that treatment and rehabilitation take a far distant backseat to punishment and control. While these limitations may appear realistic under current circumstances, the consequences are profound in terms of recidivism, victimization, and cost.

The principles of effective correctional intervention are important. However, we argue that they are the tip of the iceberg in terms of behavioral change intervention.

THE CONSEQUENCES OF INADEQUATE TREATMENT

When we consider (1) the prevalence of disorders, impairments, deficits, and situations that offenders bring into the justice system; (2) the complexity and severity of those disorders, impairments, and other crime-related circumstances; and (3) the inability of the justice system to provide effective treatment or intervention for the majority of offenders with these problems, the implications for public safety become obvious.

While there is variation across jurisdictions, the average recidivism rate is over 60 percent. Recidivism among offenders with mental illness is higher still. Research shows that prison inmates with a mental illness are much more likely to have had prior incarcerations compared to inmates who do not have a mental illness.[28] The researchers conclude:

> These findings suggest a substantially heightened risk of recidivism among released inmates with mental illness. As a result of the limited availability of community-based mental health services, mass downsizing of state psychiatric institutions, and a legal system with a limited capacity to discern mental health problems, many people with serious mental illness move continuously between crisis hospitalization, homelessness, and the criminal justice system.[29]

The evidence also shows that the recidivism of drug offenders who have been incarcerated is higher than any other type of incarcerated offenders. Moreover, drug offenders reoffend and are caught substantially more quickly after release than any other type of released offender.[30]

Between 70 and 80 percent of drug abusers commit a new crime after release, and 95 percent return to drug abuse after release from prison.[31]

There is consensus among criminologists, criminal justice experts, and behavioral health experts that the criminal justice system is not adequately addressing the mental health, substance abuse, and neurocognitive and intellectual problems of inmates, probationers, and parolees. Another consequence of inadequate care is that disordered and impaired prison and jail inmates are more likely to be involved in rule violations while incarcerated, which in turn often leads to use of force by staff. This includes use of restraints, chemical sprays, electric stun devices, and aggressive cell extractions.[32]

A common consequence of disruptive behavior by disordered inmates is solitary confinement or administrative segregation, where inmates are isolated from human contact and remain in their cells for up to twenty-three hours per day. While data on the use of segregation are limited, many experts agree that isolation is a primary management tool for the mentally ill.[33] Evidence also supports the observation that the majority of inmates in segregation are mentally disordered.[34] Moreover, the experts agree that isolation is one of the worst things that disordered offenders can experience.[35]

The courts have intervened in the use of segregation, and two major cases involving isolation in California (*Madrid v. Gomez*, 1995) and Texas (*Ruiz v. Johnson*, 1999) prison systems have initiated questioning the wisdom of segregation for mentally ill inmates. Two key observers of the use of segregation and court intervention have concluded:

> Although the court in *Ruiz* came close to ruling solitary confinement unconstitutional, we can say with confidence that we are moving toward a general consensus (which can be found across the various court decisions, consent decrees, and settlement agreements reached) that these environments are not appropriate for the mentally ill and might constitute cruel and unusual punishment for this subset of the inmate population.[36]

There are many descriptions of inadequate staffing and treatment, excessive use of restraints, excessive use of force, and keeping mentally disordered individuals in isolation for extended periods of time. The irony is that descriptions of how we treat many of our disordered prison and jail inmates today are very similar to the descriptions of how we treated mentally disordered individuals in our psychiatric hospitals in the first half of the twentieth century. A *Life* magazine exposé published in 1946, complete with photographs and disturbing descriptions, played a significant role in shuttering those hospitals, a process that contributed to where we are today, largely substituting the jail and prison for the hospital. In effect, we have replaced abusive, ineffective psychiatric hospitals with abusive, ineffective jails and prisons for many of our mentally disordered, mentally deficient, neurocognitively impaired, and addicted citizens. The voice of the experts is getting louder and louder: "The epidemic of psychiatric disorders in the U.S. prison system represents a national public health crisis."[37]

If policymakers and elected officials think they can mitigate or hide the inadequacies and failures of the public health system by keeping these disordered and impaired individuals under lock and key or on a short leash on community supervision, they are sorely mistaken. The evidence is compelling that the failure to provide appropriate and adequate treatment for disordered and impaired offenders in the community and in the justice system compromises public safety, puts everyone at risk of criminal victimization, and wastes billions of dollars every year.

This responsibility for managing and correcting disordered and impaired offenders has been forced on a system that is not designed, operated, or funded to appropriately address it. The justice system has for decades had the primary purpose of punishment, supervision, and control, something that permeates its culture. Moreover, the evidence indicates that custodial settings are not particularly conducive to therapeutic success. Interventions in community settings have significantly better clinical and recidivism outcomes.

Tinkering with the current way of doing business will not do. Simply making some changes within the existing paradigm is wholly inadequate. What we are proposing here is the much more ambitious adoption of evidence-based clinical practices for treating the key crime-related disorders, deficits, and impairments that are the primary focus of this book. As we will see shortly, we are proposing to implement these practices largely in the community rather than in correctional facilities. We are proposing a hybrid model that diverts many disordered and impaired offenders from traditional criminal prosecution and punishment to community-based settings that balance risk management, supervision, and accountability with effective, evidence-based correctional and clinical practices of treatment and intervention.

We propose a model that takes a big-picture view of each individual and makes appropriate determinations about what needs to change in order to reduce the likelihood of recidivism. Disorders and impairments are a focus here, but we want to make it clear that other factors such as homelessness, unemployment, and educational deficits are also fundamentally related to criminality and must be addressed as well. We will argue that simply addressing mental health issues or substance abuse issues, without consideration and mitigation of all relevant, primary crime-related or criminogenic conditions, will not get us to where we need to be. Recidivism is usually a function of multiple factors, and the research is quite clear that the more crime-related factors are addressed, the lower the recidivism rate.[38]

Thus, there are two critical sets of decisions—determining what are the primary crime-related circumstances, conditions, and disorders, and what are the most effective ways to mitigate them. Moreover, the research clearly shows that the earlier in the processing of criminal offenders in the justice system these decisions are made and acted upon, the better the clinical and recidivism outcomes. We also know that community-based treatment is more effective than treatment in confinement.

What we are proposing requires substantial increases in community-based capacity for treatment and intervention as well as fundamental changes to the delivery of such services. We turn to that next.

MENTAL HEALTH TREATMENT IS IN NEED OF DISRUPTIVE INNOVATION

Today, more than sixty million individuals in the United States—25 percent of the population—live with some form of mental illness (MI). Among other consequences, roughly forty thousand individuals in the United States commit suicide each year; the majority of those had acute mental health problems. Moreover, fourteen million individuals with MI have what is classified as serious mental illness (generally defined as bipolar disorder, major depression, and schizophrenia). Those who have serious mental illness, on average, die twenty-five years earlier than the general population. These fourteen million people with serious mental illness constitute the entire population of Los Angeles, Chicago, Houston, Philadelphia, Phoenix, San Antonio, and San Diego, seven of the eight largest cities in the United States.

Another way to look at this is by comparing the United States to other nations. The World Health Organization (WHO) has compiled international data on mental illness. The United States is first in terms of rates of prevalence of mental illness.[39]

Two-thirds of those with a mental disorder in the United States do not receive treatment. The question is why.

There are a number of reasons why individuals with mental illness do not receive needed, adequate treatment. One important reason is financial, due to the lack of insurance coverage, limited insurance coverage, and/or insufficient personal financial resources. Even for those with insurance coverage, only about half of all psychiatrists in the United States take insurance (compared to nearly 90 percent of other physician specialties).[40] Moreover, less than 45 percent of psychiatrists take Medicaid, which is the federal insurance for lower-income individuals.

Another reason is denial of the need for treatment services by patients who do not recognize that they have a problem or do not think it is serious enough to require professional intervention. Shame and stigma also play a role in denial of need for treatment.

Lack of treatment capacity and therefore limited access is another important reason for low treatment rates. The American Medical Association reports that between 1995 and 2013, the total number of physicians increased by 45 percent. Over that same time period, the number of psychiatrists increased by only 12 percent, while the overall U.S. population increased by nearly 40 percent. The bottom line is that there are simply too few psychiatrists to meet the need.

There is substantial variation in psychiatric capacity by state. Massachusetts, Rhode Island, Vermont, Connecticut, and New York have roughly fifteen psychiatrists per 100,000 population. Wyoming, Iowa, Mississippi, Indiana, Nevada, Idaho, and Texas have fewer than six per 100,000.[41] A recent study by the U.S. Department of Health and Human Services found that half of the 3,100 counties in the United States had no practicing mental health professionals, including psychiatrists, psychologists, or social workers.[42]

The capacity shortage is even worse for child and adolescent psychiatrists. According to the American Academy of Child and Adolescent

Psychiatry (AACAP), there are 8,300 child and adolescent psychiatrists in the United States and roughly fifteen million kids in need of treatment.[43] Moreover, there is substantial variation in capacity across states, with a low in Alaska of three per 100,000 youth to twenty-one in Massachusetts. The AACAP estimated in 1990 that the United States would need thirty thousand child and adolescent psychiatrists by 2000 to meet the demand. By way of perspective, the Columbia University National Center for Children in Poverty estimates that if every child with moderate to severe mental health disorders saw one of the existing child and adolescent mental health specialists (psychiatrists, child psychologists, behavioral pediatricians, among others), each child would be able to see one of these specialists for one hour once per year.[44]

Many states have imposed strict eligibility criteria for public mental health treatment. These criteria involve diagnosis and level of functional impairment. States have flexibility in identifying what disorders they will allow public funds to be used to treat. Generally, those diagnoses that are eligible for public treatment include schizophrenia and other psychotic disorders, and mood disorders like bipolar and major depression. States typically exclude individuals with developmental disorders and substance abuse disorders, as well as less severe mental illnesses. Eligibility is also determined by the level of functional impairment that results from a covered diagnosis. The general guidance is impairment that substantially interferes with or limits major life activities may qualify for treatment. States usually require written justification and documentation related to functional impairment.[45]

While we do not currently have specific data on how large the need-capacity gap is, all indications are that it is substantial. Moreover, absent any significant increase in capacity, the gap will just increase due to the Affordable Care Act (ACA) and the 2008 Mental Health Parity and Addictions Equity Act (MHPAEA). The ACA will result in many more individuals getting health insurance, and the MHPAEA requires equal coverage for mental health and substance abuse treatment as is provided for treatment of medical conditions. Estimates from the Congressional Budget Office indicate that about 26 million new individuals will have health insurance as a result of the ACA. About 6.5 million will be in need of mental health treatment. More than 3.5 million will be in need of substance abuse treatment.[46]

While the MHPAEA is seen by many as welcome news for the millions suffering from psychiatric, psychological, intellectual, substance abuse, and neurocognitive disorders and impairments, the reality is that we have not achieved the parity promised. An assessment of the parity situation by the Pew Charitable Trusts led to the following conclusions:

> There are many reasons why group health plans, health insurance companies and even state-run Medicaid programs are not complying with the Mental Health Parity and Addiction Equity Act of 2008, not the least of which is many states aren't enforcing parity in coverage and treatment. . . . But the federal government shares in the blame, too. Washington didn't implement rules on parity for private insurers until January 2014. Only in March 2016 did it release rules for federal- and state-funded Medicaid plans, which cover about 72 million low-income Americans.[47]

Parity is meaningless if a provider does not accept insurance. Parity is also meaningless if an individual does not have health insurance, which is the case for millions who live in states that have not expanded Medicaid. Even when individuals have insurance and a provider accepts that insurance, parity is not always the reality. A recent report by the National Alliance on Mental Illness (NAMI) found a variety of barriers to mental health care, including high rates of denial of mental health treatment, limited providers in the insurance carrier's network, high out-of-pocket costs for prescription medications, and high co-pays for mental health. One of the primary ways that private insurance companies can circumvent parity is by denial of medical necessity. The NAMI research found significantly higher rates of denial of treatment for mental health and substance abuse disorders compared to medical care, based on medical necessity criteria.[48] Moreover, as of July 2015, there had been no federal enforcement actions against an insurance carrier for violating the MHPAEA.[49]

Then there is the issue of quality or adequacy of the care for those who receive it. The Substance Abuse and Mental Health Services Administration tracks such matters and concludes:

> The available data suggest that most mental health or substance abuse treatment does not meet guidelines to be minimally adequate. Adequate treatment . . . is defined as receiving certain amounts of medica-

tion or treatment according to accepted guidelines. Estimates . . . indicate that less than one-third of adults with mental health disorders
receive a minimally adequate type or amount of treatment. Adults with
mood disorders are most likely to get levels of care that meet guidelines (39 percent), adults with anxiety disorders are slightly less likely
(34 percent), and adults with substance use disorders are the least
likely to get minimally adequate treatment (29 percent).[50]

The bigger-picture issue with the mental health system is lack of funding. Many experts have lamented the failure to properly scale and fund
local community mental health centers, which were to replace the psychiatric hospital system as a result of deinstitutionalization. The overall assessment of the public mental health system is that there was a considerable loss of capacity as a result of the transition to local care. On top of
that, the recent recession that began in 2008 has led to substantial cuts to
public mental health care. NAMI reported that between 2009 and 2011,
non-Medicaid state spending for mental health was cut by $1.6 billion.[51]
A subsequent report by NAMI documents that states cut an additional
$4.35 billion from public mental health treatment over the period
2013–2015.

Only twelve states have consistently increased mental health treatment
between 2013 and 2015. Moreover, while thirty states have expanded
Medicaid coverage to individuals and families living at or below 138
percent of the federal poverty line, twenty states have not. The result is
that the poorest in those twenty states do not have Medicaid coverage for
physical or mental health.

The primary takeaway from this discussion is that the United States
has severe constraints on the capacity of mental health treatment, both
public and private. The increase in the number of psychiatrists has not
kept pace with increasing demand. That affects public treatment as well
as private treatment. This problem is considerably worse for child and
adolescent psychiatry. Moreover, spending for public mental health treatment is far from what is required to meet demand. Beyond that, there are
serious questions about adequacy or quality of treatment for those who
receive it.

For a variety of reasons, our public mental health system is unable to
effectively address mental illness and other intellectual and cognitive
disorders (we discuss substance abuse disorders separately below). The
vast majority of expert observers have concluded that the failures of

public mental health are one of the primary reasons the criminal justice system has become the "asylum of last resort," the institution that has by default been given the responsibility to manage much of the population of disordered individuals in this country. In order to reduce the flow of disordered individuals into the justice system, the behavioral health system must be fundamentally reformed.

Fixing Mental Health Treatment

Mental health treatment is effective. About 80 percent of individuals with bipolar disorder experience improvement after appropriate treatment. Seventy percent of those who receive appropriate treatment for major depression, panic disorders, and obsessive-compulsive disorder have significant improvement. For schizophrenia, it is about 60 percent. Overall, the track record for successful treatment intervention for mental health disorders is generally the same as it is for physical health disorders.[52]

Mental health treatment is cost efficient. Research demonstrates that implementing key evidence-based treatment practices (discussed below) can reduce mental health treatment costs by $26–48 billion annually. Mental health treatment best practices can also reduce medical costs. Moreover, there are workforce implications including enhanced worker productivity and lower absenteeism.[53]

The key to successful mental health outcomes is implementing appropriate, effective interventions and funding mental health treatment at a scale in order to provide sufficient capacity. There is no lack of evidence-based recommendations for reforming the health system. We have at least two decades of research that supports key changes to dramatically enhance the accessibility, effectiveness, and cost efficiency of health care delivery. But the remedies are not piecemeal or simply fine-tuning.

The most commonly recommended change to health care delivery is premised on the following observations. Mental illness and medical disorders have high rates of comorbidity. The majority (two-thirds) of individuals with a diagnosed mental disorder have at least one general medical disorder. Nearly one-third of individuals with a medical disorder had a comorbid mental health disorder.[54] As a leading mental health care expert recently noted:

Highly prevalent mental (and addictive) disorders such as depression, anxiety and problem drinking or prescription drug abuse often first appear in primary care—either alone or co-mingling with physical illnesses, like diabetes, hypertension, heart and lung diseases and asthma. But primary care has woeful rates of diagnosing and treating mental health problems. The same population study revealed that about 15 percent of people with a serious mental disorder receive what has been called minimally adequate treatment. This is not because of bad doctors but because of how bad our current service models are. Mental health conditions are more common than heart disease or diabetes, so why aren't primary care physicians screening for them as routinely as they are cardiac abnormalities or blood glucose levels? [55]

The majority of individuals with mental or behavioral health problems receive their mental health care in a primary care setting. However, studies of primary care physicians show that they have neither the time nor the resources to provide adequate mental health treatment for their patients, although research indicates that upward of 70 percent of primary care patient visits involve a mental health concern. [56] Only one in five primary care physicians feels "very prepared" to identify or assess a substance abuse disorder. [57] As a result, while primary care settings are common venues of mental health care, the quality of that care is often suboptimal, if it occurs at all. Finally, medical care and mental health care are currently fragmented, existing in silos with a lack of communication across domains.

The names vary—collaborative care, integrated care, embedded clinic, and IMPACT (Improving Mood-Promoting Access to Collaborative Treatment)—but the point is the same. Integrated or collaborative care is a model that treats common mental health disorders such as depression, anxiety, and substance abuse in primary care, family medicine, and pediatric settings. [58] The approach consists of a team led by the primary care provider that includes a trained behavioral health case manager and consultation from a psychiatric specialist. The case manager is typically embedded in the primary care practice. The psychiatric consultant is often off-site and communicates by phone or teleconference. [59]

The evaluation evidence for collaborative care is compelling, documenting significant and substantial clinical improvements for many common mental health problems such as depression, anxiety, PTSD, and comorbid medical conditions.

Case management is an important evidence-based component of collaborative care. The case manager is often a nurse, clinical social worker, or psychologist who provides care coordination, support, and occasionally brief interventions; in some versions of collaborative care, the case manager is a trained psychotherapist who provides therapy such as cognitive behavioral therapy.

The Affordable Care Act endorses the collaborative or integrated care model. It is also identified as an evidence-based practice by the Substance Abuse and Mental Health Services Administration and has been recommended as a best practice by the President's New Freedom Commission on Mental Health, and the Surgeon General's Report on Mental Health.

Another evidence-based practice in mental health treatment is measurement-based care. The idea is simple but rarely implemented (fewer than one in five psychiatrists or one in ten psychologists routinely use it). Measurement-based care uses standardized, psychometrically validated symptom rating scales designed to measure the frequency and severity of patient symptoms. These measurements provide a reliable gauge of treatment progress or effectiveness, as well as a metric for guiding treatment modification. In a recent assessment of measurement-based care, the researchers conclude:

> MBC [measurement based care] can be conceptualized as an EBP [evidence-based practice] framework that involves systematic assessment of therapy progress and outcome to guide and adapt treatment. MBC has been shown to improve clinical outcomes, inform collaborative care efforts, enhance treatment decision-making processes, and increase client engagement in therapy. MBC can also be adapted to fit the context of the organization by matching psychometrically sound measures of appropriate length and content to the needs of clients receiving care.[60]

It is really little different from a blood pressure cuff, which is used to measure treatment effectiveness for high blood pressure. Just like the blood pressure cuff, symptom rating scales are easy to administer, easily interpretable, and sensitive—able to measure changes in symptom frequency and severity over time.[61]

These evidence-based practices have been shown to improve clinical outcomes such as symptoms and social functioning, patient and family satisfaction, and shorter hospital stays. Collaborative care has also been shown to be cost efficient.[62]

It is important to note that the vast majority of mental health treatment proposed herein is community based. We still need long-term public and private psychiatric hospitals for crisis stabilization and acute care. The capacity mix is probably somewhere around 90 percent community-based and 10 percent hospital-based.

The changes we are discussing involve both public and private physical and mental health care. While many individuals who enter the justice system are patients in the private health care system, most referrals to mental health treatment come from the justice system, and the primary payer for mental health treatment is Medicaid.

Most criminal offenders must rely on the public health system for addressing physical, mental, substance-related, neurocognitive, and intellectual disorders and impairments. Moreover, most experts, governmental commissions, nonprofits, and advocacy groups have, for decades, been documenting the gross inadequacies of public mental health and substance abuse treatment and calling for change. Today, there is little disagreement that the system is broken and a growing consensus regarding what needs to be done to accomplish the necessary reforms. Yet we have made little progress in implementing evidence-based reforms, especially in the public health care sector.

There are several reasons why elected officials have for the most part failed to adequately address these matters in the public health care sector. These include concerns that it is too expensive, a belief that the justice system is doing a reasonable job of housing many mentally disordered and addicted individuals, and the fact that the mentally ill are not as effective at lobbying Congress and state legislatures as the banking industry, oil and gas, telecommunications, technology, or any number of other interests that want a share of public resources and policy.

At the end of the day, what matters is that changing public and private health care delivery is necessary to improve the efficiency and effectiveness of treatment, in turn improving outcomes for the mentally disordered, addicted, cognitively impaired, and intellectually deficient. As the public and private health care delivery systems become more effective and public health improves, we shall see declines in the number of disordered individuals defaulting into the criminal justice system. Moreover, as the public health system improves and evidence-based practices become business as usual, the outcomes of justice-involved, disordered individuals who are connected to local, community-based treatment resources will improve through the types of diversion programs recommended in the following pages. That in turn leads to lower recidivism, victimization, and cost.

What may be persuasive to elected officials and policymakers who have failed to adequately address public health in the past is the realization that such changes will not only improve clinical outcomes and reduce criminality and recidivism but also save money by cutting criminal justice costs, making treatment more cost effective, reducing the number of people dependent on public assistance, and enhancing the productivity of many individuals who currently are heavy users of public assistance and services.

SUBSTANCE ABUSE TREATMENT IS IN NEED OF DISRUPTIVE INNOVATION

Today, over twenty-one million adults in the United States have a substance abuse disorder. The World Health Organization (WHO) data on substance abuse disorders show that the United States is third in terms of rates of substance abuse, falling behind South Africa and Ukraine.[63]

Only about 12 percent of those in need in the United States receive any specialized treatment. This is well below the rate of treatment for a variety of health conditions such as diabetes (73 percent) and hypertension (77 percent).[64] Again, the question is why.

There are many barriers to accessing appropriate and adequate substance abuse treatment, including lack of treatment capacity.[65] It is not at all unusual for individuals seeking detox and treatment to be placed on waiting lists. A shortage of treatment capacity is an issue in every state, and many experts have declared the funding and capacity shortfall a crisis.[66] For example, a recent report revealed that one in two adults and two in three adolescents seeking substance abuse treatment in New Jersey could not receive treatment because of lack of adequate capacity.[67]

Important treatment barriers also include lack of insurance and insufficient personal resources, as well as the issues discussed above regarding insurance coverage and parity, the denial of medical necessity, high patient co-pays, costs of medications, and network provisions of the insurance carrier. Other barriers or problems include the failure to use evidence-based treatment and the stigma associated with substance abuse.

Comorbidity of a psychiatric disorder with a substance abuse disorder is unfortunately common, afflicting over 40 percent of those with mental illness. About 35 percent of those with a substance abuse disorder have a comorbid psychiatric disorder. Even fewer individuals in this situation receive treatment. At the risk of sounding redundant, we ask why. In addition to the barriers mentioned above, it is also the case that mental health and substance abuse intervention involve different systems of treatment and different types of professionals providing treatment. Physicians are typically the primary care givers for mental illness, whereas a broader mix of individuals with different backgrounds are involved in substance abuse treatment. In effect, mental health treatment is a silo and substance abuse treatment another silo, and neither has the expertise to address the comorbidity. Moreover, there is a lingering bias against the use of medication among at least some substance abuse treatment providers, making it difficult to treat mental illness.

The Columbia University National Center on Addiction and Substance Abuse conducted a comprehensive analysis of the gap between practice and science in terms of substance abuse treatment. That gap is not just in terms of how many do and do not receive treatment but also in terms of the quality of care gap—the difference between services received and what the evidence indicates is quality care.

The Columbia study identified a number of factors that contribute to the gaps, including:

- inadequate integration of substance abuse treatment with mainstream medical care
- inadequate training of many substance abuse treatment providers
- inadequate accountability for substance abuse treatment providers
- lack of funding for substance abuse treatment

One of the major concerns raised by the Columbia researchers is that addiction and substance abuse treatment are largely separate from routine medical practice. One result of this is that most physicians, including primary care physicians who are the front line of medical care, are not trained in addiction and substance use disorders; thus they typically do not identify or diagnose a substance use disorder, nor do they refer individuals to treatment. Moreover, many of those individuals involved in providing substance abuse treatment are not trained or equipped to provide the range of evidence-based services necessary to provide quality treatment. Unfortunately, while addiction and substance abuse are classified as a medical disorder, the majority of treatment providers are not required to have any medical training; in fact, most states do not require advanced education like college degrees, let alone graduate degrees. The Columbia researchers conclude:

> The profound gap between the science of addiction and current practice related to prevention and treatment is a result of decades of marginalizing addiction as a social problem rather than treating it as a medical condition. Much of what passes for "treatment" of addiction bears little resemblance to the treatment of other health conditions. Much of what is offered in addiction "rehabilitation" has not been subject to rigorous scientific study and the existing body of evidence demonstrating principles of effective treatment has not been . . . integrated effectively into many of the treatment programs operating nationwide.[68]

In 1954, the American Medical Association voted to recognize alcoholism as an illness. In 1967 the AMA revised the definition to include loss of control over drinking. By 1992, the AMA recognized that addiction has genetic, environmental, and psychosocial origins. In 2011, the American Society of Addiction Medicine declared addiction a disease of the brain.

On May 17, 2016, medical students at the Harvard Medical School declared their curriculum deficient in terms of training for substance abuse disorders. Medical students from Harvard and the other medical schools in Massachusetts launched the Student Coalition on Addiction, which is in the process of identifying gaps in medical training regarding substance use disorders and their treatment.[69]

Until recently, none of the over 9,500 medical residency programs in the United States had training in addiction medicine. That is likely to change. On March 14, 2016, the American Board of Medical Specialties announced its formal recognition of it as a subspecialty. Nora Volkow, the director of the National Institute on Drug Abuse, notes that this recognition "signals the legitimacy of Addiction Medicine as a field of specialized study and practice and it will enable the accreditation and expansion

of Addiction Medicine training programs . . . [and it] raises the bar for the
quality of care in this crucial medical domain."[70]

There is another very important issue regarding substance abuse and
its treatment. The evidence links neurocognitive deficits and impairments
in executive functioning, reward processing, attention bias, and impulse
control to the development and maintenance of addiction.[71] For example,

> [t]here is a growing and consistent body of research showing that
> substance-dependent individuals usually show abnormal functioning
> in specific neural networks of the prefrontal cortex (PFC) related to
> executive cognitive function, decision-making and emotional con-
> trol . . . PFC dysfunction may impair response inhibition, impulse
> control, conflict/error monitoring and goal-driven behaviors, as well as
> contribute to poor decision-making and to the maintenance of the
> drug-seeking behavior, despite negative consequences.[72]

Cognitive impairment is quite common among substance abusing or
dependent individuals. Between 50 and 80 percent of substance abuse
treatment patients present with cognitive impairments. However, such
impairments typically remain undiagnosed and therefore untreated.[73]

While substance abuse treatment is effective, there are significant failure rates, typically in the form of dropping out of treatment and relapse
during and after treatment. Many factors play a role in treatment failure;
however, a large and growing research literature shows that neurocognitive deficits and impairments are significant predictors of treatment outcome. In particular, treatment dropout rates are linked to cognitive impairments in executive functioning, attention, and memory from a variety
of substances (cocaine, marijuana, alcohol). Executive dysfunction, cognitive disinhibition, and impulsive decision making are linked to the ability to successfully abstain from drug use after treatment.

This research has also implicated cognitive impairment with the efficacy of cognitive behavioral therapy, the primary evidence-based therapy
intervention for substance abuse.[74] It seems obvious that cognitive behavioral therapy depends on adequate cognitive functioning.[75] However,
many substance abuse treatment programs that employ the evidence-
based practice of cognitive behavioral therapy fail to consider cognitive
ability. Moreover, the evidence shows that mild cognitive impairment
may impede benefits from cognitive behavioral therapy among cocaine
abusers.[76]

Fixing Substance Abuse Treatment

Fixing substance abuse treatment involves both bigger-picture issues and very specific strategies. First, the big picture.

Substance abuse is a medical disorder. As such, the front line in terms of assessment, diagnosis, intervention, identification of comorbidities (both medical and psychiatric), and chronic disease management should be the medical community. This requires more enhanced training of physicians, especially primary care physicians, in addiction medicine and substance abuse diagnosis, treatment, and management. This training should also include non-physician health care providers. An effective, evidence-based screening protocol referred to as SBIRT (Screening, Brief Intervention and Referral to specialty Treatment) can be easily adopted in a variety of medical and other health care settings such as primary care, dental offices, emergency departments, urgent care, and mental health settings, among others. It is necessary that substance abuse assessment, treatment, and management be integrated into day-to-day medical care, such that addressing substance abuse becomes an essential part of routine medical practice.

There is tremendous variation in what passes for substance abuse treatment today and in the training and qualifications of substance abuse treatment personnel.[77] In part, this is a consequence of the historical separation of substance abuse treatment from regular medical treatment. Treatment providers need to have the knowledge and skills to provide evidence-based treatment and to address the array of conditions, including medical conditions, commonly associated with substance abuse.

Specific strategies include properly assessing the severity of the substance disorder to determine the appropriate treatment services as well as the proper dosage or initial length of treatment. Treatment must be tailored to the needs of the individual, and should address the collateral problems that often accompany substance abuse. Psychosocial interventions such as cognitive behavioral therapy, contingency management, and motivational interviewing are evidence-based strategies that are effective on at least some segments of the substance use disorder population. Medication is effective in conjunction with behavioral therapies for treating opioid addiction and abuse (methadone, buprenorphine, and naltrexone) as well as alcohol abuse (acamprosate, disulfiram). Ongoing care and relapse prevention are critical for success and should be a primary component of the treatment plan, which should be supported and monitored by primary health care providers. However, it is important to emphasize that relapse prevention strategies like twelve-step self-help groups are not treatment per se and should not be a substitute for treatment.

The National Institute on Drug Abuse has identified a variety of principles of effective substance abuse treatment.[78] They include:

- individualized treatment (individuals differ in terms of severity, substance abused, and other characteristics that impact treatment)
- readily accessible treatment (services should be available when someone decides they are ready for treatment)
- addressing multiple needs and conditions (substance abuse may be primary, but it is often not the only factor; substance abuse is commonly accompanied by psychological/psychiatric, social, employment, and legal problems)
- treatment retention for the appropriate length of time (treatment dosage is critical for success and should be based on the severity of the problem; strategies to retain patients through the treatment period should be implemented)
- behavioral therapies that are effective interventions (motivating change, drug resistance skills, problem solving, replacing drug use with other activities, improving interpersonal interaction skills, among others)
- medication in conjunction with behavioral therapies, assessment and modification of the treatment plan over time, and substance use monitoring

In light of what the evidence tells us about the propensity for neurocognitive deficits and impairment among substance abusers and how those disorders can impact the efficacy of treatment as well as treatment retention and abstinence, it is critical that a screening and assessment protocol explicitly incorporate the detection and diagnosis of neurocognitive impairments and deficits. We will discuss intervention strategies for neurocognitive impairments shortly in the section on evidence-based treatment for neurodevelopmental and neurocognitive impairments.

CO-OCCURRING SUBSTANCE ABUSE
AND MENTAL HEALTH DISORDERS

Comorbid mental illness and substance use disorders (SUDs) are common. Substance use disorders co-occur frequently with anxiety disorders, personality disorders, bipolar disorder, and depression. The interaction of mental illness and substance use disorders increases overall condition severity and often presents a complex treatment situation. Comorbidity results in higher rates of treatment noncompliance and lower rates of treatment retention.[79] Moreover, cognitive impairments commonly accompany comorbid mental illness and substance abuse, adding another layer of complexity to treatment.

For a variety of reasons, the treatment of mental illness and SUDs has occurred in silos, involving separate sets of treatment providers with different sets of credentials and expertise, and usually located separately. There are obvious concerns with treating comorbid disorders separately, and considerable evidence supports a different, integrated treatment approach. Integrated treatment is an evidence-based protocol that consists of a variety of treatment and organizational components.

Integrated treatment of comorbid psychiatric disorders and SUDs utilizes an interdisciplinary, collaborative team of experts including a dual diagnosis clinician, a physician, a nurse, a case manager, and an integrated substance abuse specialist with experience in treating dual disorder individuals. All the treatment interventions are stage-wise, meaning they are driven by the client's stage of treatment and include things like engagement, motivation/persuasion, active treatment, and ongoing care and relapse prevention.

The model involves comprehensive standardized assessments for dual diagnosis, collaborative development of an individualized treatment plan, and individualized treatment, which means that the interventions, services, and intensity are tailored to the individual's needs.

Integrated treatment involves multiple, comprehensive interventions including medicine and behavioral therapy, residential and outpatient services, illness management and recovery, family education, assertive community treatment and case management, and services and social support such as housing and employment. Treatment strategies include individual and group counseling, pharmacological treatment, participation in self-help groups like AA and NA, and strategies to promote physical health.

The goal is to address both disorders with a multidisciplinary team of professionals who understand the severity and complexity produced by the comorbidity, utilizing the array of evidence-based treatments that have proven to reduce symptoms and enhance functionality, including lower justice system involvement and fewer relapses. [80]

EVIDENCE-BASED TREATMENT FOR INTELLECTUAL DISABILITIES

Individuals with ID, depending on the severity of the disabilities, often require intervention for a variety of problems, including education, vocational training, and daily functioning. The most common therapeutic approach is cognitive behavioral therapy (CBT), which the evidence base indicates is an effective modality. [81]

The co-occurrence of intellectual disabilities and mental health problems is increasingly recognized. Best estimates indicate that roughly a third of individuals with intellectual disabilities have comorbid psychiatric disorders. Common comorbid disorders include mood disorders (depression, bipolar, and mania), anxiety disorders (panic attacks, obsessive-compulsive disorders, and PTSD), psychotic disorders (schizophrenia and schizoaffective disorder), personality disorders (borderline personality and antisocial personality disorders), and adjustment disorders.

Comorbidity can greatly impact individuals' daily functioning, as well as educational and vocational training, family relationships, and out-of-home placements, among others. Most experts agree that clinical interventions require multiple therapeutic approaches, including medication (for managing psychiatric symptoms), psychotherapy (individual, group, and family), and behavioral management. Behavioral management is used to address inappropriate behaviors and for acquisition of adaptive behaviors and skills. [82] Recent research has identified dialectical behavior therapy (DBT) as an effective, evidence-based approach for addressing challenging behaviors among comorbid individuals. DBT is a comprehensive therapeutic approach that includes elements of cognitive behavioral therapy and applied behavior analysis, in addition to contingency management, mindfulness practice, dialectical strategies, and case management. It is designed to address a broad spectrum of functional and regulatory impairments. [83]

Historically, treatment and services for mental health disorders and intellectual disabilities have been separate, meaning that administration, funding, and treatment are separate. Clearly, moving in the direction of integrated or collaborative care is appropriate.

EVIDENCE-BASED TREATMENT FOR NEUROCOGNITIVE AND NEURODEVELOPMENTAL DISORDERS AND IMPAIRMENTS

A comparative imaging study of the brains of London taxi drivers and London bus drivers revealed that taxi drivers have a larger hippocampus,[84] the area of the brain that acquires and uses complex spatial information. The reason taxi drivers have larger hippocampi is that they are routinely required to navigate through London streets, commonly utilizing the spatial ability of the brain. However, bus drivers do not utilize that part of the brain nearly as much since they drive on established routes. What does this have to do with treatment of neurocognitive disorders and impairments? Everything, since it illustrates a fundamental characteristic of the human brain—plasticity.

Plasticity is the ability of the brain to change through learning. Such changes occur with connections among neurons in the brain. New connections among neurons can form, resulting in internal changes in the structure of the brain. Such changes can lead to positive, adaptive behaviors as well as to pathological behaviors. As some of the leading neurologists in the country put it:

> Plasticity is the intrinsic property of the human brain and represents evolution's invention to enable the nervous system to escape the restrictions of its own genome and thus adapt to environmental pressures, physiologic changes and experiences . . . Such rapid, ongoing changes [in neuronal connections in the brain] . . . harbor the danger that the evolving pattern of neuronal activation may in itself lead to abnormal behavior. Plasticity is the mechanism for development and learning, as much as a cause of pathology.[85]

Traumatic brain injury and exposure to lethality, lead paint, abuse, abandonment, poverty, and a variety of other physical and emotional trauma can lead to fundamental changes in the brain through the process of plasticity. Such impairments and deficits in turn can lead to abnormal, pathological behavior, such as substance abuse, violence and aggression, and criminality. While plasticity is the process that leads to neurocognitive impairments and deficits, it is also the remedy for correcting these conditions. Deficits and impairments are largely acquired through behavior and experience. Plasticity is the process whereby neurocognitive disorders can be mitigated through learning and experience. The human brain undergoes changes throughout its lifespan; thus plasticity is characteristic of the adult brain as well as the child and adolescent brain.

While medication can be helpful in the treatment of neurocognitive disorders, including off-label applications of ADHD stimulant medication such as Ritalin and Methylin, and neuroleptics such as clozapine and risperidone, the primary, evidence-based therapy for neurocognitive impairments is cognitive rehabilitation therapy or cognitive restructuring therapy (CRT). CRT is an array of treatments that are designed to promote relearning of cognitive skills that have been lost due to brain injury, illness, and environmental trauma. The Brain Injury Interdisciplinary Special Interest Group of the American Congress of Rehabilitation Medicine defines CRT as

> a systematic, functionally-oriented service of therapeutic cognitive activities, based on an assessment and understanding of the person's brain-behavior deficits. Services are directed to achieve functional changes by (1) reinforcing, strengthening, or reestablishing previously learned patterns of behavior, or (2) establishing new patterns of cognitive activity or compensatory mechanisms for impaired neurological systems.[86]

The Cognitive Rehabilitation Task Force of the Brain Injury Special Interest Group has identified four sets of goals for CRT services, which include:

- problem awareness and goal setting (identifying and recognizing particular deficits and impairments and developing short- and long-term intervention goals);
- compensation (providing the cognitive tools for individuals to function in an effective manner);
- internalization (increasing the utilization of new cognitive strategies and skills to the point of making them more typical);

- generalization, or the application of the strategies and skills to an ever-increasing variety of situations and context to enhance day-to-day functioning.

There are two primary approaches to CRT. One involves restorative approaches that are designed to enhance the general functioning of the cognitive system to improve cognitive performance in a variety of settings and activities. Restorative approaches reinforce and strengthen previously learned behaviors. The second set of approaches is referred to as compensatory and relies on internal or external devices, strategies, and aids to support and enhance performance in spite of the presence of cognitive impairment. Compensatory approaches establish new cognitive activities and mechanisms to compensate for cognitive systems that are substantially impaired. Specific treatments include psychotherapy, medication, behavior modification, occupational therapy, and vocational training and rehabilitation, among others. These treatments can be provided in a variety of settings, such as hospitals, community-based outpatient facilities, and individuals' homes and workplaces by a multidisciplinary team of professionals in psychiatry, psychology, rehabilitation medicine, occupational therapy, neuropharmacology, vocational rehabilitation, and neuropsychology.[87]

A consensus panel convened by the National Institutes of Health concluded that evidence-based CRT interventions are "structured, systematic, goal-directed, and individualized and they involve learning, practice, social contact and a relevant context."[88] While some earlier reviews concluded that the evidence was insufficient to declare CRT an evidence-based practice, more recent analyses have determined that it is. Much of the research has been based on CRT in situations of traumatic brain injury.[89] However, others have assessed CRT in a broader set of circumstances such as mild cognitive impairment and substance abuse.[90] CRT has been accepted as a valid and effective intervention by a variety of organizations including the National Institutes of Health, the National Academy of Neuropsychology, the Society for Cognitive Rehabilitation, the Royal College of Physicians, and the British Society of Rehabilitative Medicine.

Access to rehabilitative services for cognitive impairment is a function of availability of services, cost of services, and insurance coverage. The Centers for Disease Control and Prevention notes that access to rehabilitative services for a traumatic brain injury varies by state as well as urban and rural location and availability of insurance coverage. The bottom line is much the same as it is regarding access to mental health and substance abuse treatment—capacity, cost, and insurance.

CONCLUSIONS

In light of what we know about the relationship between mental illness, substance abuse, intellectual disabilities, and cognitive impairment, on the one hand, and crime and criminal justice involvement, on the other, as well as the barriers to treatment for mental illness, SUDs, IDs, and neuro-cognitive disorders both within and outside of the criminal justice system, it should not be the least bit surprising that the recidivism rate in the United States is more than 65 percent. Criminal justice policy, including drug policy, has focused nearly exclusively on punishment and control. Common sense and the scientific evidence tell us that punishment and control do little to change the underlying disorders that characterize the majority of offenders who enter the criminal justice system.

5

CRIMINAL INTENT AND DIVERSION

Our goal in this book is to develop a front-end, gatekeeping function in the processing of criminal offenders that permits appropriate sorting of individuals into one of two categories—those who should be criminally prosecuted, and those who, because of significant psychiatric, neurological, and/or intellectual disorders, impairments, and deficits (as well as other collateral criminogenic risk factors), and because of an acceptable risk level, should be diverted to treatment and supervision/risk management. For decades the U.S. justice system has tried to punish bad behavior out of criminal offenders. That strategy has failed. It is time to accept what the evidence shows, which is that behavioral change is the appropriate path to reduced recidivism.

Mens rea, or criminal intent, is an excellent candidate for this gatekeeping purpose. Criminal intent is, in theory, an element of proof in the criminal prosecution of offenders. Lacking intent or the capacity to form intent because of a psychiatric or neurocognitive disorder or impairment should be just such a mechanism for diverting impaired offenders to treatment and risk management.

CRIMINAL INTENT IS ESTABLISHED LAW

For well over the past one hundred years, mens rea has occupied a position of sanctity in law and procedure, at least from the vantage point of legal scholars. For example, the ninth edition of *Bishop's Criminal Law* text is quite clear:

> There can be no crime, large or small, without an evil mind. It is therefore a principle of our legal system, as probably it is of every other, that the essence of an offence is the wrongful intent, without which it cannot exist.

Francis Sayre, perhaps the preeminent legal scholar of his time, wrote in 1933 of the necessity of mens rea for reflecting the sense of justice and reinforcing the legitimacy of the legal system:

> To inflict substantial punishment upon one who is morally entirely innocent, who caused injury through reasonable mistake or pure accident, would so outrage the feelings of the community as to nullify its own enforcement . . . courts can never abandon insistence upon the evil intent as a prerequisite to criminality, partly because individual interests can never be lost sight of and partly because the real menace to social interests is the intentional, not the innocent doer of harm. [1]

Morissette v. United States (1952)

One of the most important U.S. Supreme Court cases involving mens rea is *Morissette v. United States*, decided in 1952. The Supreme Court held, in one of the most widely quoted statements regarding mens rea:

> The contention that an injury can amount to a crime only when inflicted by intention is no provincial or transient notion. It is as universal and persistent in mature systems of law as belief in freedom of the human will and a consequent ability and duty of the normal individual to choose between good and evil. A relation between some mental element and punishment for a harmful act is almost as instinctive as the child's familiar exculpatory "But I didn't mean to," and has afforded the rational basis for a tardy and unfinished substitution of deterrence and reformation in place of retaliation and vengeance as the motivation for public prosecution. . . . Crime is a compound concept, generally constituted only from concurrence of an evil-meaning mind and an evil-doing hand. [2]

The *Morissette* decision very clearly established the centrality of mens rea or criminal intent as well as the requirement in most criminal proceedings that intent is something to be proven and not assumed—"the question of intent can never be ruled as a question of law, but must always be submitted to the jury."

THE AMERICAN LAW INSTITUTE'S MODEL PENAL CODE

While the Supreme Court's decision in *Morissette* was clear regarding the primacy of mens rea, there remained many problems regarding its meaning. For example, it was discovered that nearly eighty different terms were in use in existing criminal codes for describing mens rea.[3]

The American Law Institute (ALI) was organized in 1923 by a group of distinguished judges, lawyers, and law professors with the intention of clarifying and improving the law. Their primary contribution was the Model Penal Code (MPC), which, among many other things, attempted to clarify mens rea. The MPC reflects two major changes to the law of criminal intent. First is what is referred to as the culpability provision, or the general rules for criminal culpability.

The MPC reduced the mens rea terms to four: purpose, knowledge, recklessness, and negligence. As stated in the MPC, "a person is not guilty of an offense unless he acted purposely (conscious objective to cause a particular result), knowingly (not a conscious desire but a practical certainty that the conduct will cause a particular result), recklessly (a conscious disregard of a substantial risk), or negligently (unaware of a substantial risk but should have been aware)."

The MPC also addressed the matter of excuses for criminal liability. At the time that the ALI assembled the drafters of the MPC, the insanity defense was governed in over half of the states by the M'Naghten rule. The M'Naghten rule involves the requirement that at the time of the crime the defendant was "laboring under such a defect of reason, from disease of the mind, as to not know the nature and quality of the act he was doing; or, if he did know it, that he did not know that what he was doing was wrong."[4]

While M'Naghten has deep roots in American criminal justice, it was clear to the drafters of the MPC that it did not go far enough. Yes, those offenders who fit the M'Naghten criteria should not be held legally responsible and punished. However, M'Naghten is based on an extremely narrow conception of mental disorder—complete impairment. The drafters recognized that mental disorder is manifest in degrees rather than absolutes. They also recognized that criminal behavior is a matter of not only understanding the nature and quality of an act but also being able to control that behavior.

To be clear, the MPC is not law per se in any jurisdiction in the United States. While there is considerable variation in how states use the MPC, the majority (approximately two-thirds) have adopted criminal codes that reflect the four culpability levels of purpose, knowledge, recklessness, and negligence.

THE EROSION OF CRIMINAL INTENT

In 2014 in Waukesha County, Wisconsin, two twelve-year-old girls repeatedly stabbed another girl during a sleepover in an effort to please a fictional character they had found on the Internet named Slenderman. The victim survived nineteen stab wounds. The two girls who stabbed her have been transferred to adult court, are charged with attempted first-degree intentional murder, and face sixty-five years in prison if convicted. This case raises a number of important issues, but the central point at the moment is the apparent disjuncture between the law, what we know about the development of the adolescent and teen brain, and the fact that these girls stabbed the victim in an attempt to please a fictional Internet character. If nothing else, this case suggests that there are questions about the girls' neurodevelopment, their executive functioning, and consequently their ability to form the required criminal intent. The charging decisions (intentional attempted murder) and the transfer to adult court suggest that criminal intent is not an issue for the prosecutor.

While mens rea has deep roots in American jurisprudence, it is not an element of due process that has always been served well by criminal law and criminal procedure. As the late Harvard law professor William Stuntz put it:

> [F]or the most part, the concept of wrongful intent—the idea that the
> state must prove the defendant acted with a "guilty mind," the English

translation for the Latin mens rea—has gone by the boards. Criminal intent has become a modest requirement at best, meaningless at worst. . . . The upshot is that, in most cases, findings of criminal intent are automatic. The law of intent no longer serves the function it served in Morissette: a means of ensuring that only those who understand that they are engaged in serious misconduct can be criminally punished.[5]

The MPC was published in 1962. Just a handful of years after its publication, we saw the beginning of the tough-on-crime movement in the United States, which resulted in the nearly universal embrace of maximizing punishment of criminal offenders. When the goal is the prosecution, conviction, and punishment of as many criminal offenders as possible, criminal intent becomes a barrier. The justices in the *Morissette* decision were quite direct in this regard—doing away with mens rea makes criminal conviction easier.

The purpose and obvious effect of doing away with the requirement of a guilty intent is to ease the prosecution's path to conviction, to strip the defendant of such benefit as he derived at common law from innocence of evil purpose, and to circumscribe the freedom heretofore allowed juries.[6]

In theory, criminal intent functions not only as a gatekeeper at the front end of the process but also to mitigate the sentences of those who have been convicted. Presumably, offenders who are found guilty but less culpable than others should receive lesser punishment, perhaps in proportion to their diminished criminal intent or responsibility. Such sentence mitigation was a realistic possibility under indeterminate sentencing, where judges were given broad discretion in setting sentences. However, as sentencing reform shifted sentencing laws to determinate schemes, in turn effectively limiting judicial discretion, the ability to mitigate sentences in the presence of diminished intent became much more difficult.

The goals of the MPC with regard to criminal intent and the goals of the tough-on-crime agenda are in clear conflict. The bottom line is that tough on crime and retribution won, at the expense of mens rea. Even in those states that adopted elements of the MPC, legislatures created many strict liability crimes that have no intent requirement, as well as created strict liability elements for crimes that facilitated enhancing offense severity and thus the severity of the punishment. Tough on crime won not only in the statehouse and in Congress but also in the courtroom. The evidence indicates "widespread judicial endorsement of strict liability elements in MPC jurisdictions, despite state statutes that dictate presumptions otherwise."[7]

In *Elonis v. United States* (2015), Chief Justice Robert's majority opinion stipulated, among other things, that "wrongdoing must be conscious to be criminal," that the defendant must have an "awareness of some wrongdoing," and that a defendant must be "blameworthy in mind."[8] The court is quite clear in the *Elonis* case that criminal intent is the way to distinguish between criminal behavior and otherwise innocent behavior. What is troubling is that intent does not seem to fulfill that sorting function in the day-to-day prosecution and conviction of criminal defendants.

The relevance of criminal intent is substantially undermined by the process of plea negotiation. Today, in state and federal prosecutions, approximately 95 percent of all criminal indictments are disposed of through a plea bargain. All that is really required is an admission of guilt by a defendant and the deal is done. The most important part of that admission is the criminal act, and the tendency to presume intent from the facts of the criminal act itself results in little need to address mens rea in the negotiation process.

THE CONFUSING PATCHWORK OF CRIMINAL INTENT LAW

One of the primary challenges with the law of criminal intent is that there are fifty-two different penal codes in American criminal law (fifty states, the District of Columbia, and federal). Today, fourteen states have adopted key mens rea provisions from the Model Penal Code. At the same time, many other violations of state law have inconsistent, vague, and/or nonexistent mens rea provisions. Some states have backtracked from mens rea requirements. For example, in 2002 the Florida legislature removed the provision of mens rea from state drug law violations. Under the revised Florida drug law, all that the government has to prove in the prosecution and conviction of a defendant is that he or she delivered a certain substance and that the substance was a controlled substance.

Washington State also has eliminated a mens rea requirement for drug possession.

In forty-three states, one can be convicted of murder without a showing of intent to kill the victim. This is the case under the felony-murder doctrine, which holds that an individual is guilty of murder without proof of intent if that murder occurred in the context of committing another felony crime. As such, murder under the felony-murder doctrine is a strict liability crime. Moreover, the law of parties permits the conviction of someone for murder who did not kill anyone but was simply participating in a crime when an accomplice independently decided to kill someone.

In *Clark v. Arizona*, the U.S. Supreme Court upheld, among other things, an Arizona decision that psychiatric testimony about a defendant's mental condition was admissible only for its relevance to an insanity defense and could not be used in the question of mens rea. The majority opinion in *Clark v Arizona* relied on the logic that expert testimony on mental illness regarding mens rea is confusing to juries and would compel juries to free dangerous criminals. Tough on crime indeed.

Other states have similar restrictions on the admissibility of psychiatric evidence to counter intent allegations. In total, thirteen states impose significant restrictions on the use of psychiatric evidence in challenging allegations of mens rea.[9] Many other states have some provisions for admission of mental disorder evidence, but they are by no means consistent across the states.

CRIMINAL INTENT AND OVERCRIMINALIZATION

While at her father's house near Fredricksburg, Virginia, eleven-year-old Skylar Capo rescued an injured baby woodpecker from being killed by a cat. Skylar asked her mother if she could take care of the bird for a couple of days until it was well enough to release. Her mother told her that was fine. On their way home, Skylar and her mother stopped at a hardware store. They took the bird, which was in a box, into the store because they did not want to leave it in the hot car. While in the store, they were confronted by a woman who identified herself as an officer from the U.S. Fish and Wildlife Service. The woman informed them that they had violated the Federal Migratory Bird Act. Two weeks later, the same Fish and Wildlife Service officer, accompanied by a Virginia State trooper, showed up at the Capo residence and issued a $535 citation to Skylar's mother for the violation. How is one to know they have broken the law?

On September 21, 2015, Senator Orrin Hatch addressed the U.S. Senate, speaking on the problem of overcriminalization and mens rea reform:

> The overcriminalization problem manifests itself in a variety of ways. First is through the sheer number of federal crimes. There are now nearly 5,000 criminal statutes scattered throughout the U.S. Code. But statutes are only part of the story. In addition, there are an estimated 300,000 criminal regulatory offenses. [10]

Overcriminalization is defined as the misuse and overuse of criminal penalties to address societal problems. The view of many individuals and organizations is that adequate mens rea requirements are fundamental to controlling this overreach of the federal criminal justice system. The proliferation of federal criminal statutes and regulations in the absence of adequate mens rea requirements renders problematic the phrase "ignorance of the law is no excuse."[11]

How big is the federal problem? By way of example, in 2009 the Heritage Foundation and the National Association of Criminal Defense Lawyers[12] found that nearly two-thirds of the nonviolent criminal offenses enacted by the 109th Congress (which sat from 2005 to 2006) lacked an adequate intent requirement.

The late Justice Antonin Scalia described the mens rea problem in the following way:

> It should be no surprise that as the volume increases, so do the number of imprecise laws. . . . Fuzzy, leave-the-details-to-be-sorted-out-by-the-courts legislation is attractive to the Congressman who wants credit for addressing a national problem [without addressing] the nitty gritty. [13]

The American Bar Association (ABA) is clear regarding its concern about inadequate mens rea requirements. Mens rea is necessary because it provides the normative criterion that punishment should be proportional to and limited by culpability or blameworthiness. The failure to include adequate mens rea requirements risks punishing morally blameless or morally innocent individuals. The ABA position likewise warns that the "erosion of the mens rea requirements threatens individuals with punishment for making honest mistakes or engaging in conduct that was not sufficiently wrongful *to give notice of criminal responsibility* [emphasis added]."[14]

A significant concern with inadequate mens rea requirements is the additional discretion and leverage it affords prosecutors. The road to conviction is clearly expedited when the government often does not have to be concerned with intent. Moreover, inadequate or missing intent provides the government wide latitude to prosecute cases that prosecutors see fit. In a recent (2011) book titled *Three Felonies a Day*, a Boston civil liberties attorney estimates that the average adult in the United States unwittingly and unknowingly commits three felonies daily because of vague, poorly written, and obscure laws.

Most of the discussion and concern about overcriminalization is focused on the federal government. However, states are not immune to the proliferation of crimes and regulations that have criminal consequences and ill-defined or absent criminal intent requirements. A state-by-state survey of the mens rea requirements highlights the wide variation in how states address criminal intent.[15] When a particular criminal statute does not specify a mens rea requirement, nineteen states have no relevant general mens rea provision. Three more states' codes do not define which crimes require mens rea.

The bigger-picture problem with laws that fail to specify an intent requirement is that it facilitates tough-on-crime policies. Lack of an intent requirement is an accelerated path to indictment and conviction and precludes any discussion of mitigation. That includes consideration of any disorders, impairments, and deficits a defendant may have.

WHY SUCH LAX TREATMENT OF MENS REA?

The answer to the question of why criminal intent took such a backseat in criminal proceedings lies at least partially in the culture and political climate of crime policy. It is not difficult to link the strict liability preferences of Congress, state legislatures, prosecutors, and judges to the nearly all-encompassing political environment of tough on crime.[16] Tough on crime has carried with it substantial political advantage for elected officials, which includes legislators, prosecutors, and state judges.

The variety of ways that has played out is not easy to know, but it is reasonable to think it has influenced lawmakers' decisions regarding mens rea requirements in criminal statutes. It certainly has had a major influence in the day-to-day prosecution of criminal cases. The goal is to increase prosecutions, convictions, and the processing of as many cases as efficiently as possible. Minimizing the impact of criminal intent is a way to facilitate accomplishment of these prosecutorial goals. Plea negotiation makes it that much easier to bypass intent considerations.

Another reason is that the appellate courts, especially the U.S. Supreme Court, have sent mixed messages about criminal intent. On the one hand, we have *Morissette* and *Elonis*, which affirm the importance of mens rea. On the other, we have cases like *Clark v. Arizona* that send different messages.

It seems likely that criminal intent is a complex matter that few lawyers really understand. While the Model Penal Code has simplified the language by reducing it to intentional, knowing, reckless, and negligent, it still involves matters of will, volition, consciousness, moral blameworthiness, and evil mind, among others. These can be difficult concepts to understand for philosophers and behavioral experts, not to mention prosecutors, judges, defense counsel, and juries.

MENS REA AND CRIMINAL JUSTICE REFORM

For a variety of reasons discussed above, mens rea has not and we believe cannot today serve its intended purpose as a procedural gatekeeper for differentiating, in the words of the U.S. Supreme Court in *Elonis*, those who are guilty of a crime and those who are otherwise innocent. In a culture of tough on crime, retributive, just deserts punishment policies, mens rea can be an inconvenient procedural requirement. Finding someone innocent who committed a crime but lacked the capacity for intent is counterproductive in a system based on maximizing punishment. What is tough about cutting someone loose who committed a serious crime simply because of some "technicality" regarding intent?

We began this analysis with the goal of using mens rea as it was designed to be used—as the mechanism for differentiating those who are criminally liable and those who are not. However, for a variety of reasons, the state of criminal intent law and the erosion of mens rea in criminal proceedings render it relatively useless for this purpose. That is not to say that mens rea reform should not be a priority. Efforts toward that end should focus on providing intent requirements to crimes, with very limited exceptions. Congress should take the lead in revising intent law for federal crimes, and especially federal regulations with criminal implications. Much of the current status of criminal intent is linked to tough-on-crime policies. As we come to recognize that tough on crime is counterproductive, we should also appreciate the importance of mens rea and use it as intended.

We believe that the state of intent law and the erosion of its use in criminal proceedings present an advantage in our effort to craft a path to meaningful diversion. We suggest that intent asks the wrong question. Intent focuses on whether someone is culpable or blameworthy. When someone is found to be or assumed to be blameworthy, that usually leads directly to the questions of how much harm was done when they committed the crime, and thus how much punishment is due. Blameworthiness implies retribution and just deserts. We argue that rather than focusing on blameworthiness and intent, and thus the reflexive matter of how much punishment (a harm-based, just deserts question), the goal should be how to reduce the likelihood of recidivism (an outcome-based question).

Our proposed alternative involves a shift in thinking about crime, punishment, and criminal offenders. We propose that prosecutors focus on what can be done to reduce the likelihood an individual will reoffend. The rationale is that this approach takes us away from the relatively universal, but failed, policy of blameworthiness, retribution, and punishment and places the business of criminal justice squarely on outcomes, the primary being reducing recidivism and enhancing public safety.

In many cases, incarceration, not rehabilitation, should be the first priority because of the nature of the crimes committed (for example, a violent offender or a predatory sex offender), or because an offender has an extensive criminal history. That is how we should use prison, for incapacitating those we truly fear, those who simply deserve retribution and punishment, and those who experts believe cannot be rehabilitated and should be physically separated from society.

We propose a diversion process on a scale unimagined in U.S. history. It is one that has as the primary goal the reduction of recidivism by means of a balance between risk management/supervision, on the one hand, and evidence-based clinical intervention and rehabilitation, on the other.

6

THE PATH FORWARD

Diverting Disordered Offenders

[handwritten margin note: no rehabilitation because they deserve consequence for breaking law.]

THE LOGIC

A regime focused primarily on the blameworthiness of offenders has arguably led to a primary emphasis on the retributive aspect of punishment, with other goals such as rehabilitation rarely considered. This is understandable, since blameworthiness is inevitably linked with what an offender *deserves* as a consequence of his law breaking. Such an approach has largely failed to take into consideration mitigating factors in offending such as mental illness (short of insanity), addiction, and intellectual and cognitive impairments and deficits. So we have continued to incarcerate more and more people for longer periods of time with little regard to whether there is any beneficial effect of this strategy beyond satisfying a punitive urge, and notwithstanding the enormous costs, both financial and human. The virtually reflexive use of incarceration and punishment as the primary response to offending has been made with little understanding of the effects of this mode of punishment on recidivism or the inevitable release of unrehabilitated offenders back into the community. Here, briefly, is what we know.

First, mentally ill individuals are no more likely to be violent than anyone else. It is unfortunate that media coverage of extreme situations has defined the link between mental illness and violence for the public. Incidents such as the Planned Parenthood shooting in Colorado Springs,

Colorado; the Fort Hood shooting in Texas; the Newtown school shooting in Connecticut; the Aurora theater shooting in Colorado; and the
shooting of Representative Gabby Giffords and the killing of six others,
where there is evidence that the perpetrator was mentally ill, often lead to
the conclusion that most mentally ill individuals are violent.

The evidence indicates precisely the opposite. Yes, some mentally ill
individuals are violent. But when we consider mentally ill individuals in
general,[1] and mentally ill criminal offenders in particular, the data just do
not support the conclusion that mentally ill individuals tend to be violent.
The Vera Institute, one of the leading criminal justice policy and research
organizations in the world, has comprehensively studied mental illness
and crime. They and dozens of other mental health and justice research
organizations, as well as nearly all researchers in the nation, conclude that
the vast majority of mentally ill offenders commit low-level, nonviolent
crimes.[2]

A widely cited 2006 study by the U.S. Department of Justice, Bureau
of Justice Statistics, shows that while nearly 50 percent of state prison
inmates with a mental illness were convicted of a violent crime, an essentially equal percentage (47 percent) of inmates without a mental illness
were convicted of a violent crime. The same patterns hold for federal
prison inmates and local jail detainees. Moreover, 50 percent of state
prison inmates with a mental illness were convicted of nonviolent crimes,
including property crimes, drug offenses, and public order offenses. The
vast majority of federal prison inmates with a mental illness were convicted of nonviolent crimes (over 50 percent for drug crimes). Finally, the
majority of mentally ill jail inmates (75 percent) were arrested for nonviolent offenses. The same study also looked at use of a weapon in the
commission of a crime and found no difference between mentally ill and
not mentally ill state prison and local jail detainees regarding use of a
weapon.

Mentally ill inmates released from prison on parole supervision are
twice as likely to return to prison as parolees who are not mentally ill.[3]
Mentally ill parolees are much more likely (than those without a mental
illness) to be returned to prison for a violation of the conditions of supervision, often as a result of untreated mental illness affecting their ability
to comply with the conditions of parole.[4] In some cases, the mental ill-
ness-recidivism link is direct, meaning the mental illness is the reason for
revocation or it interferes with their ability to comply. In other cases, it is

a result of mental illness being associated with other crime-related factors, such as unemployment, substance abuse, and homelessness. There is also evidence for the criminalization of mental illness, whereby supervision officers, parole authorities, and judges use lower thresholds for revoking mentally ill individuals.[5] The evidence is also clear that individuals with substance abuse problems recidivate at a significantly higher rate than those without a substance abuse disorder.[6]

The situation is worse for those with severe mental illness and co-occurring disorders.[7] Recidivism rates are substantially higher for those with a variety of serious Axis 1 disorders, including bipolar disorder, major depression, schizophrenia, and schizophreniform disorder, in combination with a substance abuse disorder.[8] Additional research shows that this pattern of recidivism also holds for mild mental illness and co-occurring substance abuse disorders.[9]

While the majority of mentally ill justice-involved individuals are nonviolent, they do recidivate at a greater rate and thus are a public safety risk as well as a burden on and a cost to the criminal justice system, including local law enforcement, jails, prosecutors, public defenders, the courts, and corrections. As unfortunate as this situation is for all involved, it is the reality of the day. The criminal justice system is the unwitting repository of many disordered individuals, including the mentally ill and those with substance abuse disorders and neurocognitive and intellectual disorders, deficits, and impairments.

Logic tells us that treating offenders for mental illness should reduce the risk of rearrest. The evidence supports this logic—treatment for mental illness reduces the likelihood of rearrest by nearly 50 percent for individuals released from prison.[10] The evidence is also clear that treating offenders for substance abuse significantly reduces the risk of recidivism.[11]

Despite the corner that criminal justice and behavioral health policies have been painted into, continuing down the same road is not likely to produce any better results than we have seen in the past. Moreover, there is considerable consensus among informed observers that current behavioral health and justice policies are unacceptable. Most media outlets in the United States have featured stories about the mental health crisis and the inappropriate use of jails and prisons as asylums. There has been a lot of talk, but not much action.

It is before this backdrop that we propose a new and rather radical approach (in terms of recent U.S. justice policy) to dealing with many of those accused of committing criminal offenses. This is a model based on outcomes, particularly recidivism reduction, not blameworthiness and just deserts. The approach shifts the focus from a largely exclusive assessment of moral responsibility and harm done, which usually leads automatically to how much punishment, to an emphasis on the best way to resolve a criminal situation and reduce the likelihood of an individual reoffending.

Resolving the criminal situation as we suggest involves the concept of problem solving. An offender's criminality should be thought of as a problem in need of resolution, not just quick legal disposition. Appropriate problem solving requires investigation of the crime as well as of the circumstances of the offender. It then requires the development of a plan most likely to produce a positive outcome (public safety, reduction in recidivism). Sometimes that involves traditional criminal prosecution, conviction, and punishment. In some cases incarceration is a necessary choice. But we need to recognize that the deeper an offender goes into the criminal and juvenile justice systems, the lower the likelihood of a positive outcome.

There is plenty of blame to go around for our high recidivism rates. Much of it is on the offender. But it doesn't (and shouldn't) stop there. It is important that the government (including elected officials, policymakers, prosecutors, judges, and corrections officials, among others) recognizes its role and accepts its share of responsibility for the revolving door of the justice system.

We assert that for most eligible cases (individuals with significant mental health and substance use disorders and/or neurocognitive and intellectual deficits and impairments), the best way to reduce the probability of recidivism is by diverting appropriate individuals into community-based programs focused on evidence-based behavioral change coupled with risk management strategies. Granted, "do the crime, do the time" and "lock 'em up and throw away the key" sound tough, proactive, and reassuring, but the reality is that such practices are a very poor investment in terms of recidivism, victimization, and cost. Why should we accept policies that compromise public safety, needlessly and avoidably put all of us at risk of criminal victimization, and waste hundreds of billions of dollars annually?

We propose in outline form the structure of such a system of diversion. In so doing, we acknowledge the institutional, political, and cultural challenges to be overcome. We also recognize that there certainly are ways to modify and improve what we propose that we have failed to incorporate. However, we are convinced by the overwhelming evidence of the need for comprehensive, systematic change and are confident that what we propose is a very productive direction in which to head.

What we propose then is an approach that first takes into consideration the risk of an offender in order to determine whether he or she is a reasonable candidate for diversion. Clearly, public safety is the end game. If an individual has significant impairments or disorders (the second criterion) but poses an unacceptably high risk of reoffending, that person presumably would not qualify. For those eligible by the risk criterion, a meaningful inquiry is made as to whether behavioral factors such as mental illness, addiction, and neurocognitive and/or intellectual deficits and impairments played a role in the offense, and, if so, whether interventions can reduce the probability of reoffending.

With this information, we can then tailor a response to a particular offense that may include diversion from traditional prosecution and punishment to programs that prioritize risk management and rehabilitation. Once the decision is made to divert an individual, he or she are then directed to well-resourced, evidence-driven, community-based programs of supervision and treatment that are designed and implemented with the specific goal of reducing the likelihood the defendant will reoffend, primarily through interventions aimed at behavior change and symptom management. At the same time, mechanisms must be in place to manage risk and ensure compliance. We discuss these mechanisms below.

Diversion is, of course, not a novel concept. Most prosecutors employ some mechanism for diverting certain defendants from the pipeline to incarceration, whether on an ad hoc basis or pursuant to a formalized process. Informal diversion, where a prosecutor simply decides that a particular offender should be spared the prospect of prosecution and likely incarceration, is usually done "off the books." That is, these decisions are made by individual prosecutors on a case-by-case basis, often with little guidance or accountability. There is no articulation of the criteria employed, little transparency or consistency, and no formal follow-up to determine whether the defendant reoffended. There are, of course, prosecutor's offices where more formalized practices exist, often incorporating special diversion programs that may include the type of evaluation and resources we are proposing. Referral to a drug court is a common example. But even these programs usually suffer from inherent limitations. For example, drug courts are generally effective in reducing recidivism and relapse. However, they are quite limited in resources, with the capacity to meet about 5–10 percent of the need.[12] The fact remains, whether by means of a formal or informal diversion process, that prosecutors are already identifying cases that don't belong in the pipeline to punishment. But they face several challenges when trying to identify offenders who they suspect might be appropriate for diversion.

First, prosecutors are lawyers, and generally lack substantial training and expertise in behavioral health, including assessing mental illness, addiction, and cognitive and intellectual disorders. As such, prosecutors are not in a good position to identify those who might in fact be good candidates for diversion. They may miss or misinterpret cues. For example, some individuals who suffer from mental illness may not exhibit typical indicia of remorse or may not at the time of arrest appear to be prime candidates for diversion. Moreover, it is often difficult to uncover the existence of mental illness or other behavioral disorders as a factor in criminality. And even when prosecutors see indications of behavioral or cognitive disorders that might suggest that a response other than incarceration is appropriate, they may lack confidence in their observations, causing them to be too conservative in endorsing alternatives. It is difficult, then, to know whether the "right" offenders are being diverted (those who have a reasonable likelihood of being rehabilitated), much less whether the diversion policies are successful in lowering rates of recidivism.

Second, prosecutors currently have little institutional support in deciding which offenders to divert from traditional prosecution and imprisonment. Because they alone have the responsibility of determining the appropriate disposition of the cases that are presented to them, prosecutors know that they likewise bear the responsibility for diverting an offender from the traditional path to prison if the person ultimately reoffends. By incorporating a formal diversion mechanism as a part of the system, prosecutors will not only be able to rely on the expertise of others to identify individuals appropriate for diversion (more on that shortly) but also have confidence that these individuals will get the treatment, services, and supervision that will maximize the likelihood they will stay out of the system. As we have observed, while many diversion programs have achieved significant results and serve as illustrations for the approach we are advocating, such programs are not uniformly available and frequently suffer from a shortage of resources. Even formal diversion programs that involve supervision and treatment are under-resourced and are not given the attention and status of the programs that are more directly related to the primary mission of a prosecutor's office—pursuing and obtaining criminal convictions. As a result, diversion programs are not vested with the status of a legitimate, essential component of the criminal justice system.

Finally, prosecutors usually lack reliable alternatives upon which they can rely, such as well-established and well-resourced intervention and treatment programs. From our own discussions with prosecutors and law enforcement officials, we are confident that most would embrace alternatives to incarceration for appropriate offenders if they had confidence in the programs to which they would be diverted. As we have observed elsewhere, prosecutors and law enforcement officials understand better than anyone that, except when a life sentence is imposed, offenders who are incarcerated *will eventually be released*. We advocate, then, a system in which we capitalize on the potential not only to rehabilitate but also to provide the treatment and support necessary to achieve those goals *up front.* We believe that some programs exist that offer a significant opportunity to address factors underlying criminal behavior and get offenders out of the cycle of reoffending. Moreover, we know how to build successful programming that can substantially change behavior and reduce the likelihood of recidivism.

We propose that a new, formal diversionary option be added to the criminal justice system, in which the expertise of a variety of professionals be brought to bear both on the identification of individuals appropriate for diversion and on the development and implementation of programs to keep them out of the traditional correctional system in the long run. We propose a system that includes a more formalized sorting process with defined criteria and the involvement of not only prosecutors but also experts in a variety of relevant disciplines. These experts, acting as a team and following an established protocol, would be presented with offenders whose offense conduct and background suggest that they might be candidates for diversion from prosecution. These teams would make assessments early in the process—post-arrest but typically pre-indictment. And they would have the ability to make a recommendation to the prosecuting authority that an appropriate individual be put on a different path from the one that would otherwise lead to incarceration or simply punishment, one that would involve a program of treatment and supervision appropriate to their needs. Likewise, we propose that the programs to which offenders are diverted be interdisciplinary and separately funded from prosecuting authorities to ensure that minimizing recidivism remains at the core of their mission. We maintain there is strong reason to believe that fully funded programs run by experts in the field using evidence-based programs and practices have the prospect of substantially lowering recidivism rates.

The primary sense in which our proposal differs from the current response to offending is the focus on outcomes. Most punishment decisions are now made with regard to matching the seriousness of the punishment with the seriousness of the crime. Once the threshold state of mind requirement is met or presumed (mens rea), there is generally little inquiry into the effect of mental illness, addiction, or cognitive and intellectual impairment. While we do not, as a philosophical matter, wish to contest the premise that people who commit bad acts deserve their just punishment, we do suggest that other very important factors be considered in fashioning a response to criminal conduct. And we do make the claim that the focus on punishment and incarceration as the primary response to crime has caused us to miss opportunities to realize other worthy goals. We are not recommending amnesty for offenders. We envision a system in which those clearly deserving of punishment are suitably punished. Instead, we are proposing a commonsense reevaluation of criminal justice policy other than simple, reflexive punishment. And we believe this will lead us to conclude that there are other outcomes equally, if not more, desirable.

To be sure, we advocate a response to offending that ensures that those who deserve punishment, whether by virtue of the nature of their crime (for example, violent crime) or their history of offending (for example, chronic, habitual offenders), face the appropriate consequences for their acts. But we also propose that a compelling case can be made for an approach that asks important questions about whether, in appropriate cases, responses other than incarceration or punishment would fully serve the community's interests as well as give offenders the opportunity and resources to become productive members of society.

We are fortunate that the tools necessary to bring about fundamental change to behavioral health care delivery and treatment outcomes are largely known and have been evaluated. There is a large and growing repository of evidence-based treatments and interventions for individuals with mental health disorders, substance use disorders, neurodevelopmental and neurocognitive impairments, intellectual deficiencies, and comorbid disorders. These practices, many of which we reviewed earlier in these pages, have been ordained as evidence-based practices (EBPs) by organizations such as the American Psychiatric Association, the American Psychological Association, the Substance Abuse and Mental Health Services Administration, the American Medical Association, the Treatment Advocacy Center, the National Alliance on Mental Health, the National Institute on Drug Abuse, the Association for Cognitive and Behavioral Therapies, and the University of Washington's Alcohol and Drug Abuse Institute, among many others.

As we know from our discussion earlier, while we have much of the knowledge, we lack the infrastructure on the ground to follow through on these evidence-based practices. The lack of infrastructure is a consequence of a lack of funding and a lack of the political will required to implement the necessary changes and to adequately resource the public health system. While it seems ludicrous, an outsider might look at this situation and conclude that policymakers must think it is okay for the criminal justice system to "manage" much of behavioral health in this country.

Many of the efforts that are necessary to achieve the outcomes of reducing crime, recidivism, victimization, and expenditures include a variety of agencies, organizations, and institutions involved with public health, encompassing treatment for mental health, substance abuse, cognitive and intellectual disorders, and physical health, as well as federal agencies and organizations, like Medicare and Medicaid, Veterans Affairs, Housing and Urban Development, and many more state and local organizations. All of these must be key players going forward.

The goal is to reduce justice system involvement and enhance treatment and rehabilitation of disordered offenders. We know that the deeper an offender goes in the criminal and juvenile justice systems, the worse the outcome, meaning a higher risk of recidivism. What we propose is an up-front diversion process that identifies appropriate individuals at the front end of processing arrestees and diverts them from deeper penetration into the court and correctional system to appropriate supervision and treatment.

A PROPOSED DIVERSION MODEL

> Safe and humane mental health and substance use treatment should be provided in the least-restrictive environment, namely, communities and neighborhoods not jails or prisons. . . . Diversion and alternatives to incarceration for people with mental illness and addictions should become overarching public health goals of a new, responsive mental health system. Jails are no place for people with serious illnesses of any kind, yet they have become the largest institution for people with mental disorders in this country. [13]

Not only is community-based treatment for mental illness and substance abuse preferable from the perspective of mental health experts, but it has also been found to be more effective than treatment in an incarceration setting. [14] In fact, federal law codifies the fact that prison is not an appropriate venue for rehabilitation. In 18 U.S. Code § 3582 (Imposition of a Sentence of Imprisonment), the federal code states:

> The court, in determining whether to impose a term of imprisonment, and, if a term of imprisonment is to be imposed, in determining the length of the term, shall consider the factors set forth in section 3553(a) to the extent that they are applicable, recognizing that imprisonment is not an appropriate means of promoting correction and rehabilitation. [15]

Moreover, the incarceration of offenders with mental illness or substance abuse, or the combination of the two, is often a return ticket to prison.

Prosecutors currently play the primary role in determining which offenders are diverted from the traditional path of prosecution and punishment. For the reasons discussed above, we believe that a program of effective, evidence-based diversion must begin with the expertise of a variety of other professionals. In place of the current system of prosecutors unilaterally making diversion decisions according to unknown or imprecise criteria, there would be a separate, quasi-independent entity designed and staffed by behavioral health experts with the special purpose of determining the fitness of a given offender for a program of diversion. We believe that the participation of these experts should be formalized and that the proceedings of the panels be non-adversarial. We also recommend that the panelists are appointed by local prosecutors and judges.

Although this might be accomplished in a variety of ways, we propose that the most straightforward and transparent model would provide for a panel or committee of specially qualified and trained professionals that would include social workers, psychiatrists, psychologists, and other mental health, addiction, and neurocognitive professionals. This panel of experts would bring to bear the most reliable diagnostic and predictive tools to assess the extent to which an individual offender's risk of reoffending is suitable for diversion, and to ascertain whether he or she has significant impairments and disorders that are likely linked to their offending. The panel would also offer their judgment regarding the likelihood that treatment would reduce the probability of recidivism.

The initial assessment of disorder and risk is stage one of the panel's decision-making role. Obviously, there is a trade-off between what is preferable or beneficial from a treatment or clinical perspective and the threat to public safety posed by an offender with a significant risk of reoffending. So, one consideration is whether an offender poses such a risk that he or she needs to be incarcerated (incapacitated) to prevent reoffending or whether that individual's risk can be sufficiently managed in a community-based setting. Public safety is the priority, but that includes both short-term and long-term public safety. What may seem like an appropriate response in the interest of short-term public safety (incarceration, for example) may in fact increase the long-term risk of reoffending repeatedly.

Once a determination is made that the risk is at a level that is appropriate for diversion, the panelists then assess the presence and severity of any disorders, impairments, and deficits. The next question is how to optimize the outcome of the case—that is, what can be done to reduce the likelihood of reoffending? The point is to shift the thinking and decision making to how to achieve the most favorable outcome in terms of recidivism reduction. Having said that, it may be tempting or logical for the panelists to want to consider criminal responsibility or culpability as an element of the totality of the evidence. However, we caution against putting too much weight on this because of the inherent difficulties in aligning clinical evidence and decision making with culpability. That is partly why we rejected the use of mens rea as a key element in the diversion decision. If questions of responsibility or culpability arise, we recommend they be answered in general, commonsense, layperson terms, focusing on the question of whether any assessed disorders, impairments, and deficits probably mitigate responsibility.

If the panel finds that the individual is an acceptable public safety risk and has significant disorders and/or impairments that are likely contributing to criminality, and that treatment would probably be helpful in reducing recidivism, we would expect the panel at that point to refer the case to the prosecutor for diversion. If the prosecutor accepts the recommendation, the panel can further assess the individual and develop a recommendation for diversion and a preliminary treatment plan. The panel could also recommend risk management strategies such as level and frequency of supervision and imposition of particular conditions of supervision. Obviously, the prosecutor could also set supervision conditions and risk mitigation strategies.

Prosecutors retain the ultimate authority over cases. They can identify cases that are categorically ineligible for diversion by the nature or severity of the crime or the individual's extensive prior criminal history or failed prior attempts at diversion and rehabilitation. These are the types of cases for which there are really no other viable options than separation from society. In some cases, that decision may be motivated by retribution. In other instances it could be based on the goal of incapacitation. Both are appropriate motivations for incarceration. Those cases would not even go to the panel. Moreover, the panel's recommendations are advisory, meaning prosecutors have veto power over its recommendations. In the event that the recommendation is rejected, we contemplate that the prosecuting authority would identify the justification for failing to follow the recommendation, both for the sake of transparency and to provide data for evaluative use. Finally, the defendant also has the right to reject a diversion offer. In all three of these circumstances, cases would be prosecuted and sentenced in the traditional manner.

We anticipate that the panels would develop procedural guidelines and adopt professional standards in conducting their assessments and making their recommendations. We do not offer such standards here since they should be developed by the panelists themselves. We also anticipate that the panelists will be able to review all the relevant information that is available about a particular individual. In some cases, they may require additional information such as psych evaluations or other testing. Resources should be available for such eventualities. We would also expect the panels to develop a protocol for voting on individual cases regarding recommendations for and against diversion.

Diversion can take several forms—traditional probation, specialized probation, deferred adjudication, deferred prosecution, dismissal of charges, or the various types of diversion used in problem-solving courts like drug and mental health courts. While different jurisdictions may adopt whatever strategies are acceptable, we recommend that the diversion decision is pre-conviction and pre-indictment whenever possible. The rationale is that, at least in some cases, the advantages of not having a criminal conviction and not having an indictment can not only serve as leverage or incentive for a defendant to agree to diversion but also provide motivation while in treatment.

To be clear, the panel's decisions are based on likelihood—this individual probably poses an acceptable risk for diversion, this individual is probably sufficiently impaired, the disorders and deficits probably played a significant role in his or her criminal offending, and there is a reasonable chance that effective intervention will reduce the likelihood of reoffending. All these decisions are probabilities, and, as such, some cases will result in failures. The goal is to accept that there will be failures, but to minimize them as the experts gain experience and learn from prior errors.

It is important to note that we do not envision a diversion assessment procedure in which an offender would have any due process rights. In that the diversion panels will be operating as an extension of, and subject to the discretion of, the prosecuting authority, it is our intention that their function would exempt them from due process requirements as an exercise of prosecutorial discretion. That is, offenders will have neither a right to the assessment nor the right to any due process during assessment. Nor would they be able to seek legal review of the recommendation of a diversion panel or a prosecutor's decision to reject a recommendation of diversion. We believe this is an important feature of the system, and its design and articulation should be crafted in such a manner as to foreclose claims that an offender would have any due process rights. This is important for several reasons. First, prosecutors must believe, and be correct in believing, that they are retaining full prosecutorial discretion. They must see diversion panels as valuable assets in assisting them in making just and appropriate decisions about the fate of an offender. Further, it is important that the diversion assessment process not become a procedural bureaucracy in which offenders stage mini-trials in hopes of avoiding incarceration. In a very real sense, we consider the diversion panels to be a part, albeit a formalized one, of the exercise of prosecutorial discretion. Again, offenders would have the right to reject diversion, which could result in formal criminal prosecution.

The offender's rejection of diversion is not the desired outcome. The goal here is to get appropriate individuals away from criminal prosecution and into treatment. One way that offenders can be persuaded to accept diversion is the threat of criminal prosecution and punishment if the offer is rejected, as well as the inducement of dismissal of charges if diversion is accepted and completed. This is part and parcel of the plea negotiation process, and the threat or incentive may motivate some who would otherwise reject the offer of diversion.

JUVENILE OFFENDERS

Juvenile offenders and the juvenile justice system present a particularly important opportunity for reducing crime and recidivism. However, this requires fundamental changes as to how we go about the business of processing, sentencing, and punishing juveniles.

For much of the history of the juvenile justice system, the emphasis was on rehabilitation. However, beginning in the early 1990s, we saw a dramatic shift away from rehabilitation toward punishment. Tough on crime came to characterize how we dealt with juvenile offending. This led to an increasing alignment of the juvenile justice system with the criminal justice system. Retributive punishments, mandatory sentences, and liberal laws governing transferring juvenile offenders to adult court and adult punishment came to define the juvenile justice system. As I concluded in 2016:

> [W]e lead the world in the use of incarceration for youthful offenders. The juvenile incarceration rate in the United States is roughly six times that of the Netherlands, seven times that of the United Kingdom, twelve times that of Australia and Germany, over sixteen times that of France, twenty-seven times that of Italy, seventy-five times that of Finland and Sweden, and three hundred times that of Japan.[16]

One of the results of this heavy reliance on incarceration is that juvenile detention centers in the United States have become, as is the case with adult prisons, the repository for many disordered and impaired kids, for whom there are few other options.

Another similarity between the adult and juvenile justice systems is the extraordinarily high recidivism rate. Rearrest of juveniles released from custody ranges between 75 and 90 percent. Reconviction rates average around 70–80 percent after three years of release. These metrics indicate a highly risk-prone, disordered, impaired population of offenders, a substantial lack of effectiveness in correcting/treating juvenile offenders, or (more likely) a combination of both.

These policies have important downstream consequences since involvement with the juvenile justice system is a very strong predictor of adult criminality. A National Academies of Sciences report from 1986 estimated that 50–60 percent of adult offenders had juvenile justice involvement.[17] More recent research puts the probability of being arrested as an adult at four times higher for those who were arrested as a juvenile, compared to those who were not arrested as a juvenile.[18] Moreover, those with juvenile justice involvement who were rearrested as adults were much more likely to have multiple adult arrests, compared to those who were arrested as adults but had no prior juvenile involvement. In fact, this latter group is very likely to be arrested only once.

Not only is there a pipeline from the juvenile justice system to adult criminality and criminal justice involvement, but the evidence is also clear that how we go about the business of juvenile justice substantially increases the flow of offenders into adult criminality. While a juvenile arrest significantly increases the likelihood of adult criminality, juvenile justice interventions (incarceration, supervision) increase the probability of adult crime by a factor of nearly 38. There is no deterrent effect, and the experience of juvenile justice involvement dramatically heightens the risk that juvenile offenders will persist into adult criminality.[19]

A similar worsening of long-term outcomes appears to result from the transfer of juveniles to adult court. The research shows that adult prosecution, conviction, and punishment of juveniles does not reduce recidivism but instead increases it.[20] The result is that one of the tougher tough-on-crime strategies for juvenile offenders has extraordinarily negative consequences.

A variety of factors play into juvenile criminality, not the least of which are mental illness, substance abuse, intellectual deficiencies, and neurodevelopmental and neurocognitive impairments and deficits. As is the case with adult offenders, punishment likely aggravates these disorders and deficits. In fact, a recent assessment of juvenile crime and juvenile justice involvement led to the following conclusions:

> [T]he weight of the evidence suggests that involvement with the juvenile justice system does more harm than good, with negative effects magnified as punishments become harsher. . . . In light of the neuroscientific evidence on developmental immaturity, it is a distinct possibility that punitive settings disrupt adolescent development in ways that increase the likelihood of subsequent crime.[21]

The evidence is clear that there are short-term and long-term consequences associated with what we do with juvenile offenders. We have made rather radical, systemic, evidence-based recommendations regarding how to reduce recidivism among adult offenders. We make even stronger recommendations for juvenile offenders.

The U.S. Supreme Court has told us that the death penalty and life without parole sentences for juvenile offenders are unconstitutional, because of the special circumstances involving mental, emotional, and neurocognitive development of youth. We take this logic a good bit further. We recommend that incarceration of juveniles should be limited to situations where the goal is retribution or incapacitation. Either the nature of the crime (for example, a particularly violent crime) or the determination that an individual is a serious public safety threat (and the only way to mitigate that risk is through incapacitation) should be the reasons for incarceration. We need to abandon ideas about deterrence. The evidence is clear that the severity of punishment does not deter. Thus, the toughest punishment should be reserved for cases where the circumstances of the crime or the offender substantially outweigh the likely greater harm done by incarceration. Consistent with our recommendation for adults, the remainder of juvenile offenders should have minimal contact with the juvenile justice system, and should be diverted to treatment and risk management. We also envision a process for juveniles that is the same as for adults—panels of professional behavioral experts that screen and assess individual offenders for suitable risk and presence of crime-related mental, substance use, neurocognitive, and/or intellectual disorders and impairments. These panels then recommend cases for diversion to prosecutors. Presumably, decisions about diversion versus further criminal prosecution will be made in light of the clear evidence indicating that contact with the juvenile justice system considerably increases the risk of reoffending.

RISK MANAGEMENT AND COMPLIANCE

Regardless of the type of diversion, a very important component is risk management. Risk management refers to strategies that reduce the likelihood that a diverted offender will reoffend while on diversion. At the same time, interventions must be deployed that address crime-related factors such as mental illness, homelessness, unemployment, substance abuse, and neurocognitive and intellectual disorders, among others. It is this delicate balance between control and risk management, on the one hand, and therapeutic interventions, on the other, that is critical for this population of offenders.

As we mentioned earlier, the link between mental illness and crime is largely indirect. Much of what looks like a direct effect of mental illness on crime is in fact other crime-related factors associated with mental illness, including conditions, circumstances, deficits, and disorders such as substance abuse, unemployment, homelessness, family problems, antisocial personality patterns (low self-control, sensation seeking), and antisocial cognition (thoughts, beliefs, attitudes, and values that are conducive to crime and include misinterpreting social behavior as threatening, instant gratification, and lack of empathy). The evidence is compelling that while mental illness may be the most obvious marker, it is these related risk factors that lead to criminal behavior much more often than mental illness.[22] Moreover, mentally ill offenders tend to have more risk factors than non–mentally ill offenders.

Mentally ill offenders have a higher likelihood of return to prison or jail, but are no more likely to be rearrested than non–mentally ill offenders. What this means is that mentally ill offenders have higher rates of revocation off probation and parole for violating the conditions of supervision, known as technical violations. The typical scenario is that a supervision officer learns that an offender on probation or parole has violated one or more conditions of supervision. When that occurs, it is generally at the discretion of the officer whether to initiate revocation proceedings. The evidence indicates that supervision officers are more likely to revoke a mentally ill offender on community supervision for a technical violation. There is also evidence that supervision officers watch mentally ill offenders more closely, in turn increasing the likelihood that they will discover violations of conditions.[23]

This line of research leads to two important conclusions about mentally ill offenders on community supervision. First, recidivism reduction of mentally ill offenders must include interventions and programming that address the crime-related conditions and disorders associated with mental illness. That does not, however, mean that we can ignore mental illness. Some criminality is directly related to psychiatric symptoms. Second, mental health treatment and symptom management can facilitate intervention strategies targeting other risk factors and reduce the likelihood of mentally ill offenders committing technical violations of supervision.[24]

We do not have a hard and fast recommendation regarding who should conduct supervision and risk management of diverted offenders. There are advantages and disadvantages to various scenarios. Probation officers are an obvious choice, but assuming diversion occurs prior to conviction, and realizing that probation is a post-conviction sentence, it probably would have to be a special type of probation unit for diversion. Moreover, it would require substantial training and cultural changes of supervision officers. One of the problems with probation is the imbalance between programs and services designed to reduce reoffending and strategies to enhance success while on probation, on the one hand, compared to the supervision and control function, on the other. If probation had responsibility for supervision of the individuals we propose diverting, there would have to be substantial realignment of the roles, responsibilities, beliefs, and attitudes of supervision officers that result in outcome-based supervision strategies, with recidivism reduction as the top priority. Pretrial services, the agency that is in charge of pre-trial release, could also be a candidate. Or perhaps it's an entirely new agency in the criminal justice system.

In the end, who is less important than how. The "how" part is derived from evaluation research on probation and parole supervision of mentally ill offenders. While we are not implicitly recommending probation and parole officers for supervising diverted offenders, there are evaluation findings about strategies of supervision that are transferrable to other settings. Here is what the research indicates are effective supervision, risk management strategies.

Specialty mental health probation evolved out of traditional probation to address the challenges of supervising mentally ill offenders sentenced to probation. Specialty probation is characterized by several key features. One is reduced caseload, from the traditional caseload of more than one hundred to fewer than fifty for a specialty caseload, as well as more frequent contacts between probationers and officers. A second characteristic is that specialty caseload officers receive specialized training relevant to understanding mental illness. Third, specialty supervision officers make efforts to integrate and align internal probation resources and external treatment resources. The point is to attempt to meld supervision and treatment where the officer can become more involved in treatment decision making and the treatment process. Compliance is more generally accomplished with problem solving and incentives, rather than the traditional approach of threats, sanctions, and revocation. Revocation and jail are often measures of success for traditional probation, but they are a last resort for specialty supervision of mentally ill offenders, largely because of a recognition that functional impairments of mentally ill offenders make violations more frequent and that revocation does not generally have a good outcome. Finally, specialty supervision officers attempt to develop fair, firm, and understanding relationships with offenders, rather than the more typical authoritarian posture for regular probation.[25] While all this sounds reasonable, the obvious question is: Does it work? Is specialty probation supervision of mentally ill offenders effective?

The bottom line is that specialty probation supervision is effective in terms of intermediate goals such as enhancing access to psychiatric treatment and reduction in violation reports. The evidence indicates that positive compliance strategies (rather than sanctions) as well as establishing a good relationship with those they supervise were key in reducing violations of conditions. While the frequency of supervision contacts made officers more often aware of violations of conditions, well-trained officers engaged problem-solving strategies to resolve situations, rather than revocation to prison, which is more characteristic of traditional probation.

Another approach for offenders with mental illness is called Forensic Assertive Community Treatment (FACT). FACT is an adaptation of Assertive Community Treatment, or ACT, which is an evidence-based psychosocial intervention for individuals with severe mental illness. The

ACT model includes a mobile, multidisciplinary team consisting of psychiatrists, nurses, addiction specialists, vocational rehabilitation, and housing assistance, among others, who are available around the clock. The team is responsible for all treatment services, and the majority of services are provided in the community. Caseloads are small, facilitating frequent contact and community outreach and engagement.[26]

FACT adds to the ACT model interfaces with the justice system, enrollment of those with prior arrests and jail time, integrating law enforcement and probation officers into the team, encouraging referrals from the justice system, and prioritizing recidivism reduction as the key goal. The evaluation research on FACT is sparse, but one study in particular provides strong evidence documenting that FACT participants had reduced jail detentions and hospital stays and more frequent outpatient contacts.[27] Another evaluation found that a FACT program focusing on homelessness, intensive community-based recovery services, and reduced justice system involvement resulted in reduced jail bookings and days in jail, and reduction in inpatient psychiatric services.

The FACT and specialty probation models, as well as components of each, are certainly worth considering in developing supervision strategies for diverted disordered offenders. The key drivers in those decisions should be the substantial challenges these individuals present in terms of the number and complexity of risk factors, their treatment/intervention needs, and the impact of their disorders, impairments, and deficits on treatment success, compliance, and retention, and day-to-day functioning.

In general, the use of sanctions and punishment on mentally ill offenders is a last resort. However, sometimes it is necessary. Moreover, the use of sanctions on other types of disordered offenders (for example, substance abusers or the neurocognitively impaired) may be helpful in enhancing compliance. What some evidence indicates is worth considering as a sanction approach is what is called a swift and certain sanction court. While severity of punishment is not an effective deterrent to reoffending, some limited evidence supports the swiftness and certainty of mild punishment as an effective way to enhance compliance with supervision conditions. Swift and certain sanction courts are a version of problem-solving courts. The prototype was developed in Hawaii in 2004 and is called the HOPE Court (Hawaii's Opportunity Probation with Enforcement). The HOPE Court was designed to increase accountability and compliance among probationers who are in drug treatment. The method is really quite simple. Rather than relying on the severity of punishment, this approach maximizes the certainty and swiftness of modest punishment to enhance compliance. The evaluation research indicates that while severe punishment has very limited behavior-altering effects, swift and certain but modest punishment—a night or two in jail—may be quite effective in getting individuals who violate the conditions of probation to follow the rules. The threat of such sanctions is also a key element in increasing compliance. The HOPE Court concept has mainly been applied to a variety of offenders on probation. Today, at least sixty jurisdictions in more than eighteen states have HOPE court–based swift and certain sanctioning courts for probationers. The point here is that swift and certain sanctioning is one tool among several that supervision officers can use. It is important, however, that we understand the circumstances of offenders in order to know whether sanctioning is appropriate and whether the threat of sanctioning is a realistic deterrent.

While keeping individuals engaged and participating in treatment is the objective, there will be cases where offenders drop out or otherwise quit participating. When other strategies such as swift and certain sanctioning have failed, revocation and criminal prosecution are available when appropriate. Presumably, such decisions would be made in collaboration with an offender's treatment team.

PROCEDURES FOR IDENTIFYING DISORDERED OFFENDERS: DIAGNOSIS VERSUS DYSFUNCTION

One of the most important objectives in what we propose is accurately identifying who should be criminally prosecuted and who should be diverted. We propose that the prosecutor should be able to rule out for diversion certain offenses (for example, certain violent crimes) and certain types of offenders (for example, chronic habitual offenders). Presumably, those that do not meet the prosecutor's exclusion criteria should be eligible for diversion. A very important question is: How are the expert panelists to determine who should be recommended for diversion?

The nearly universal protocol for doing that is by determining a diagnosis utilizing the criteria provided in the *Diagnostic and Statistical Manual of Mental Disorders* (DSM). While determining a diagnosis is the common method for defining disorders, there is little about the label of bipolar that helps us address how bipolar disorder is linked to crime and recidivism, and in turn what to do about it. Rather, what seems much more relevant are the behavioral and cognitive dysfunctions that are associated with (or consequences of) mental illness, neurocognitive and neurodevelopmental disorders, substance abuse, and intellectual deficiencies. It is these dysfunctions, rather than the diagnosis per se, that have clear implications for behavior and thus criminality.

The DSM has been characterized as a checklist of symptoms that allows professionals to attach labels to their patients' mental disorders. As Thomas Insel, director of the National Institute of Mental Health from 2002 to 2015, put it in 2013:

> The goal of this new manual [the DSM-5], as with all previous editions, is to provide a common language for describing psychopathology. While DSM has been described as a "Bible" for the field, it is, at best, a dictionary creating a set of labels and defining each. The strength of each of the editions of DSM has been "reliability"—each edition has ensured that clinicians use the same term in the same ways. The weakness is its lack of validity. Unlike our definitions of ischemic heart disease, lymphoma or AIDS, the DSM diagnoses are based on a consensus about clusters of clinical symptoms, not any objective laboratory measure. In the rest of medicine, this would be equivalent to creating diagnostic systems based on the nature of chest pain or the quality of fever. Indeed, symptom-based diagnosis, once common in other areas of medicine, has been largely replaced in the past half century as we have understood that symptoms alone rarely indicate the best choice of treatment. [28]

Insel is not alone in this characterization of the DSM, as many behavioral health experts have expressed similar concerns with the DSM and diagnostic procedures. [29] Concerns with the DSM have led the National Institute of Mental Health to develop a new framework for conducting research on mental disorders. The NIMH has developed what it calls research domain criteria that create an interdisciplinary view of psychopathology that incorporates biology and neuroscience and links disorder and behavior.

Even though there are significant limitations, the DSM provides common language for discussing mental illness among psychiatrists and psychologists as well as government agencies such as the courts, prisons, and social service providers. The DSM diagnoses are also used for insurance reimbursements.

We are not recommending that behavioral health professionals stop using the DSM. Rather, we propose a framework that utilizes the DSM for guiding the identification of particular disorders and comorbidities, but then focuses more directly and intensely on identifying the collateral behavioral, cognitive, or intellectual dysfunctions that are present. The goal is to identify the behavioral implications of various disorders and impairments, and in turn develop the most appropriate treatment plan. As Craddock and Mynors-Wallis recommend:

> A good psychiatrist (as any good doctor) must be aware of the limitations of the diagnostic categories used and decisions made. It is important to think beyond diagnosis and make assessments of causation, the range and pattern of symptoms, severity and impairment in functioning (sometimes called "domains of psychopathology"). The key is to produce a formulation that goes beyond a simple list of facts and that complements the diagnosis by including information about important clinical variables that have relevance for the management plan. [30]

While diagnosis as represented in the current version of the DSM is one useful and common language to speak with regard to mental health evaluations, it is perhaps not the most important communication for our purposes. Sometimes experienced therapists speak of how easy it is to diagnose individuals upon a first meeting, but as you get to know them over weeks and months, it becomes harder to place them in the available DSM categories. Human beings are capable of appreciating nuances of personality and functioning in another that defy categories. Nuanced narratives summarize the complex integration of issues and derivatives more accurately and usefully than diagnostic categories. Two twenty-year-old intellectually disabled males may have identical IQs, but one may need help with anger control and be prone to hitting when frustrated, while the other wanders the neighborhood without a concept of private property. Both may come into contact with the criminal justice system but for very different reasons, and both require vastly different interventions to prevent reoccurrences. The goal is not just labeling people using diagnoses from the DSM but also determining the functional impairments impacting behavior.

Below we provide an outline of what we believe is a more comprehensive view of the behavioral consequences of the disorders, impairments, and deficits that we have been discussing. We refer to this framework as "spheres of psychological dysfunction." These spheres describe deficits and dysfunctions of multiple etiologies and include, but are not limited to, the language of the DSM. We assert that a better approach to recidivism reduction and enhancing the functionality of offenders in the community is one that is not exclusively linked to traditional labels or diagnoses. Rather, the bigger picture of criminality is one that investigates the dysfunctions that offenders present with in order to develop more precise and effective interventions.

We want to emphasize that this approach is a work in progress and is certainly subject to modification and revision. However, we believe this framework provides the necessary perspective for understanding the behavioral implications of various disorders and impairments by directing attention to treating not just symptoms but also the behavioral risk factors associated with crime and recidivism. We provide examples of common disorders that are associated with each sphere to illustrate the connections between traditional DSM diagnoses and their behavioral and cognitive consequences or dysfunctions.

Severe Emotional Dysregulation

Think of a two-year-old who is having a temper tantrum. This is a classic picture of a moment when an individual has no capacity to regulate anger or the behavior associated with it. Now imagine a similar emotional "blind rage" in a fifteen-, eighteen-, twenty-five-, or forty-five-year-old. We see through usual brain development an increase in the ability to regulate emotions due to changes in the developing brain that produce specialized neuronal tracks and more cortex (thinking help) inhibition of pure emotional outbursts. Anyone who has been around a twelve- to thirteen-year-old knows that they feel small things very deeply and have issues redirecting or modulating these feelings. While this usually gradually improves with natural brain development, some neuropsychiatric conditions such as executive dysfunction may limit the capacity to develop adequate modulation.

Emotional dysregulation is often associated with the diagnoses of major depression, bipolar disorder, disruptive mood dysregulation disorder, and post-traumatic stress disorder.

Social Perception Impairments/ Failure to Have Empathetic Capacities

Empathy is the ability to imagine accurately what another person feels, thinks, and experiences in a particular situation. Empathy is different from sympathy, which involves feeling badly for another person for what they are going through. Experiencing an empathic moment involves an emotionally intimate connection with another person and having the capacity of abstract thinking to do a "brain experiment" with a considerable degree of accuracy. Empathy is arguably the mental health professional's most useful tool. Under the best of circumstances, and even with the most skilled "empathizers," accuracy is not 100 percent, and one must be ready to modify empathic positions based on new data received and new experiences with the subject. Empathy does not always involve positive feelings and experiences. It is possible to be empathic with a person who has little conscience or care about the harm caused by his or her preferred actions. This is still useful empathy, but it leads one to caution and feelings of danger instead of warmth.

Common diagnoses associated with social perception impairments/ failure to have empathetic capacities include autism spectrum disorder, bipolar disorder, borderline personality disorder, narcissistic personality disorder, and intellectual disability.

Impulse Control

Certain mental conditions predispose to acting before thinking about the consequences of the action. This impulsivity may take the form of risk taking behaviors that are not well thought through or drug taking behavior in a belief that it will enhance one's bravado with peers. Some folks with the rapid thinking and grandiosity associated with bipolar disorder will take impulsive actions that seem perfectly logical when they are manic. Impulsive sexual actions and spending money one does not have can also be characteristic of a manic state.

Antisocial personality disorder, bipolar disorder, intermittent explosive disorder, and disruptive mood dysregulation disorder are commonly associated with impulse control problems.

Intellectual Impairments That Impair Judgment

Adaptive functioning (judgment) does not necessarily have a linear correlation with level of IQ in intellectual disabilities and is a separate evaluation from an IQ determination. We must also note that socioeconomic factors may play a role in a family's ability to protect the intellectually disabled family member from consequences of their poor judgment.

Executive Dysfunction

This sphere includes foreseeable knowledge of consequence of an action or sequence of actions. It also includes impairments in planning and executing a series of actions to produce a desired goal or result. Examples include a child who might do her homework but can never find it in her backpack to turn it in, or possibly doesn't remember that turning it in is part of the sequence for getting a good grade. It is not unusual for the individual with poor executive functioning to be perplexed at lack of success, blame others, and have low self-esteem.

This sphere can cut across many conditions including attention deficit hyperactivity disorder, autism spectrum disorder, intellectual disability, and learning disorders.

Distortions of Reality

When someone has a true "command hallucination" telling them to commit a harmful action, it is very difficult to convince the person it is a false message and to not act on the voice command.

Distortions of reality tend to be associated with schizophrenia, delusional disorder, bipolar disorder, and major depression with psychotic features.

Distortions of Sense of Self

We all have certain identifiers by which we describe ourselves. Certain identifiers become so important to us that the thought of losing them causes depression and anxiety. An ordinary example of this is the process people face as they contemplate retirement. If, for example, one has been a successful lawyer, it is not uncommon to think that losing the identifier of a functioning attorney might lead to a loss of self-esteem and a derailed sense of existential purpose. Many of us hang our identity significantly on our job or profession. We all have a list of self-identifiers that make up our sense of self or identity.

A person with chronic, severe depression over many decades may develop an identity predominated by "I am a depressed person." If this is a core belief, as opposed to seeing depression as a problem to be wrestled with, overcome, or managed, then treatment does not go well until other self-identifiers can take precedence. The same pitfall may exist for someone who is bipolar or whose identity is based on having been a victim of abuse or other maltreatment.

Substance dependency and abuse, anorexia nervosa, borderline personality disorder, and bipolar disorder are commonly associated with distortions of sense of self.

There are two more sets of conditions that tend to cut across the other spheres; thus they are not really spheres of dysfunction as we have developed the concept here. However, they are quite common disorders, and because of their importance, we include them in this discussion. They are reactions to trauma and abuse, and addiction behaviors.

Reactions to Trauma/Abuse

There has been a long history in the mental health field of underestimating the frequency and impact of abuse experiences. Only in recent years, due largely to the efforts of the Substance Abuse and Mental Health Services Administration and trauma-informed care, has behavioral health more broadly appreciated the presence and impacts of trauma.

As we discussed earlier, trauma is a very common experience among criminal offenders. Poverty is related to trauma through a variety of channels including poor parenting, violence, traumatic brain injury, and environmental toxins. Trauma has a variety of psychological, psychiatric, and neurological consequences. Because it is quite common among criminal offenders, consideration of the consequences of trauma is very important in the bigger picture of criminality.

Addiction Behaviors

As we mentioned earlier, addiction involves an inability to control behavior, and it has a variety of emotional, cognitive, and social dysfunctions. Repeated drug use also has important consequences for the structure and functioning of the brain. The sheer number of offenders with substance use disorders underscores the importance of incorporating substance-related consequences in the bigger picture of assessment and treatment.

Our goal in presenting these spheres of dysfunction is to provide the logic for going beyond the classification of individuals per the DSM diagnoses by drilling down deeper to gain a comprehensive understanding of the behavioral consequences or dysfunctions of various disorders. Then we are in a position to develop appropriate treatment plans.

A bigger picture of this assessment process, in addition to diagnosis and identification of dysfunctions, is the bio-psycho-social workup. The bio-psycho-social assessment, as the name implies, considers biological, psychological, and social factors and the interactions of our genetic endowment with the environment. Biological factors include genetic predisposition and physical illness. Examples include neuropsychiatric disorders, addiction, intellectual disorders, seizure disorders, and hypoglycemia. These are the factors that are inherent in an individual's anatomy and physiology that can significantly change one's thermostat for impulsive actions, misperception of threats from others in social interactions, tendencies to experience rage with minor provocations, or compulsive actions that are independent of gain or negative consequences. Psychological factors to look at might include sadness to the level of depression on a chronic or acute basis, compulsive suicidal thoughts, chronic panic episodes or a situation that induces panic, psychological response to a recent loss or mourning, psychological responses to a present or past trauma, or a recent failure with a significant other. Social factors include poverty, trauma (physical, sexual, emotional, event witnessing, perceived threat), exposure to lead paint, diet/nutrition, divorce, and the death of a close role model, child, or sibling, among others.

DISORDERED OFFENDERS IN PRISON, JAIL, PROBATION, AND PAROLE

While our attention has been on diverting suitable offenders from criminal prosecution and punishment, we have not lost sight of those who end up incarcerated or sentenced to traditional probation. It is reasonable to expect that many of them will have mental health, substance abuse, and neurocognitive and intellectual disorders and impairments. We do not believe these disorders and impairments should be ignored. Most of these offenders will one day be released from prison and discharged from probation. It is clearly in the interest of public safety to do what can be done to mitigate crime-related factors to reduce the risk of recidivism.

We certainly appreciate the challenges associated with providing evidence-based treatment in custodial settings like prison and jail. Security is the priority, and such considerations can make behavioral interventions difficult, as can the punishment and control culture of prison and jail. Moreover, funding for in-prison treatment has been radically cut in recent decades, partly in response to tough-on-crime initiatives that prioritize punishment and more recently as a result of the recession, which caused states to cut funding.

Several experts have called for a new generation of correctional interventions that address not only mental illness and substance abuse (presumably neurocognitive disorders and intellectual deficiencies as well, despite their not being included in those discussions) but also the primary collateral risk factors that often accompany them.[31]

Correctional mental health experts have compiled inventories of evidence-based practices and programs, as well as those that are "promising," which with more evaluation may become EBPs. These apply in a variety of correctional settings, including prison, jail, pre-trial diversion, probation, and parole.[32] The programs and practices include those we discussed earlier, such as integrated mental health, substance abuse treatment, psychopharmacology, Assertive Community Treatment, motivational enhancement therapy, and cognitive behavioral therapy. The Counsel on State Governments Justice Center in collaboration with the SAMHSA GAINS Center put together a comprehensive inventory of EBPs and other promising practices that should inform the development of intervention policy in correctional settings.

CONCLUSIONS

One means by which the success of a retributivist model of punishment can be measured is by the toll taken on the offender. The tougher the sentence, the more successful. And by that measure, we have become more and more successful. However, what the current system of mass incarceration fails to take into account is that, sooner or later, incarcerated offenders will be released back into the community. While those with a retributivist bent may receive some degree of satisfaction from an offender's lengthy prison sentence, it is time to admit the well-understood fact that severe punishment does not deter reoffending. In many cases, it has the opposite effect. As we have observed, the costs have been borne not only by the offenders but also by taxpayers who are paying dearly for the privilege of exacting vengeance in this way. The public also pays with higher rates of recidivism and victimization. We see no way of avoiding the conclusion that punitive policies result in a very poor return on investment. We will expand on this point in the concluding chapter.

We have attempted to imagine a criminal justice system that, as an alternative to the reflexive and expensive incarceration of offenders or punitive supervision and control, effectively addresses some of the underlying drivers of criminal behavior, resulting in fewer people reoffending. We have focused on the benchmark of rates of recidivism for a variety of reasons. First, the optimal goal of any system of punishment should be the return of an offender to the status of a law-abiding citizen. The evidence is clear that the way to do that for hundreds of thousands of offenders is through concerted, evidence-based rehabilitation. Second, there is an obvious economy to identifying offenders who can be diverted from incarceration at the outset (initial savings) and given the treatment or other means to stay out of prison forever (ultimate savings). Finally, recidivism is a measurable outcome, and the effectiveness of the sorting process and the diversion programs can be determined and maximized.

We believe that it is time to use what we know about what contributes to criminal behavior to make a serious attempt not just to punish but also to seek to prevent reoffending by means of effective, informed decision making and diverting appropriate offenders to programs that have the reasonable likelihood of yielding significantly lower recidivism. We believe that such sorting of offenders is feasible, and that programs can be fashioned to yield measurably improved public safety outcomes. To continue to incarcerate hundreds of thousands of nonviolent offenders without asking whether, in light of the role of significant disorders, impairments, and deficits, we might use established expertise and resources to address the issues underlying their behavior, would be both unjust and fiscally imprudent.

Given the social and institutional commitment to tough-on-crime policies as well as a criminal justice culture that prioritizes punishment, we are not naïve about the inertia that will have to be overcome. Elected officials are rarely disposed to try approaches that are not largely punitive. Yet we are convinced that, given the failure of our current policies on many levels, both policymakers and those involved in the criminal justice system should be open to developing new approaches to addressing criminal behavior. There are many difficulties in going down this road, and we will discuss challenges and barriers in the last chapter.

It is important to point out that there has been a significant shift in thinking about criminal justice policy in the United States, with more and more discussion about reducing mass incarceration and the exorbitant cost of punishment. At the same time, the public is behind initiatives to reduce incarceration, divert nonviolent offenders to more effective alternatives, and save money. It is unfortunate that elected officials cannot seem to muster what it takes to implement important, substantive changes.

To be clear, we are not advocating closing U.S. prisons and jails and diverting everyone. This is not a "get-out-of-jail free" card. Clearly, dangerous adults and juveniles with and without disorders and deficits need to be locked up, separated from society. However, what we propose is a substantial departure from business as usual. It is, as we say in the title, disruptive innovation. Our goal is to reduce the needless and expensive warehousing of individuals in prison, to improve decision making, and to get the right people to the right places. At the end of the day, we expect lower recidivism, victimization, criminal justice expenditures, and the social and economic costs of crime.

7

COSTS, BENEFITS, AND CHALLENGES

It is clear today that the public and many policymakers believe that we have too many people in prison. The media echo this sentiment on a regular basis in stories and editorials on mass incarceration. And we have seen some states modestly reducing prison populations in response to the recent recession and the cost of incarceration. We have yet to see, however, a sustained trend in the direction of significant reductions in prison populations. And the 2016 election of tough-on-crime, law-and-order Donald Trump is not a good sign for reform efforts.

There is also growing consensus that all this punishment has not been terribly effective. There are good reasons why punishment severity does not deter. First, the effects of punishment are relatively short lived. When offenders leave the justice system, they return to the realities of their lives, but often in worse shape than when they came in, and with restrictions on things like employment, housing, and owning and driving a car, among others. As we know, many have identifiable disorders, impairments, and deficits that rarely are better and often are worse when they leave the system. They also have a variety of detrimental life circumstances (poor education, family disruptions, homelessness, employment problems) that don't typically improve while they are in the justice system. The result is high recidivism. From a purely financial perspective, our hyper-punitive approach to public safety has wasted massive amounts of public dollars and has failed to provide the crime reduction dividends that most would (or should) consider a reasonable return on investment.

We view what we have proposed as a starting point. We certainly expect local jurisdictions to experiment, problem solve, and innovate. We expect recalibration of processes as indicated by feedback and evaluation.

THE COST-BENEFIT OF INCARCERATION

Many cost-benefit analyses have been conducted on incarceration in the United States. The consensus among economists is that prison as currently used in the United States is not economically efficient.[1] That conclusion directly implicates sentencing laws and practices, and retribution as a rationale for incarceration.

The cost-benefit problem associated with mass incarceration is one of the basic principles in economics, the law of diminishing marginal return. The reason that increased incarceration has such a small effect on crime and recidivism is that our rate of incarceration is very high. That high incarceration rate already includes many serious violent offenders; thus each additional offender we incarcerate is more likely to be a less serious, less risky, nonviolent offender. In turn, the value in terms of public safety of incarcerating less risky offenders is low, and thus the cost exceeds the benefits.

This rationale applies to decisions to incarcerate as well as the length of the sentence imposed and the length of sentence served. To be sure, we have increased prison sentences and time served across the board. Analyses by the Pew Center on the States show that time served in prison for drug offenders who were released in 2009 increased by 36 percent compared to time served in 1990. Time served for property offenders and violent offenders over the same time period increased by 24 percent and 37 percent, respectively.[2]

Since the evidence is clear that more severe punishment does not appear to have much of a deterrent effect, longer sentences and longer time served are wasted on many offenders, with perhaps the exception of incapacitating those who are likely to reoffend. However, the relative value of incapacitation is based on who we incapacitate. Again, as the incarceration rate increases, we imprison less risky, nonviolent offenders. The cost of incarceration exceeds the benefit of incapacitating less risky, nonviolent offenders for longer periods of time. Moreover, there is the replacement or substitution effect that mitigates the crime-reducing impact of incapacitation. Take drug dealers, for example. Convicting and incarcerating drug dealers, as we have done consistently for decades, does not eliminate the crime that dealer was committing. It is quite likely that someone will take that incarcerated dealer's place in the drug market.

The bottom line is that sentencing based on retribution, deterrence, and in many cases incapacitation has substantial direct costs to the criminal justice system. As more offenders are being incarcerated for longer periods of time, the marginal benefit of incarceration declines and costs exceed benefits. That is where we are today and where we have been for some time. Unfortunately, that is only part of the broader cost of incarceration.

In a recently released study (July 2016), researchers at Washington University in St. Louis provide estimates of the cost of incarceration. This work goes beyond that of others by taking a bigger-picture perspective of cost by including not only costs to the criminal justice system but also other collateral social costs to incarcerated individuals, their families and children, and communities. All told, the study attaches monetary value to twenty-two different costs associated with incarceration. The bottom line is a quite sobering figure of $1 trillion annually. This represents the annual financial burden of incarceration and reflects the broad array of collateral costs. For every dollar the United States spends on incarceration, there is an additional $10 in social costs.[3] Examples of these collateral costs include lost wages to incarcerated individuals, reduced lifetime earnings of those who have been incarcerated, adverse health and mental health effects, increased criminality of the children of incarcerated individuals, recidivism associated with the incarceration experience, and divorce, among others.

Granted, such an analysis requires many assumptions. The $1 trillion figure is an estimate, and there is without doubt error in that estimate. But even if it is off by 25 percent, or as much as 50 percent, we are still looking at an enormous price tag for our penchant for punishment. Dollar figures aside, this study focuses attention on the variety of ways that punishment impacts not only offenders and the justice system but also society at large, including neighborhoods, families, and children.

DIVERSION

Research has documented the negative consequences associated with involvement in the criminal justice system. Obviously, there are many circumstances in which an offender needs to be in the justice system, including prison. Prison should be used to incapacitate or separate certain offenders from society. Prison can be used for simple retribution as well. But we need to understand and appreciate the consequences, including the limitations and costs associated with these decisions. Retribution has limited utility in terms of public safety. The crime control impacts of incapacitation are limited by our ability to incapacitate the right people. Violent offenders are obvious candidates, as are habitual offenders. Unfortunately, we use incarceration for hundreds of thousands of nonviolent offenders. We also imprison offenders when information is limited regarding whether they are habitual offenders. We have gotten angry at criminals, and that anger has all too often directed decision making around criminal sentences and parole release decisions, among others.

One of the major contributors to the failure of our hyper-punitive approach to public safety is that we do little to address or remedy the circumstances and conditions associated with criminality. While there are many such circumstances and conditions, we are particularly focusing here on psychiatric and substance use disorders, and neurocognitive and intellectual impairments and deficits—for two primary reasons. First, collectively these characterize the vast majority of offenders in state and federal correctional systems. The second reason is that punishment does nothing to change these conditions or interrupt the cycle of justice involvement and, in many situations, simply perpetuates it.

We have attempted to make the case that selective diversion from harsh punishment is an evidence-based practice that should have a much larger presence in the day-to-day administration of criminal justice. The evidence clearly shows much more positive outcomes associated with diversion, compared to punishment as usual. Those positive outcomes include lower recidivism, crime, victimization, and cost.

Diversion or problem-solving courts are the most common type of intervention or rehabilitation-focused diversion programs other than probation. The typical problem-solving court embodies some balance between accountability and risk management, on the one hand, and therapeutic intervention, on the other. As we noted earlier, the evaluation research supports the concept of a diversion court as an evidence-based program when properly designed, implemented, and operated. For that reason, problem-solving courts could be a viable option for the diversion we are proposing here. In order to fulfill that need, however, some significant changes would need to occur.

First, problem-solving courts have very limited capacity and numbers of participants. The majority (60 percent) of drug and mental health courts have a capacity of fewer than 50 individuals.[4] Juvenile courts are considerably smaller than adult courts. Many operate under capacity. Obviously, to have a discernable impact, we need to substantially increase the capacity of these courts.

Second, while there are over 3,050 problem-solving courts in the United States, nearly half are drug courts. Only 11 percent are mental health courts. Less than 15 percent of these courts serve juveniles (the vast majority are drug courts; there are only about thirty-five juvenile mental health courts).[5] Given what we know about the diversity of disorders, deficits, and impairments, we would need to see the development of courts that serve a broader array of problems.

A related issue is comorbidity. Most problem-solving courts tend to focus on one condition, disorder, or impairment. However, it is the rare disordered offender who presents with only one primary condition. As the collaborative care model of health delivery is the evidence-based model, it makes sense to attempt to mimic that logic in diversion courts. What is preferable here are diversion courts that have the capacity and expertise to address multiple conditions.

Probation can be a reasonable model for delivering the kinds of services we are proposing. However, probation as we generally know it is a post-conviction sentence, which means there can be long-term consequences associated with a criminal conviction. Let's be clear that probation is an entirely appropriate sentence for many offenders. It is certainly preferable to prison for many offenders suitable for community supervision. However, hybrids like deferred adjudication or deferred prosecution could be more appropriate options for many of the types of cases we are considering here.

Whether the choice is traditional probation (and thus avoiding incarceration) or deferred adjudication or deferred prosecution (avoiding a criminal conviction), community supervision as we know it must change.[6] There needs to be a substantial expansion of intervention programs and services, as well as changes in the training of supervision officers and the culture of community supervision. Training and culture need to reflect the primary purpose of community supervision, which is recidivism reduction achieved by a balance of supervision and risk management, on the one hand, and comprehensive programs and services, on the other.

We also recommend the use of swift and certain sanction courts in conjunction with community supervision. These have been found to be quite effective in enhancing compliance and reducing violations and recidivism while on supervision. We recommend that problem-solving courts adopt the principles of these sanction courts to address compliance and violations. The Washington State Institute for Public Policy has conducted cost-benefit analyses of sanction courts and found that benefits far exceed costs.[7]

The Cost-Benefit of Diversion

Most of the research on diversion courts has been conducted on drug courts. Here is what we know. Drugs courts are effective at reducing recidivism when properly designed and operated.[8] Researchers estimate that treating the roughly 55,400 offenders each year in drug courts for substance use disorders prevents approximately 34 million drug crimes and 170,000 other crimes. Simulation research shows that ramping up the capacity of drug courts and relaxing some of the eligibility criteria, resulting in about 215,000 offenders treated in drug courts, could prevent 117 million drug crimes and 650,000 non-drug crimes.[9]

Cost studies from a variety of sources including the Washington State Institute for Public Policy, the U.S. Department of Justice, the Justice Policy Institute, the Center for Court Innovation, and RTI International all show the substantial financial advantages of drug treatment using the drug court diversion model. For example, the RTI research reports that diverting 10 percent of eligible offenders from prison to community-based treatment would save nearly $5 billion annually in direct criminal justice costs. Diverting 40 percent of eligible offenders would save $13 billion.[10]

An analysis by the Center for Court Innovation shows a cost-benefit ratio for diversion to drug court for treatment is as high as 1:4 (for every dollar invested in drug court treatment, the criminal justice system benefit due to reduced recidivism is $4). Adding in the costs associated with avoided victimizations raises the ratio to 1:7.[11] The Washington State Institute for Public Policy cost-benefit analysis estimates a cost-benefit ratio for drug courts at 2.61, or $2.61 in criminal justice system benefits for every dollar invested in drug court diversion.[12]

A recent simulation analysis estimates the lifetime benefits of diverting drug offenders from prison to community-based treatment. This is an important contribution since prior cost-benefit analyses do not project the benefits over the entire lifetime of an offender. Moreover, the lifetime financial impact of rehabilitation is something that policymakers rarely seem to consider. This research incorporates "the episodic and recurrent nature of substance abuse and the multiple episodes of drug abuse treatment, crime commission and reincarceration in jail or prison."[13] The results are based on a single cohort of offenders incarcerated in 2004 under the assumption that 10 percent and 40 percent of eligible offenders are diverted from prison. The lifetime societal net benefits are $22.5 billion if 40 percent are diverted to treatment and $8.5 billion if 10 percent are diverted.

Diversion of mentally ill individuals has been demonstrated to be effective in reducing jail time as well as short-term and long-term recidivism for both violent and nonviolent crimes.[14] Diversion is also cost efficient for mentally ill and cognitively impaired offenders.[15] Mental health courts have an estimated cost-benefit ratio of $6.22, meaning that for every dollar invested in mental health courts, a fiscal benefit of $6.22 is realized by reductions in recidivism.[16] Post-arrest jail diversion also has significant net monetary benefits.[17] Providing supportive housing and Assertive Community Treatment (expensive options for mentally ill individuals) are also less expensive than incarceration in jail.[18]

Juvenile diversion programs are both effective and cost beneficial. Effectiveness of diversion is due in part to limited contact with the juvenile justice system, thus avoiding the negative consequences of deeper involvement in that system. This conclusion is supported by comparisons of recidivism with youth who had limited contact with the juvenile justice system and those who had more extensive contact before diversion. All in all, diversion resulted in lower recidivism compared to traditional processing in the juvenile justice system.[19]

The Washington State Institute for Public Policy has conducted cost-benefit analyses for a variety of juvenile diversion programs. Juvenile drug courts have an estimated $1.53 cost-benefit ratio.[20] While it did not compute cost-benefit ratios for diversion with services and diversion without services, in both cases there are sizable net financial benefits.[21]

One of the most compelling analyses regarding the importance of interventions with juvenile offenders was conducted on the long-term cost implications of not intervening. As Cohen and Piquero note:

> [O]ne of our most important findings is that while juvenile offending behavior accounts for a small fraction of total costs, if those juveniles can be prevented from becoming career criminals, savings may be enormous. For example, the typical career criminal imposes $65,000 in costs through age 12 and $230,000 through age 14. However, throughout a lifetime, these costs total nearly $5.7 million. Thus, early interventions targeting high risk youth can have high payoffs if they are effective.[22]

Conclusions

Adult and juvenile diversion is more productive in terms of reducing recidivism than traditional criminal prosecution, conviction, and punishment. Moreover, diversion avoids the negative consequences of more extensive contact with the criminal and juvenile justice systems. There are both short-term and long-term financial benefits to diversion. The most important long-term benefit is the reduction in chronic offending and the interruption of criminal careers that are a result of intervention. As we look longer term, the cost savings associated with mitigating crime-related circumstances and disorders are enormous.

It is important to point out that the beneficial recidivism and cost outcomes discussed above are often the result of intervening with only one crime-related risk factor such as drug abuse or mental illness. The evidence is clear that there is a strong relationship between the number of risk factors successfully addressed and recidivism reduction. This underscores the importance of not only substantially expanding diversion programming but also identifying all the relevant primary dysfunctions that play a role in an individual's criminality, appreciating the complexity of disorders and dysfunctions that some will present with, and providing all the required interventions, programs, and services needed to mitigate those primary conditions.

The stark reality of reducing recidivism is dramatically ramping up our efforts to address crime-related problems. This involves much greater effort and expertise in screening and assessing individuals to accurately determine the primary issues, developing comprehensive treatment plans that address all relevant, primary conditions, and providing sufficient risk management and supervision that is also conducive to therapeutic interventions. We need to get more sophisticated in terms of tailoring the interventions to the needs of individuals. It is a waste of resources to provide thirty days of substance abuse treatment to someone requiring ninety days of treatment. It is equally counterproductive to address one mental health or neurocognitive disorder but ignore a comorbid disorder. Many offenders have quite complex situations. Our interventions should identify and address that complexity.

It is evident to us that what we are proposing requires substantial changes to the criminal and juvenile justice systems. These changes involve revisions of statutes such as sentencing laws, modifying criminal procedure (such as implementing expert panels to advise prosecutors regarding criminal prosecution versus diversion to treatment), developing diversion procedures and resources, and balancing risk management and rehabilitation programming.

This will also require changes to the roles and responsibilities of prosecutors, judges, and corrections officials as well as the culture of American criminal justice. Prosecutors, judges, and corrections officials all need to accept primary responsibility for reducing recidivism. We need to change how we think about crime and punishment. Our policies, practices, attitudes, and beliefs need to catch up with the science, much in the same way that evidence from climate science is altering our thinking and policies regarding global warming.

It is also evident that changing the criminal and juvenile justice systems is necessary but not sufficient to accomplish significant reductions in recidivism. There are many other moving parts that come into play in what we propose. Dramatically ramping up appropriate community-based resources and changing how we go about the business of public health are two key components that are directly implicated in the success of this effort.

There are many, many details to be worked out. Much of this will be negotiated at the local level. That is where diversion has been successfully implemented and where we believe it needs to be implemented going forward. Needless to say, this will also require the alignment of state-level policymakers and elected officials in implementing necessary changes to laws, procedures, funding, and other resources as well as the delivery of public health. It will also require an appreciation by state officials of the big picture of what can be accomplished—reductions in crime, recidivism, criminal victimizations, and spending. That is what we want and expect government to do. We believe we have provided a general framework for accomplishing that task.

There is nothing easy about what we propose, and we do not take lightly what is required to get this right. We now turn to some of the major challenges this effort faces.

CHALLENGES GOING FORWARD

Prosecutors

Our proposal requires a fundamental re-ordering of the current practices and procedures for assessing offenders' conduct, background, and attributes in order to determine the most appropriate use of resources in response to their offending. This necessitates an additional formal step in the processing of offenders, involving determining which offenders will be criminally prosecuted and which will be diverted. That decision will be made by behavioral experts, who determine risk and the presence of significant crime-related disorders and impairments.

Clearly, this will impinge on prosecutorial discretion. While we envision procedures that give final authority to prosecutors to define classes of offenders who are ineligible for diversion, as well as giving prosecutors veto power over recommendations made by the experts, this will amount to a significant departure from business as usual.

Convincing prosecutors to embrace what we propose will in many cases be quite difficult. It is natural for individuals to hesitate giving up power and discretion. Moreover, this will involve a rather dramatic change in prosecutors' thinking about crime and punishment. As punishment has been the primary tool for trying to accomplish public safety, and tough on crime has worked well at least in terms of political resonance, one of the major challenges going forward is asking prosecutors to embrace the idea that their primary responsibility is reducing recidivism, and that the best way to get there in many, many instances is behavioral change through interventions other than punishment. This requires a shift in thinking to recidivism outcomes, not just criminal convictions and meting out severe punishment. It involves a redefinition of success, from getting someone off the street to effectively reducing the likelihood they will return to the justice system.

This change in perspective includes acknowledging that psychiatric, addiction, neurocognitive, and intellectual disorders can be and often are related to criminal offending and that evidence-based treatment interventions can reduce the likelihood of recidivism better than punishment. This will require a new balance in thinking about crime, including an explicit commitment to rehabilitation and evidence-based recidivism reduction along with punishment as legitimate and primary goals of the criminal justice system.

There are likely to be ideological, philosophical, and political objections to this new path we propose. And there clearly are risks that likely will give prosecutors pause.

Why should prosecutors be persuaded by what we propose? Today, the majority of cases that typical local prosecutors deal with are recidivists. Much of the heavy caseloads that characterize metropolitan prosecutors are due to repeat offenders. Prosecutors should find our proposal appealing because it will reduce recidivism, and in turn caseloads. It will slow the revolving door, and it will promote public safety. It will also reduce victimization and cost. In short, it will produce better outcomes. After all, enhancing public safety is what prosecutors are supposed to do. What we are proposing is shifting from failed policies to providing prosecutors with a broader array of options. Punishment, such as incarceration, is an option. It just need not be the primary option, as we have seen in the past.

While we see prosecutors playing a primary role going forward, it is essential that the entire justice system, including policymakers, elected officials, police, prosecutors, judges, public defenders, pre-trial services, and corrections officials get on board. One important incentive will be the reduction in recidivism, which will be felt across the justice system as caseloads decline. Another important benefit, especially for elected officials, is saving public money.

Criminal Justice Costs

Another challenge arises from the fact that criminal justice costs are paid
from different pots of money. Some of it is local, some state, and some
federal money. It is generally the case that local counties (and county
equivalents) pay for courts, prosecutors, public defenders, jail, pre-trial
supervision, and probation. State government typically pays for prison
and parole release supervision, and it may cover some of the costs of
probation. In some states, the state government pays some or most of the
cost of community supervision. The federal government pays for the
federal criminal justice system in addition to providing funding (for example, grant money) for justice-related programing and infrastructure at
the state and local levels.

Because different state and local governments pay for different components of criminal justice, there is the obvious question of who realizes
the financial costs and benefits of diversion resulting in reductions in
recidivism. We suggested earlier that most of the diversion effort should
be at the local level, decided by local panels of experts and local prosecutors and judges, diverting individuals to local, community-based programming. This produces substantial cost burdens on counties and raises
the question of how we should fund diversion going forward.

Since prisons are by far the most expensive component of corrections
(90 percent of all corrections expenditures are for prisons), states stand to
benefit the most financially from reductions in incarceration. One very
appealing approach for funding evidence-based, recidivism-reducing diversion programming is through performance incentive funding. As of
2014, eight states had implemented performance incentive funding,
which reallocates money to local jurisdictions for successfully diverting
offenders to probation rather than incarceration.[23] Some of the money
saved by reducing revocations, and thus incarceration is distributed to
local jurisdictions that contributed to the decline in revocations.

The logic of performance incentive funding could be adopted to partially fund the diversion programming proposed here. Those counties that
successfully implement expanded diversion programs could receive state
funding proportional to their reduction in overall state incarceration.

Another funding model is justice reinvestment. The justice reinvestment initiative (JRI) was launched in 2010 by the Bureau of Justice
Assistance, in collaboration with the Pew Charitable Trusts. The goal of

JRI is to identify ways to reduce spending on corrections by designing and implementing new evidence-based policies, practices, and programs that reduce recidivism, jail and prison populations, and costs. In turn, portions of the money saved by those policies, practices, and programs are reinvested by jurisdictions in evidence-based programs that have been proven to reduce recidivism. Officials in twenty-four states and seventeen local communities have implemented JRI.

The performance incentive funding and justice reinvestment models can provide significant funding and serve to motivate local jurisdictions to develop, implement, and operate evidence-based diversion programs that reduce recidivism. While these are important initiatives, they will be insufficient to adequately fund this effort. State legislatures will need to allocate criminal justice funding to local communities over and above current funding levels and the funding provided by JRI and performance incentive funding. We envision diversion on an unprecedented scale; thus funding should be proportional to the scale in each jurisdiction. Obviously, funding increases should come from county and city governments as well, since a substantial portion of the benefits, including many of the collateral social costs we discussed earlier, will be realized in local communities.

Intervention Costs

What we propose will result in a substantial increase in the number of offenders diverted to treatment, requiring a considerable ramp-up in treatment capacity and supervision. We appreciate what is involved here but underscore that the success of these efforts will depend on the availability of and access to appropriate, adequate, evidence-based intervention capacity. We wrote chapter 4 to provide a broad road map for the direction that community-based behavioral health interventions need to go to align with evidence-based practices. While we acknowledge the considerable investment this will require, the economics indicate that there will be commensurate short-term and especially long-term savings as a result of reduced recidivism and lower incarceration rates. Substantial savings are also associated with the reduction in the social costs of crime.

The long-term trend in financing mental health care in the United States is troubling. Over the past thirty-five years, state spending on mental health treatment has eroded dramatically. When adjusted for inflation and population growth, state spending on mental health treatment today is about 12 percent of what it was in 1955. Some of that decline has been offset by increases in federal Medicaid spending. Today, the majority (52 percent) of mental health treatment funding is federal dollars, mainly Medicaid.[24]

There is considerable variation across the states regarding access to mental health treatment services. For example, an analysis by Mental Health America on access to care demonstrates that in the best case, meaning the states that ranked highest in terms of access to care, only 57 percent of those individuals in need of mental health services received any treatment. That figure for the lowest 10 states in access ranking is 30 percent.[25]

One of the drivers of access to care is insurance coverage. There is a strong correlation between access to mental health services and insurance coverage rates. Those states that are ranked highest in terms of access to services have the highest insurance coverage rates. Those states ranked lowest in access have the lowest insurance coverage rates.[26]

Thirty-one states and the District of Columbia have expanded Medicaid as of this writing. Nineteen have not. There is a strong correlation between access to services and expansion of Medicaid. Nearly all of the top-ranked states in access to mental health services expanded Medicaid. Nearly all of the lowest-ranked states in access to services did not expand Medicaid.[27] However, a caution is necessary here since some states (for example, Rhode Island, Massachusetts, Michigan, Arkansas, Hawaii, and Kentucky) expanded Medicaid but reduced state spending on mental health care.

The Affordable Care Act (ACA) has had a significant impact on increasing insurance coverage for justice-involved individuals. Roughly half of justice-involved individuals were estimated to be eligible for insurance coverage through the ACA. As of 2014, the ACA resulted in a 13 percent decline in the uninsured among the justice-involved population, and Medicaid expansion led to a 10 percent decline in the uninsured. However, the uninsured rate among the justice-involved population is still over 16 percentage points higher that the non-justice-involved.[28]

Private insurance through the ACA and Medicaid expansion will go a long way in funding access to care for diverted offenders. Clearly, states that have refused to expand Medicaid need to set aside politics and make decisions based on the best evidence of need and the benefits in terms of public safety and public spending. However, Medicaid expansion should not be an invitation to states to roll back general fund allocations for treatment. Rather, states should conduct needs assessments of the demand for mental health and substance abuse treatment, including estimates of the diverted justice-involved population, in order to determine realistic capacity needs and the requisite funding.

Additional general revenue funding for interventions for diverted offenders should come from the cost savings due to lower incarceration rates. Those savings can be used to fund direct treatment costs as well as supervision costs of diverted offenders through performance incentive funding and justice reinvestment initiatives.

The bottom line regarding funding is that all levels of government need to come to the table and make community-based, public treatment of mental illness, substance abuse, neurocognitive disorders, and intellectual disabilities of justice-involved individuals a priority. If we are serious about public safety being a public good, then it is time to get serious about reducing crime, recidivism, and victimization. That involves adequately funding those evidence-based strategies and programs that have been proven to accomplish those goals.

We elect public officials to be stewards of public resources. It is time to hold these officials accountable for how they spend criminal justice money. It is time for them to be responsible with public expenditures on criminal justice. It is time for them to be wise investors.

Politics

It seems safe to say that at the moment (November 2016), federal criminal justice reform is dead. As modest as the proposals were, the fear that has paralyzed Congress and the law and order mantra of president-elect Trump and his surrogates led to its demise. This is unfortunate not only because it keeps federal criminal justice policy on the tough-on-crime track that has characterized it for decades but also because it precludes Congress from setting an example of reform for the states.

Observers expressed optimism when some states recently began reducing the size of their prison populations. These reductions were small, but perhaps they spelled a new phase in correctional policy, one that would put us on a course of shrinking our prisons. What was born out of a concern over revenue and spending due to the recent recession has failed to gain the traction of meaningful change. There is little evidence that we have embarked on a significant, sustained downsizing of mass incarceration.

It is not for a lack of effective alternatives. There is more than sufficient evidence to justify a new direction toward much-enhanced public safety, substantial reductions in recidivism and victimization, and sizable reductions in public spending. There is also compelling evidence of a variety of collateral benefits that can accrue, such as avoiding numerous social costs of crime and the long-term negative consequences of justice system involvement.

Perhaps it is political fear or the paralysis of partisan politics that is keeping us from turning around what is probably the greatest policy failure in U.S. history. It seems that there are fewer overt tough-on-crime advocates today, but the politics of crime and punishment still resonates in electoral politics. As Bill Keller of the Marshall Project recently wrote:

> Proponents of reform . . . say it has become safer for politicians to be "smart on crime" rather than merely tough on crime. But the soft on crime smear is still a staple in election campaigns for judgeships and prosecutor positions, and many members of Congress remain wary of the subject.[29]

What is remarkable is that there is considerable bipartisan political support for significant criminal justice reform. From Charles Koch, Newt Gingrich, Grover Norquist, John Kasich, and Right on Crime on the conservative side to Barack Obama, Eric Holder, the ACLU, and the Center for American Progress on the liberal side, reform has many high-profile advocates.

Moreover, there is substantial bipartisan public support for justice reform. Very recent surveys (2015 and 2016) show that the vast majority (87 percent) believe that drug addicts and the mentally ill should not be in prison, but rather in treatment facilities. The majority also believe that reducing the prison population will make communities safer.[30] Another poll found that the majority (79 percent) believe mandatory minimum sentences for drug offenders should be eliminated, and a majority believe too many drug offenders are incarcerated.[31]

An interesting survey of crime victims reveals very strong support for reform. Victims, by a margin of 3 to 1, believe that incarceration increases recidivism. Compared to incarceration, crime victims prefer investments in mental health treatment (7 to 1), drug treatment (4 to 1), education (15 to 1), job creation (10 to 1), and holding offenders accountable through rehabilitation, mental health treatment, drug treatment, community supervision, and community service (3 to 1).[32]

With all this support, we still can't seem to set a course to real criminal justice reform.

We appreciate that politics is a considerable barrier. But as the public and politicians become better educated about the evidence for reform, especially the potential for significant cost savings, the path should become more compelling and more difficult to obstruct with inaccurate and outdated political rhetoric.

THE CULTURE OF CRIMINAL JUSTICE

American criminal justice has operated for nearly five decades with one primary purpose: punishment. One of the essential elements necessary to support that overarching goal was a culture of punishment. Police, prosecutors, judges, and corrections officials all operated in a culture of tough on crime. We can make the changes to laws, policies, procedures, and funding necessary for moving to reality what we propose. However, without changes in how we think about crime and punishment—changes to the culture of the criminal justice system—these efforts will fall short.

Changing the culture requires clarifying the goals of the system and developing an incentive structure that rewards accomplishing those goals. Going forward, reducing recidivism through diversion to treatment for appropriate offenders will be the primary goal. The new "brand" of the criminal justice system involves problem solving and recidivism reduction. Prosecutors, because they are key to what we propose, are expected to shift their thinking and roles and responsibilities from punisher to problem solver and recidivism reducer. That change in thinking applies to all involved, from law enforcement to treatment providers and everyone in between. Changing the culture requires that everyone involved in this enterprise understand that and "live the brand" of reducing recidivism.

CHANGE IS LOCAL

Each county in the United States is a criminal justice system. Courts, prosecutors, jails, probation, drug courts, and other diversion programs are operated at the county level. Clinical intervention also occurs locally.

Most of the effort in what we propose will fall on local communities, and will require leadership and innovation. There are many moving parts at the local level, including various criminal justice agencies as well as a variety of community-based treatment and intervention programs and organizations, some government and some private and nonprofit. Getting the right parties to the table will require considerable effort and skillful leadership.

Some jurisdictions will develop innovative, effective programs that will serve as models for adoption in other jurisdictions. Diffusion of innovation is essential and can be greatly facilitated by a variety of governmental and nonprofit organizations. These include the Bureau of Justice Assistance, the Office of Juvenile Justice and Delinquency Prevention, the National Institute of Justice, Mental Health America, the Treatment Advocacy Center, the Justice Center at the Council on State Governments, the Vera Institute, the Center for Court Innovation, the Urban Institute, the Pew Public Safety Performance Project, SAMHSA, and many more. These organizations provide expertise and technical assistance. Some of these and other organizations provide funding as well.

The Justice Center at the Council on State Governments, in collaboration with the Bureau of Justice Assistance, the National Association of Counties, the American Psychiatric Association Foundation, and others, has launched a program called the Stepping Up Initiative, which is designed to reduce the number of mentally ill and substance abusing adults in local jails by diverting them to evidence-based programs. It engages a diverse array of organizations and individuals with justice and treatment expertise, including law enforcement, judges, prosecutors, jail administrators, community corrections administrators, mental health and substance abuse treatment program directors, individuals with mental illness, and others.

Key to the success of this initiative is providing a forum for the emergence of strong, diverse, and committed leaders from a variety of agencies and organizations (including state-level policymakers) to assess the treatment needs of disordered offenders in a local community, determine treatment capacity, identify strategies for reducing barriers to treatment, develop a plan to divert individuals to treatment, implement the plan, and assess outcomes. The Justice Center provides a variety of technical assistance tools to facilitate assessment, implementation, and evaluation.

STATE VERSUS FEDERAL

It is likely that the proposals we offer in this book will have greater applicability in state criminal justice systems than in the federal context. Most federal criminal cases are elective in nature—that is, they involve crimes for which the accused could also be prosecuted in state court, and likely would be, in the event that federal authorities declined to pursue them. And federal prosecution and penal resources have traditionally been reserved for more serious offenders, as measured by the seriousness of the offense or extensive criminal history. As a result, many, if not most, federal defendants would, by virtue of their crimes or backgrounds, not be suitable for the diversionary options we have outlined. Stated another way, the kinds of cases that might be diverted according to our protocol would likely not rise to the level of seriousness that would warrant federal prosecution in the first instance.

FINAL THOUGHTS

It is difficult to think of a better time to get serious about change. There is substantial bipartisan energy and enthusiasm behind reform. The public, including crime victims, clearly support the direction we propose. We have evidence-based alternatives that have been shown to cost effectively reduce recidivism. It is time to write the obituary for tough on crime and turn to the business of doing what the justice system is supposed to do. Piecemeal change will not get us to where we need and can be. We need to think big.

While we may be wrong on some of the details, we believe that true criminal justice reform is too important to ignore. It should be unacceptable that we avoidably expose hundreds of thousands of Americans every year to criminal victimization. It should be irresponsible to continue running a system with such high recidivism rates. It should be unthinkable that we continue to waste vast amounts of money every year, both on direct criminal justice costs and on the collateral social costs of crime and punishment. If nothing else, the financial benefits from what we propose should be compelling to the new regime in Washington.

NOTES

INTRODUCTION

1. Executive Office of the President of the United States, "Economic Perspectives on Incarceration and the Criminal Justice System."
2. McLaughlin et al., "Economic Burden of Incarceration."
3. Shim, "How Committed Are We to Improving Our Nation's Mental Health?"

1. THE GREAT AMERICAN PUNISHMENT EXPERIMENT

1. World Prison Brief, "Highest to Lowest Prison Population Total."
2. Kelly, *The Future of Crime and Punishment*.
3. Arceneaux, "Why Are the Three Largest Mental Health Care Providers Jails?"
4. Wartna et al., "Recidivism Report."
5. Subramanian and Shames, "Sentencing and Prison Practices," 7.
6. Allen, "Reducing the Use of Imprisonment."
7. Subramanian and Shames, "Sentencing and Prison Practices."

2. FOUR MAJOR THREATS TO RECIDIVISM REDUCTION

1. *Texas Tribune*, "Mentally Challenged Teen Faces 100 Years in Prison."

2. American Psychiatric Association, *Diagnostic and Statistical Manual of Mental Disorders*, 5th ed.

3. Ellis and Walsh, "Crime, Delinquency and Intelligence."

4. Salekin et al., "Offenders with Intellectual Disability"; Blume et al., "Convicting Lennie"; Jones, "Persons with Intellectual Disabilities."

5. Everington and Keyes, "Diagnosing Mental Retardation."

6. Blume et al., "Convicting Lennie."

7. Blume et al., "Convicting Lennie," 958.

8. *McCarver v. State of North Carolina*, Amicus Brief.

9. *Atkins v. Virginia*, 536 U.S. 304 (2002).

10. *Atkins v. Virginia*, 536 U.S. 304 (2002).

11. *Atkins v. Virginia*, 536 U.S. 304 (2002).

12. *Atkins v. Virginia*, 536 U.S. 304 (2002).

13. Einfield et al., "Comorbidity of Intellectual Disability."

14. Prasher and Routhu, "Epidemiology of Learning Disability."

15. United Nations Office on Drugs and Crime, *World Drug Report 2015*.

16. Kilmer et al., *How Big Is the U.S. Market for Illegal Drugs?*

17. Huffpost Politics, "The War on Drugs Has Failed, So Let's Shut It Down."

18. See Kelly, *Criminal Justice at the Crossroads*, and Kelly, *The Future of Crime and Punishment*, for more detailed assessments of U.S. drug control policies.

19. Kelly, *Criminal Justice at the Crossroads*; Kelly, *The Future of Crime and Punishment*.

20. American Society of Addiction Medicine, "Definition of Addiction."

21. Hyman, "The Neurobiology of Addiction."

22. Duncan, "Current Perspectives on the Neurobiology of Drug Addiction," 6.

23. Hyman, "The Neurobiology of Addiction."

24. Volkow, "Neurobiologic Advances," 367.

25. Kessler et al., "Lifetime Co-occurrence of DSM-III-R Alcohol Abuse."

26. Ross et al., "The Prevalence of Psychiatric Disorders."

27. Grant, "Comorbidity Between DSM-IV Drug Use Disorders."

28. Kennert et al., "Drug Addiction," 1068.

29. Bates et al., "Cognitive Impairment Influences Drinking Outcome."

30. Kelly, *Criminal Justice at the Crossroads*; Kelly, *The Future of Crime and Punishment*.

31. Jarmolowicz et al., "Executive Dysfunction in Addiction."

32. Nyberg, "Cognitive Impairments in Drug Addicts," 235.

33. Volkow and Fowler, "Addiction, A Disease of Compulsion and Drive."

34. Gould, "Addiction and Cognition"; Bernardin et al., "Cognitive Impairments in Alcohol-Dependent Subjects"; Pau et al., 2002, "The Impact of Heroin on Frontal Executive Functions"; Hester and Garavan, "Executive Dysfunction in Cocaine Addiction"; van der Plas et al., "Executive Control Deficits in Substance-Dependent Individuals."

35. Bechara, Noël, and Crone, Chapter 15: "Loss of Willpower: Abnormal Neural Mechanisms of Impulse Control," 228.

36. Burns and Bechara, "Decision Making and Free Will."

37. *Robinson v. California*, 370 U.S. at 667.

38. Kelly, *Criminal Justice at the Crossroads*, 103.

39. Kelly, *Criminal Justice at the Crossroads*, 105.

40. Raine, "The Biological Crime."

41. Raine and Yang, "Neural Foundations," 205–6.

42. Redding, "The Brain-Disordered Defendant"; Lamparello, "Neuroscience, Brain Damage, and the Criminal Defendant."

43. Harmon, "Brain Injury Rate 7 Times Greater."

44. Raine, "The Biological Crime," 2.

45. Redding, "The Brain-Disordered Defendant."

46. Redding, "The Brain-Disordered Defendant," 70.

47. Klaming and Koops, "Neuroscientific Evidence."

48. Sapolsky, "The Frontal Cortex"; Klaming and Koops, "Neuroscientific Evidence."

49. Kiehl and Hoffman, "The Criminal Psychopath."

50. Blair, "The Amygdala and Ventromedial Prefrontal Cortex."

51. Brooks, "New Insight into the Psychopathic Brain."

52. Ogilvie et al., "Neuropsychological Measures."

53. Meijers et al., "Prison Brain?"

54. Meijers et al., "Prison Brain?" 4.

55. Wortzel and Arciniegas, "A Forensic Neuropsychiatric Approach."

56. Glenn and Raine, "Neurocriminology."

57. Barzman et al., "Does Traumatic Brain Injury Cause Violence?"

58. Wortzel and Arciniegas, "A Forensic Neuropsychiatric Approach," 278.

59. Centers for Disease Control, "Traumatic Brain Injury in Prisons and Jails."

60. Brooks-Gunn and Duncan, "The Effects of Poverty on Children."

61. Kelly, *Criminal Justice at the Crossroads*.

62. Noble et al., "Family Income, Parental Education and Brain Structure."

63. Boutwell et al., "The Intersection of Aggregate-Level Lead Exposure."

64. Walsh and Bolen, *The Neurobiology of Criminal Behavior*, 163–64.

65. Reavis et al., "Adverse Childhood Experiences and Adult Criminality."

66. Ibid.

67. Kessler et al., "Prevalence, Severity and Comorbidity of Twelve-Month DSM-IV Disorders."

68. Center for Behavioral Health Statistics and Quality, *Behavioral Health Trends in the United States.*

69. Hartz et al., "Comorbidity of Severe Psychotic Disorders."

70. NAMI, "Numbers of Americans Affected by Mental Illness."

71. Wang et al., "Twelve-Month Use of Mental Health Services."

72. Pan, "MAP: Which States Have Cut Treatment for the Mentally Ill the Most?"

73. James and Glaze, "Mental Health Problems of Prison and Jail Inmates."

74. Sarteschi, "Mentally Ill Offenders Involved with the U.S. Criminal Justice System."

75. Travis et al., *The Growth of Incarceration in the United States.*

76. Lurigio et al., "Standardized Assessment"; Prins, "Prevalence of Mental Illnesses in U.S. State Prisons."

77. National Institute of Mental Health. "Inmate Mental Health."

78. Peterson et al., "How Often and How Consistently Do Symptoms Directly Precede Criminal Behavior."

79. Mears, "Mental Health Needs and Services."

80. Elbogen and Johnson, "The Intricate Link Between Violence and Mental Disorder"; Peterson et al., "How Often and How Consistently Do Symptoms Directly Precede Criminal Behavior"; Fazel et al., "Bipolar Disorder and Violent Crime."

81. Fazel et al., "Schizophrenia, Substance Abuse"; Peterson et al., "How Often and How Consistently Do Symptoms Directly Precede Criminal Behavior"; Elbogen and Johnson, "The Intricate Link Between Violence and Mental Disorder."

82. Peterson et al., "How Often and How Consistently Do Symptoms Directly Precede Criminal Behavior"; Elbogen and Johnson, "The Intricate Link Between Violence and Mental Disorder."

83. Sirotich, "Correlates of Crime and Violence."

84. Stuart, "Violence and Mental Illness."

85. Schwartz et al., "Posttraumatic Stress Disorder among African-Americans"; Donley, "Civilian PTSD Symptoms and Risk."

86. Schwartz et al., "Posttraumatic Stress Disorder among African-Americans."

87. Donley, "Civilian PTSD Symptoms and Risk."

88. Peters et al., "Co-Occurring Substance Use and Mental Disorders."

89. Mallik-Kane and Visher, "Health and Prisoner Reentry"; Cloyes et al., "Time to Prison Return for Offenders"; Baillargeon et al., "Psychiatric Disorders and Repeat Incarcerations."

90. Lurigio, "People with Serious Mental Illness," 74S.

91. Peterson et al., "How Often and How Consistently Do Symptoms Directly Precede Criminal Behavior."

3. THE SPECIAL CASE OF
THE JUVENILE BRAIN

1. National Research Council, *The Science of Adolescent Risk-Taking.*

2. Dahl, "Adolescent Brain Development."

3. Office of the Surgeon General, "Youth Violence."

4. Steinberg, "A Social Neuroscience Perspective"; Casey et al., "The Adolescent Brain."

5. American Medical Association and the American Academy of Child and Adolescent Psychiatry, as Amici Curiae in *Miller v. Alabama*, 23.

6. American Medical Association and the American Academy of Child and Adolescent Psychiatry, as Amici Curiae in *Miller v. Alabama.*

7. American Medical Association and the American Academy of Child and Adolescent Psychiatry, as Amici Curiae in *Miller v. Alabama*, 35.

8. Van Voorhees and Scarpa, "The Effects of Child Maltreatment"; National Scientific Council on the Developing Child, "Working Paper No. 3."

9. Irigaray et al., "Child Maltreatment and Later Cognitive Functioning"; Hilt et al., "Emotion Dysregulation."

10. McCrory et al., "The Impact of Childhood Maltreatment."

11. McEwen and Morrison. "The Brain on Stress."

12. Loughan and Perna, "Neurocognitive Impacts for Children of Poverty and Neglect"; de Bellis, "The Psychobiology of Neglect"; DePrince et al., "Executive Function Performance"; Chugani et al., "Local Brain Functional Activity."

13. Child Welfare, "Issue Brief."

14. Jednoróg et al., "The Influence of Socioeconomic Status."

15. Jednoróg et al., "The Influence of Socioeconomic Status"; Noble et al., "Neural Correlates of Socioeconomic Status."

16. Luby et al., "The Effects of Poverty"; Noble et al., "Neural Correlates of Socioeconomic Status."

17. Noble et al., "Neural Correlates of Socioeconomic Status"; Hanson et al., "Association Between Income and the Hippocampus"; Luby et al., "The Effects of Poverty."

18. Azma, "Poverty and the Developing Brain," 41.

19. Luby et al., "The Effects of Poverty"; Hanson et al., "Association Between Income and the Hippocampus"; Noble et al., "Family Income, Parental Education and Brain Structure."

20. Noble et al., "Family Income, Parental Education and Brain Structure."

21. Kishiyama et al., "Socioeconomic Disparities."

22. Hanson et al., "Family Poverty Affects the Rate of Human Infant Brain Growth."

23. Noble et al., "Neurocognitive Correlates of Socioeconomic Status"; Farah et al., "Childhood Poverty."

24. Azma, "Poverty and the Developing Brain."

25. Hanson et al., "Family Poverty Affects the Rate of Human Infant Brain Growth."

26. Holz et al., "The Long-Term Impact of Early Life Poverty."

27. Danese and McEwen, "Adverse Childhood Experiences."

28. Anda et al., "The Enduring Effects of Abuse."

29. Kelly, *Criminal Justice at the Crossroads*.

30. *Roper v. Simmons* (2005) at 15–16.

31. *Graham v. Florida* (2010) at 17.

32. *Miller v. Alabama*, 567 U.S. (2012), at 15.

33. American Academy of Pediatrics, "Adverse Childhood Experiences and the Lifelong Consequences of Trauma"; Centers for Disease Control, "Child Abuse and Neglect."

34. Anda et al., "The Enduring Effects of Abuse," 174.

35. Reavis et al., "Adverse Childhood Experiences and Adult Criminality."

36. Raine et al., "Neurocognitive Impairments in Boys," 46.

37. Moffitt et al., "Males on the Life-Course Persistent and Adolescent-Limited Antisocial Pathways"; Raine et al., "Neurocognitive Impairments in Boys"; Moffitt, "Life-Course-Persistent versus Adolescence-Limited Antisocial Behavior."

38. Moffitt et al., "A Gradient of Childhood Self-Control," 2697.

39. Stagman and Cooper, "Children's Mental Health."

40. Fox et al., "Prevalence of Youth Drug Use."

41. Murphey et al., "Access to Mental Health Care."

42. Stagman and Cooper, "Children's Mental Health."

43. Stagman and Cooper, "Children's Mental Health."

44. Murphey et al., "Access to Mental Health Care."

45. Stagman and Cooper, "Children's Mental Health," 6.

46. Shufelt and Cocozza, *Youth with Mental Health Disorders in the Juvenile Justice System*.

47. Cuellar et al., "Mental Health and Substance Abuse Treatment"; Odgers et al., "Misdiagnosing the Problem"; National Center on Addiction and Substance Abuse, "Criminal Neglect"; Schubert et al., "Influence of Mental Health and Substance Use Problems"; Abram et al., "Comorbidity and Continuity of Psychiatric Disorders"; Shufelt and Cocozza, "Youth with Mental Health Disorders";

Coker et al., "Crime and Psychiatric Disorders Among Youth"; Teplin et al., "Prevalence and Persistence of Psychiatric Disorders."

48. Odgers et al., "Misdiagnosing the Problem."

49. Shufelt and Cocozza, "Youth with Mental Health Disorders."

50. The National Center on Addiction and Substance Abuse, "Criminal Neglect."

51. Schubert and Mulvey, "Behavioral Health Problems"; Schubert et al., "Serious Juvenile Offenders"; Schubert et al., "Influence of Mental Health and Substance Use Problems."

52. Abram et al., "PTSD, Trauma and Comorbid Psychiatric Disorders."

53. Baglivio et al., "The Prevalence of Adverse Childhood Experiences"; Schilling et al., "Adverse Childhood Experiences."

54. Schilling et al., "Adverse Childhood Experiences."

55. Abram et al., "Comorbidity and Continuity of Psychiatric Disorders"; Teplin et al., "Prevalence and Persistence of Psychiatric Disorders."

56. U.S. Department of Health and Human Services, "Report of the Surgeon General's Conference on Children's Mental Health," 1.

57. Abram et al., "Perceived Barriers to Mental Health Services."

58. International Society of Psychiatric Mental Health Nurses, "Meeting the Mental Health Needs of Youth"; Swift, "Lack of Expertise, Inadequate Funding"; Underwood and Washington, "Mental Illness and Juvenile Offenders"; Abram et al., "Perceived Barriers to Mental Health Services."

4. THE PATH FORWARD

1. The phrase *disruptive innovation* was literally stolen by us from Lloyd Sederer. He used it in a *U.S. News and World Report* op-ed called "Tinkering Can't Fix the Mental Health Care System," March 20, 2015. Our theft was motivated by how appropriate this phrase is regarding the U.S. criminal justice system.

2. Cullen, "Taking Rehabilitation Seriously," 110.

3. Schnittker et al., "Out and Down: Incarceration"; Baillargeon et al., "Psychiatric Disorders and Repeat Incarcerations."

4. Schnittker et al., "Out and Down: Incarceration," 459.

5. *Ruiz v. Estelle*, 503 F. Supp. 1265 (1980) at 1339.

6. *Brown v. Plata*, 563 U.S. (2011) at 3, 5, and 6.

7. Christine Sarteschi, "Mentally Ill Offenders."

8. President's New Freedom Commission, "Achieving the Promise," 1.

9. James and Glaze, "Mental Health Problems of Prison and Jail Inmates"; Human Rights Watch, "Ill Equipped."

10. Cloud and Davis, "Treatment Alternatives to Incarceration for People with Mental Health Needs," 1.

11. Kim et al., "The Processing and Treatment of Mentally Ill Persons"; Morgan et al., "Treating Offenders with Mental Illness."

12. Snyder, "Nothing Works, Something Works."

13. Morgan et al., "Treating Offenders with Mental Illness."

14. Vanderplasschen et al., "Therapeutic Communities for Addictions"; Chandler et al., "Treating Drug Abuse."

15. Substance Abuse and Mental Health Services Administration, "Screening and Assessment," 28.

16. Kelly, *Criminal Justice at the Crossroads*; Kelly, *The Future of Crime and Punishment*.

17. James and Glaze, "Mental Health Problems of Prison and Jail Inmates"; Byron, "Criminals Need Mental Health Care."

18. Treatment Advocacy Center, "Consequences of Non-Treatment."

19. Kim et al., "The Processing and Treatment of Mentally Ill Persons"; Mumola and Karberg, "Drug Use and Dependence."

20. Steadman, "When Political Will Is Not Enough."

21. NAMI, "Jailing People with Mental Illness."

22. Substance Abuse and Mental Health Services Administration, "Mental and Substance Use Disorders."

23. Tuominen et al., "Neurocognitive Disorders"; Marceau et al., "Neuropsychological Assessment."

24. Bronson et al., "Disabilities Among Prison and Jail Inmates."

25. Frost et al., "Prevalence of Traumatic Brain Injury."

26. Hughes, "Neurodisability in the Youth Justice System."

27. Kelly, *Criminal Justice at the Crossroads*; Kelly, *The Future of Crime and Punishment*.

28. Baillargeon et al., "Psychiatric Disorders and Repeat Incarcerations."

29. Baillargeon et al., "Psychiatric Disorders and Repeat Incarcerations," 105.

30. Spohn and Holleran, "The Effect of Imprisonment."

31. National Association of Drug Court Professionals, "Facts on Drugs and Crime in America," retrieved from www.nadcp.org/sites/default/files/nadcp/Facts%20on%20Drug%20Courts%20.pdf.

32. Human Rights Watch, "Callous and Cruel"; Frost and Monteiro, "Administrative Segregation."

33. Frost and Monteiro, "Administrative Segregation."

34. American Civil Liberties Union of Colorado, "Out of Sight, Out of Mind"; Frost and Monteiro, "Administrative Segregation."

35. Frost and Monteiro, "Administrative Segregation."

36. Frost and Monteiro, "Administrative Segregation," 11.

37. Baillargeon et al., "Psychiatric Disorders and Repeat Incarcerations," 103.

38. Kelly, *Criminal Justice at the Crossroads*; Kelly, *The Future of Crime and Punishment*.

39. World Health Organization, "Mental Health Atlas."

40. Bishop et al., "Acceptance of Insurance."

41. Crary, "A Serious Shortage of Psychiatrists."

42. Fields and Dooren, "For the Mentally Ill."

43. American Academy of Child and Adolescent Psychiatry, "Workforce Issues."

44. National Center for Children in Poverty, "No Easy Fixes."

45. U.S. Department of Health and Human Services, "Medicaid and Permanent Supportive Housing."

46. U.S. Department of Health and Human Services, "Examining Substance Use Disorder Treatment."

47. Pew Charitable Trusts, "Enforcement of Mental Health Care," 2.

48. NAMI, "A Long Road Ahead."

49. Gold, "Health Insurers Face Little Enforcement."

50. Substance Abuse and Mental Health Services Administration, "Behavioral Health Equity," 23–24.

51. NAMI, "State Mental Health Cuts."

52. National Council for Behavioral Health, "The Business Case for Effective Mental Health Treatment."

53. Ibid.

54. Druss and Walker, "Mental Disorders and Medical Comorbidity."

55. Sederer, "Tinkering Can't Fix the Mental Health Care System," 2.

56. NAMI, "State Mental Health Legislation 2015."

57. Kennedy Forum, "Fixing Behavioral Health Care in America."

58. Patel et al., "Grand Challenges"; Kennedy Forum, "Fixing Behavioral Health Care in America"; Unützer et al., "The Collaborative Care Model"; Sederer and Sharfstein, "Fixing the Troubled Mental Health System"; Appelbaum, "How to Rebuild America's Mental Health System"; Sederer, "Tinkering Can't Fix the Mental Health Care System."

59. Kennedy Forum, "Fixing Behavioral Health Care in America"; Unützer et al., "The Collaborative Care Model"; Cochrane Reviews, "Collaborative Care"; University of Washington AIMS Center, "Evidence Base for Collaborative Care."

60. Scott and Lewis, "Using Measurement-Based Care," 8.

61. Kennedy Forum, "Fixing Behavioral Health Care in America."

62. Unützer et al., "The Collaborative Care Model."

63. Walton, "Why More Americans Suffer from Mental Disorders."

64. U.S. Department of Health and Human Services, "Examining Substance Use Disorder Treatment."

65. Hyde, "Report to Congress."

66. Hwang, "Rising Access to Substance Abuse Treatment."

67. NCAAD New Jersey, "Access to Treatment."

68. National Center on Addiction and Substance Abuse at Columbia University, "Addiction Medicine," 4.

69. Bailey, "Medical Students Demand Better Training."

70. Volkow, "A Major Step Forward."

71. Pedrero-Perez et al., "Cognitive Remediation"; Campanella, "Neurocognitive Rehabilitation"; Rezapour et al., "Perspectives on Neurocognitive Rehabilitation"; Rezapour et al., "Neuro Cognitive Rehabilitation"; Sofuoglu et al., "Cognitive Enhancement"; Passetti et al., "Neuropsychological Predictors."

72. Cunha et al., "The Frontal Assessment Battery," 875.

73. Sofuoglu et al., "Cognitive Enhancement."

74. Tolin, "Is Cognitive Behavioral Therapy More Effective?"

75. Aharonovich et al., "Cognitive Impairment"; Aharonovich et al., "Cognitive Deficits."

76. Aharonovich et al., "Cognitive Impairment."

77. Miller et al., "Disseminating Evidence-Based Practices."

78. National Institute on Drug Abuse, "Principles of Drug Addiction Treatment."

79. Kelly and Daley, "Integrated Treatment."

80. Drake et al., "Implementing Dual Diagnosis"; Kelly and Daley, "Integrated Treatment."

81. Bhaumik et al., "Psychological Treatments"; Didden et al., "Intellectual Disabilities."

82. National Association for Persons with Developmental Disabilities, "Information on Dual Diagnosis."

83. Brown et al., "Treating individuals with Intellectual Disabilities."

84. Maguire et al., "London Taxi Drivers."

85. Pascual-Leone et al., "The Plastic Human Brain Cortex," 377.

86. Halligan and Wade, *The Effectiveness of Rehabilitation*, 13.

87. Koehler et al., *Cognitive Rehabilitation Therapy*.

88. National Institutes of Health, "Consensus Development Conference Statement."

89. Koehler et al., *Cognitive Rehabilitation Therapy*; Cicerone et al., "Evidence-Based Cognitive Rehabilitation."

90. Miotto et al., "Cognitive Rehabilitation"; Hampstead et al., "Cognitive Rehabilitation"; Pedrero-Perez et al., "Cognitive Remediation"; Campanella,

"Neurocognitive Rehabilitation"; Halligan and Wade, *The Effectiveness of Rehabilitation.*

5. CRIMINAL INTENT AND DIVERSION

1. Sayer, "Public Welfare Offenses," 56, 68.
2. *Morissette v. United States*, 342 U.S. 246 (72 S. Ct. 240, 96 L.Ed. 288).
3. National Commissions on Reform of the Federal Criminal Law, S. REP. NO. 605, Part 1, 95th Cong., 1st Sess. 55 (1977).
4. M'Naghten Case, 1 C. & K. 130: 4 St. Tr. N.S. 947 (1843).
5. Stuntz, *The Collapse of American Criminal Justice*, 260, 262.
6. *Morissette v. United States*.
7. Brown, "Criminal Law Reform," 297.
8. *Elonis v. United States*, 575 U.S.
9. Amit Patel, "Mens Rea as an Element of Crime," 49.
10. Hatch, "It's Time."
11. Malcolm, "Point/Counterpoint: Criminal Justice Reform and Mens Rea."
12. Walsh and Joslyn, "Without Intent: How Congress Is Eroding the Criminal Intent Requirement in Federal Law."
13. *Sykes v. United States*, 131 S. Ct. 2267, 2288 (2011) (Scalia, J. dissenting).
14. Testimony of Stephen A. Saltzburg on behalf of the American Bar Association for the Hearing on the Adequacy of Criminal Intent Standards in Federal Prosecutions.
15. Baker, "Mens Rea and State Crimes."
16. Brown, "Criminal Law Reform."

6. THE PATH FORWARD

1. Health and Human Services, Mental Health.gov, Mental Health Myths; American Psychological Association, "Mental Illness Not Usually Linked."
2. Cloud and Davis, "Treatment Alternatives."
3. Skeem et al., "Correctional Policy."
4. Ostermann and Matejkowski, "Exploring the Intersection"; Skeem et al., "Correctional Policy."
5. Skeem et al., "Correctional Policy."
6. Hall et al., "Predictors of General and Violent Recidivism."
7. Baillargeon et al., "Parole Revocation."

8. Baillargeon et al., "Risk of Reincarceration."

9. Jaffe et al., "Drug-Abusing Offenders"; Hall et al., "Predictors of General and Violent Recidivism."

10. Hall et al., "Predictors of General and Violent Recidivism."

11. American Psychological Association, "Inmate Drug Abuse"; National Institute on Drug Abuse, "Principles of Drug Addiction Treatment."

12. Kelly, *Criminal Justice at the Crossroads*; Kelly, *The Future of Crime and Punishment*.

13. Sederer and Sharfstein, "Fixing the Troubled Mental Health System."

14. Andrews and Bonta, *The Psychology of Criminal Conduct*.

15. Legal Information Institute, "Imposition of a Sentence of Imprisonment."

16. Kelly, *The Future of Crime and Punishment*, 190–91.

17. Blumstein, *Criminal Careers*.

18. Piquero et al., "Criminal Career Patterns."

19. Monahan et al., "Juvenile Justice Policy and Practice."

20. Monahan et al., "Juvenile Justice Policy and Practice."

21. Monahan et al., "Juvenile Justice Policy and Practice," 597.

22. Skeem et al., "Offenders with Mental Illness"; Sarteschi, "Mentally Ill Offenders."

23. Skeem et al., "Offenders with Mental Illness."

24. Skeem et al., "Offenders with Mental Illness."

25. Manchak et al., "High-Fidelity Specialty Mental Health Probation."

26. Phillips et al., "Moving Assertive Community Treatment"; Morrissey, "Forensic Assertive Community Treatment."

27. Morrissey, "Forensic Assertive Community Treatment."

28. Insel, "Directors Blog."

29. Kozak and Cuthbert, "The NIMH Research Domain Criteria"; McTeague, "Reconciling RDoC and DSM Approaches"; Craddock and Mynors-Wallis, "Psychiatric Diagnosis"; Regier et al., "DSM-5 Field Trials."

30. Craddock and Mynors-Wallis, "Psychiatric Diagnosis," 3.

31. Skeem et al., "Correctional Policy for Offenders"; Epperson et al., "Envisioning the Next Generation."

32. Morgan et al., "Treating Offenders"; Blandford and Osher, "A Checklist for Implementing Evidence-Based Practices"; Osher, "Integrating Mental Health"; Fontanarosa et al., "Interventions for Adult Offenders."

7. COSTS, BENEFITS, AND CHALLENGES

1. Welsh et al., "Benefit-Cost Analysis"; Marsh et al., "Do You Get What You Pay For?"; Furman and Holtz-Eakin, "Why Mass Incarceration Doesn't Pay."

2. Pew Center on the States, "Time Served."

3. McLaughlin et al., "The Economic Burden of Incarceration."

4. Strong et al., "Census of Problem-Solving Courts."

5. Ibid.

6. See Kelly, *Criminal Justice at the Crossroads*; Kelly, *The Future of Crime and Punishment*.

7. Washington State Institute for Public Policy, "Swift and Certain Sanctions."

8. Bhati and Roman, "Simulated Evidence"; Zarkin et al., "Lifetime Benefits and Costs"; Roman, "Cost-Benefit Analysis of Criminal Justice Reforms"; McVay et al., "Treatment or Incarceration?"

9. Bhati and Roman, "Simulated Evidence."

10. RTI International, "Study: Replacing Prison Terms with Drug Abuse Treatment."

11. Waller et al., "Testing the Cost Savings of Judicial Diversion."

12. Washington State Institute for Public Policy, "Drug Courts Benefit-Cost Estimates."

13. Zarkin et al., "Lifetime Benefits and Costs," 830.

14. Steadman and Naples, "Assessing the Effectiveness of Jail Diversion"; Sirotich, "The Criminal Justice Outcomes"; McNiel and Binder, "Effectiveness of a Mental Health Court"; Steadman et al., "Effect of Mental Health Courts"; Liebowitz et al., "A Way Forward."

15. McCausland, "People with Mental Health Disorders"; Kiehl and Hoffman, "The Criminal Psychopath."

16. Washington State Institute for Public Policy, "Mental Health Courts."

17. Washington State Institute for Public Policy, "Jail Diversion Programs"; Cloud and Davis, "Treatment Alternatives."

18. Liebowitz et al., "A Way Forward."

19. Wilson and Hoge, "The Effect of Youth Diversion Programs."

20. Washington State Institute for Public Policy, "Drug Courts."

21. Washington State Institute for Public Policy, "Diversion, No Services"; "Diversion with Services."

22. Cohen and Piquero, "New Evidence on the Monetary Value," 47.

23. Lawrence, "Managing Corrections Costs."

24. Bazelon Center, "Funding for Mental Health Services."

25. Mental Health America, "Parity or Disparity."

26. Ibid.

27. Ibid.

28. Winkelman et al., "Health Insurance Trends."

29. Keller, "Criminal Justice Reform: An Obituary."

30. ACLU, "ACLU Nationwide Poll on Criminal Justice Reform."

31. Arkin, "Poll: Majority Supports Prison and Justice Reform."

32. Alliance for Safety and Justice, "Crime Survivors Speak."

REFERENCES

Abram, Karen, Leah D. Paskar, Jason J. Washburn, Linda A. Teplin, Naomi A. Zwecker, and Nicole M. Azores-Gococo. "Perceived Barriers to Mental Health Services Among Detained Youth." *Juvenile Justice Bulletin*, Washington, DC: Office of Juvenile Justice and Delinquency Prevention, 2015.

Abram, Karen M., Naomi A. Zwecker, Leah J. Welty, Jennifer A. Hershfield, Mina K. Dulcan, and Linda A. Teplin. "Comorbidity and Continuity of Psychiatric Disorders in Youth After Detention: A Prospective Longitudinal Study." *JAMA Psychiatry* 72, no. 1 (2015): 84–93. doi: 10.1001/jamapsychiatry.2014.1375.

Abram, Karen, Linda A. Teplin, Devon C. King, Sandra L. Longworth, Kristin M. Emanuel, Erin G. Romero, Gary M. McClelland, Mina K. Dulcan, Jason J. Washburn, Leah J. Welty, and Nichole D. Olson. "PTSD, Trauma, and Comorbid Psychiatric Disorders in Detained Youth." *Juvenile Justice Bulletin*, Washington, DC: Office of Juvenile Justice and Delinquency Prevention, 2013.

ACLU National Prison Project. "Know Your Rights: Medical, Dental and Mental Health Care." Last updated July 2012.

ACLU. "ACLU Nationwide Poll on Criminal Justice Reform." www.aclu.org/other/aclu-nationwide-poll-criminal-justice-reform. Accessed October 3, 2016.

Aharonovich, Efrat, Adam C. Brooks, Edward V. Nunes, and Deborah S. Hasin. "Cognitive Deficits in Marijuana Users: Effects on Motivational Enhancement Therapy Plus Cognitive Behavioral Therapy Treatment Outcome." *Drug and Alcohol Dependence* 95, no. 3 (2008): 279–83.

Aharonovich, Efrat, Deborah S. Hasin, Adam C. Brooks, Xinhua Liu, Adam Bisaga, and Edward V. Nunes. "Cognitive Deficits Predict Low Treatment Retention in Cocaine Dependent Patients." *Drug and Alcohol Dependence* 81, no. 3 (2006): 313–22.

Aharonovich, Efrat, Edward Nunes, and Deborah Hasin. "Cognitive Impairment, Retention and Abstinence among Cocaine Abusers in Cognitive-Behavioral Treatment." *Drug and Alcohol Dependence* 71, no. 2 (2003): 207–11.

Allen, Rob. "Reducing the Use of Imprisonment." Criminal Justice Alliance. May 2012. http://www.prisonpolicy.org/scans/CJA_ReducingImprisonment_Europe.pdf.

Alliance for Safety and Justice. "Crime Survivors Speak: The First-Ever National Survey of Victims' Views on Safety and Justice." 2012.

American Academy of Child and Adolescent Psychiatry. "Workforce Issues." February 2016. http://www.aacap.org/aacap/resources_for_primary_care/Workforce_Issues.aspx. Accessed July 21, 2016.

American Academy of Pediatrics. "Adverse Childhood Experiences and the Lifelong Consequences of Trauma." 2014. https://www.aap.org/en-us/Documents/ttb_aces_consequences.
pdf.

American Bar Association. Testimony of Stephen A. Salzburg on behalf of the American Bar
Association for the hearing on The Adequacy of Criminal Intent Standards in Federal
Prosecutions before the Committee on the Judiciary of the US Senate. January 20, 2016.

American Civil Liberties Union (ACLU) of Colorado, and United States of America. "Out of
Sight, Out of Mind: Colorado's Continued Warehousing of Mentally Ill Prisoners in Solitary
Confinement." 2013. no. 14–280.

American Medical Association and the American Academy of Child and Adolescent Psychiatry, as Amici Curiae in *Miller v. Alabama*, 132 S. Ct. 2455, 567 U.S., 183 L. Ed. 2d 407
(2012).

American Psychiatric Association. "Comprehensive Mental Health Reform in the 114th Congress." 2016. https://www.psychiatry.org/psychiatrists/advocacy/federal-affairs/comprehen
sive-mental-health-reform. Accessed July 26, 2016.

American Psychiatric Association. *Diagnostic and Statistical Manual of Mental Disorders*. 5th
ed. Washington, DC: American Psychiatric Publishing, 2013.

American Psychiatric Association. *DSM-5 Intellectual Disability Fact Sheet*. Washington, DC:
American Psychiatric Publishing, 2013. https://www.psychiatry.org/psychiatrists/practice/
dsm/dsm-5.

American Psychiatric Association. "Substance-Related and Addictive Disorders" (*DSM-5*).
Washington, DC: American Psychiatric Publishing, 2013. http://dsm.psychiatryonline.org/
doi/abs/10.1176/appi.books.9781585624836.jb16.

American Psychological Association. "Inmate Drug Abuse Treatment Slows Prisons Revolving
Door." March 23, 2014. http://www.apa.org/research/action/aftercare.aspx.

American Psychological Association. "Mental Illness Not Usually Linked to Crime." 2014.
http://www.apa.org/news/press/releases/2014/04/mental-illness-crime.aspx.

American Society of Addiction Medicine. "Definition of Addiction." http://www.asam.org/
qualitypractice/definition-of-addiction.

Anda, R., V. Felitti, D. Bremner, J. Walker, C. Whitfield, B. Perry, S. Dube, and W. Giles.
"The Enduring Effects of Abuse and Related Adverse Experiences in Childhood." *European
Archives of Psychiatry and Clinical Neuroscience* 256, no. 3 (2006): 174–86.

Andrews, Donald, and James Bonta. *The Psychology of Criminal Conduct*. New York: Rutledge, 2011.

"Any Disorder Among Children." NIH. http://www.nimh.nih.gov/health/statistics/prevalence/
any-disorder-among-children.shtml. Accessed June 20, 2016.

Appelbaum, Paul S. "How to Rebuild America's Mental Health System in 5 Big Steps." 2014.
https://www.theguardian.com/commentisfree/2014/may/29/-sp-fix-america-mental-health-
system-ideas. Accessed July 2, 2016.

Arceneaux, Michael. "Why Are the Three Largest Mental Health Care Providers Jails?" *News-
one*, 2013. https://newsone.com/2744141/prisons-mental-health-providers/.

Arkin, James. "Poll: Majority Supports Prison and Justice Reforms." Real Clear Politics. February 11, 2016. www.realclearpolitics.com/articles/2016/02/11/poll_majority_supports_
prison_and_justice_reforms_129635.html.

Ash, Peter. "The Adolescent Brain Is Different." *Psychiatric Times*. October 26, 2012. http://
www.psychiatrictimes.com/special-reports/adolescent-brain-different.

Atkins v. Virginia, 536 U.S. 304, 318, 122 S. Ct. 2242, 2250 (2002). https://www.law.cornell.
edu/supremecourt/text/536/304. Accessed April 25, 2016.

Azma, Sheeva. "Poverty and the Developing Brain: Insights from Neuroimaging." *Synesis: A
Journal of Science, Technology, Ethics, and Policy* 4, no. 1 (2013): G40–G46.

Baglivio, Michael T., Nathan Epps, Kimberly Swartz, Mona Sayedul Huq, Amy Sheer, and
Nancy S. Hardt. "The Prevalence of Adverse Childhood Experiences (ACE) in the Lives of
Juvenile Offenders." *Journal of Juvenile Justice* 3, no. 2 (2014): 1.

Bailey, Melissa. "Medical Students Demand Better Training to Tackle Opioid Crisis." *STAT
News*. May 17, 2016. www.statnews.com/2016/05/17/opioid-addiction-medical-schools/.

Baillargeon, Jacques, Brie A. Williams, Jeff Mellow, Amy Jo Harzke, Steven K. Hoge, Gwen Baillargeon, and Robert B. Greifinger. "Parole Revocation Among Prison Inmates with Psychiatric and Substance Use Disorders." *Psychiatric Services* 60, no. 11 (2009): 1516–21.

Baillargeon, Jacques, Ingrid Binswanger, Joseph Penn, Brie Williams, and Owen Murray. "Psychiatric Disorders and Repeat Incarcerations: The Revolving Prison Door." *American Journal of Psychiatry* 166 (2009): 103–9.

Baillargeon, Jacques, Joseph V. Penn, Kevin Knight, Amy Jo Harzke, Gwen Baillargeon, and Emilie A. Becker. "Risk of Reincarceration Among Prisoners with Co-Occurring Severe Mental Illness and Substance Use Disorders." *Administration and Policy in Mental Health and Mental Health Services Research* 37, no. 4 (2010): 367–74.

Baker, John. "Mens Rea and State Crimes." White Paper, The Federalist Society, September 4, 2012. Retrieved from http://www.fed-soc.org/publications/detail/mens-rea-and-state-crimes.

Bargh, John A. "Bypassing the Will: Toward Demystifying the Nonconscious Control of Social Behavior." *The New Unconscious* (2005): 37–58.

Bargh, John A. "Our Unconscious Mind." *Scientific American* 310, no. 1 (2014): 30–37.

Bargh, John A., and Ezequiel Morsella. "The Unconscious Mind." *Perspectives on Psychological Science* 3, no. 1 (2008): 73–79.

Baroff, George S. "In Memory of John Jacobson, PhD: On the Mitigating Nature of Intellectual Disability (ID) in the Offender with Developmental Disability." *NADD Bulletin* 8, no. 2 http://thenadd.org/modal/bulletins/v8n1a2~.htm.

Barr, Alasdair M., William J. Panenka, G. William MacEwan, and Allen E. Thornton. "The Need for Speed: an Update on Methamphetamine Addiction." *Journal of Psychiatry & Neuroscience* 31, no. 5 (2006): 301.

Barzman, Drew, John Kennedy, and Manish Fozar. "Does Traumatic Brain Injury Cause Violence?" *Current Psychiatry*, April 1, 2002. http://www.mdedge.com/currentpsychiatry/article/66123/somatic-disorders/does-traumatic-brain-injury-cause-violence.

Bates, Marsha, and Anthony Pawlak. "Cognitive Impairment Influences Drinking Outcome by Altering Therapeutic Mechanisms of Change." *Psychology of Addiction Behavior* 20, no. 3 (2006): 241–53.

Bazelon Center for Mental Health Law. "Funding for Mental Health Services and Programs." Updated June 2011. http://www.bazelon.org/LinkClick.aspx?fileticket=GzmAbAweikQ%3D&tabid=436.

Beauchaine, Theodore P., Emily Neuhaus, Sharon L. Brenner, and Lisa Gatzke-Kopp. "Ten Good Reasons to Consider Biological Processes in Prevention and Intervention Research." *Development and Psychopathology* 20 (2008): 745–74. doi: 10.1017/S0954579408000369.

Bechara, Antoine. "Decision Making, Impulse Control and Loss of Willpower to Resist Drugs: A Neurocognitive Perspective." *Nature Neuroscience* 8, no. 11 (2005): 1458–63.

Bechara, Antoine, and Hanna Damasio. "Decision-Making and Addiction (part I): Impaired Activation of Somatic States in Substance Dependent Individuals when Pondering Decisions with Negative Future Consequences." *Neuropsychologia* 40, no. 10 (2002): 1675–89.

Bechara, Antoine, Sara Dolan, and Andrea Hindes. "Decision-Making and Addiction (part II): Myopia for the Future or Hypersensitivity to Reward?" *Neuropsychologia* 40, no. 10 (2002): 1690–1705.

Bechara, Antoine, Sara Dolan, Natalie Denburg, Andrea Hindes, Steven W. Anderson, and Peter E. Nathan. "Decision-Making Deficits, Linked to a Dysfunctional Ventromedial Prefrontal Cortex, Revealed in Alcohol and Stimulant Abusers." *Neuropsychologia* 39, no. 4 (2001): 376–89.

Bechara, Antoine, and Eileen M. Martin. "Impaired Decision Making Related to Working Memory Deficits in Individuals with Substance Addictions." *Neuropsychology* 18, no. 1 (2004): 152.

Bechara, Antoine, Xavier Noël, and Eveline A. Crone. "Loss of Willpower: Abnormal Neural Mechanisms of Impulse Control and Decision Making in Addiction." *Handbook of Implicit Cognition and Addiction* (2006): 215–32.

Bensing, Russ. "Mens Rea Reform." *The Briefcase: Musings by an Ohio Criminal Lawyer* (blog). January 27, 2016. http://briefcase8.com/2016/01/mens-rea-reform.html.

Bernardin, Florent, Anne Maheut-Bosser, and François Paille. "Cognitive Impairments in Alcohol-Dependent Subjects." *Frontiers in Psychiatry* 5 (2014): 78.

Bhati, Avinash Singh, and John K. Roman. "Simulated Evidence on the Prospects of Treating More Drug-Involved Offenders." *Journal of Experimental Criminology* 6, no. 1 (2010): 1–33.

Bhaumik, Sabyasachi, Satheesh Gangadharan, Avinash Hiremath, and Paul Swamidhas Sudhakar Russell. "Psychological Treatments in Intellectual Disability: The Challenges of Building a Good Evidence Base." *British Journal of Psychiatry* 198, no. 6 (2011): 428–30.

Bishop, T., M. Press, S. Keyhani, and H. Pincus. "Acceptance of Insurance by Psychiatrists and the Implications for Access to Mental Health Care." *JAMA Psychiatry* 71, no. 2 (2014): 176–81.

Blair, R. J. R. "The Amygdala and Ventromedial Prefrontal Cortex: Functional Contributions and Dysfunction in Psychopathy." *Philosophical Transactions of the Royal Society B: Biological Sciences* 363, no. 1503 (2008): 2557–65.

Blandford, Alex M., and Fred C. Osher. "A Checklist for Implementing Evidence-Based Practices and Programs for Justice-Involved Adults with Behavioral Health Disorders." Substance Abuse and Mental Health Services Administration GAINS Center (2012).

Blume, J., S. Johnson, and S. Millor. "Convicting Lennie: Mental Retardation, Wrongful Convictions, and the Right to a Fair Trial." Cornell Law Faculty Publications, Paper 603, 2012.

Blumstein, Alfred, ed. *Criminal Careers and "Career Criminals."* Vol. 2. Washington, DC: National Academies Press, 1986.

Boodman, Sandra G. "Few Doctors Know How to Treat Addiction. A New Program Aims to Change That." *Washington Post.* September 3, 2012. https://www.washingtonpost.com/national/health-science/few-doctors-know-how-to-treat-addiction-a-new-program-aims-to-change-that/2012/08/31/d43f85bc-db27-11e1-bd1f-8f2b57de6d94_story.html.

Boutwell, Brian B., Erik J. Nelson, Brett Emo, Michael G. Vaughn, Mario Schootman, Richard Rosenfeld, and Roger Lewis. "The Intersection of Aggregate-Level Lead Exposure and Crime." *Environmental Research* 148 (2016): 79–85.

Brady, Kathleen T., Kevin M. Gray, and Bryan K. Tolliver. "Cognitive Enhancers in the Treatment of Substance Use Disorders: Clinical Evidence." *Pharmacology Biochemistry and Behavior* 99, no. 2 (2011): 285–94.

Bronson, Jennifer, Laura Maruschak, and Marcus Berzofsky. "Disabilities Among Prison and Jail Inmates, 2011–12." Washington, DC: Bureau of Justice Statistics, U.S. Department of Justice, 2015.

Brooks, Megan. "New Insight into the Psychopathic Brain." Medscape, February 5, 2015. www.medscape.com/viewarticle/839307.

Brooks-Gunn, Jeanne, and Greg J. Duncan. "The Effects of Poverty on Children." *The Future of Children* (1997): 55–71.

Brower, Montgomery C., and B. H. Price. "Neuropsychiatry of Frontal Lobe Dysfunction in Violent and Criminal Behaviour: A Critical Review." *Journal of Neurology, Neurosurgery & Psychiatry* 71, no. 6 (2001): 720–26.

Brown, Darryl. "Criminal Law Reform and the Persistence of Strict Liability." *Duke Law Journal* 62 (2012): 285–338.

Brown, Julie F., Milton Z. Brown, and Paige Dibiasio. "Treating Individuals with Intellectual Disabilities and Challenging Behaviors with Adapted Dialectical Behavior Therapy." *Journal of Mental Health Research in Intellectual Disabilities* 6, no. 4 (2013): 280–303.

Brown v. Plata, 563 U.S. (2011).

Burns, Kelly, and Antoine Bechara. "Decision Making and Free Will: A Neuroscience Perspective." *Behavioral Sciences & the Law* 25, no. 2 (2007): 263–80.

Byron, Robert. "Criminals Need Mental Health Care." *Scientific American* (2014). Retrieved from https://www.scientificamerican.com/article/criminals-need-mental-health-care/.

Campanella, S. "Neurocognitive Rehabilitation for Addiction Medicine: From Neurophysiological Markers to Cognitive Rehabilitation and Relapse Prevention." *Progress in Brain Research* 224 (2016): 85–103.

Casey, B. Jones, Rebecca M. Jones, and Todd A. Hare. "The Adolescent Brain." *Annals of the New York Academy of Sciences* 1124, no. 1 (2008): 111–26.

Casey, B. J. "The Teenage Brain: An Overview." *Current Directions in Psychological Science* 22, no. 2 (2013): 80–81.

Casey, B. J., and Kristina Caudle. "The Teenage Brain Self Control." *Current Directions in Psychological Science* 22, no. 2 (2013): 82–87.

"Causes & Effects of Intellectual Developmental Disorder." *Millcreek.* http://www.millcreekofmagee.com/disorders/intellectual-disability/signs-causes-symptoms.

Center for Behavioral Health Statistics and Quality. *Behavioral Health Trends in the United States: Results from the 2014 National Survey on Drug Use and Health* (HHS Publication No. SMA 15-4927, NSDUH Series H-50). (2015). Retrieved from www.samhsa.gov/data/.

Centers for Disease Control and Prevention. "Child Abuse and Neglect: Consequences." http://www.cdc.gov/violenceprevention/childmaltreatment/consequences.html. Accessed April 23, 2016.

Centers for Disease Control and Prevention. "Traumatic Brain Injury in Prisons and Jails: An Unrecognized Problem." 2007.

Chandler, Redonna, Bennett Fletcher, and Nora Volkow. "Treating Drug Abuse and Addiction in the Criminal Justice System: Improving Public Health and Safety." *Journal of the American Medical Association* 301, no. 2 (2010): 183–90.

Child Welfare. "Issue Brief Understanding the Effects of Maltreatment on Brain Development." Washington, DC: U.S. Department of Health and Human Services, 2009.

Chugani, H., M. Behen, O. Muzik, C. Juhasz, F. Nagy, and D. Chugani. "Local Brain Functional Activity Following Early Deprivation: A Study of Postinstitutionalized Romanian Orphans." *Neuroimaging* 14, no. 6 (2001): 1290–1301.

Cicerone, Keith, Harvey Levin, James Malec, Donald Stuss, and John Whyte. "Cognitive Rehabilitation Interventions for Executive Function: Moving from Bench to Bedside in Patients with Traumatic Brain Injury." *Journal of Cognitive Neuroscience* 18, no. 7 (2006): 1212–22.

Cicerone, Keith D., Donna M. Langenbahn, Cynthia Braden, James F. Malec, Kathleen Kalmar, Michael Fraas, Thomas Felicetti, et al. "Evidence-Based Cognitive Rehabilitation: Updated Review of the Literature from 2003 through 2008." *Archives of Physical Medicine and Rehabilitation* 92, no. 4 (2011): 519–30.

Clark v. Arizona, 548 U.S. 735. No. 05-5966. Argued April 19, 2006. Decided June 29, 2006.

Cloud, David, and Chelsea Davis. "Treatment Alternatives to Incarceration for People with Mental Health Needs in the Criminal Justice System: The Cost-Savings Implications." *Research Summary*, Vera Institute of Justice (2013).

Cloyes, K., B. Wong, S. Latimer, and J. Abarca. "Time to Prison Return for Offenders with Serious Mental Illness Released from Prison: A Survival Analysis." *Criminal Justice and Behavior* 37, no. 2 (2010): 175–87.

Cochrane Reviews. "Collaborative Care for People with Depression and Anxiety." 2012. Retrieved from http://www.cochrane.org/CD006525/DEPRESSN_collaborative-care-for-people-with-depression-and-anxiety.

Cohen, Mark A., and Alex R. Piquero. "New Evidence on the Monetary Value of Saving a High Risk Youth." *Journal of Quantitative Criminology* 25, no. 1 (2009): 25–49.

Coker, Kendell L., Philip H. Smith, Alexander Westphal, Howard V. Zonana, and Sherry A. McKee. "Crime and Psychiatric Disorders Among Youth in the US Population: An Analysis of the National Comorbidity Survey–Adolescent Supplement." *Journal of the American Academy of Child & Adolescent Psychiatry* 53, no. 8 (2014): 888–98.

Compton, David M. "The Consequences of Neglect in Children: Neurocognitive Comparisons Among Conduct Disordered and Non-Conduct Disordered Youth Residing in Foster-Care with that of Children from Intact Families." *Psychology and Behavioral Sciences* 2, no. 3 (2013): 96–105.

Consensus Conference. *Rehabilitation of Persons with Traumatic Brain Injury.* NIH Consensus Development Panel on Rehabilitation of Persons with Traumatic Brain Injury. 1999.

Cooper, Janice L., Peter S. Jensen. NCCP. "No Easy Fixes: Disparities in How America Addresses Children's Mental Health Abound." http://www.nccp.org/media/releases/release_99.html. Access July 2, 2016.

Cornet, Liza JM, Catharina H. de Kogel, Henk LI Nijman, Adrian Raine, and Peter H. van der Laan. "Neurobiological Factors as Predictors of Cognitive–Behavioral Therapy Outcome in Individuals with Antisocial Behavior A Review of the Literature." *International Journal of Offender Therapy and Comparative Criminology* 58, no. 11 (2014): 1279–96.

Craddock, Nick, and Laurence Mynors-Wallis. "Psychiatric Diagnosis: Impersonal, Imperfect and Important." *British Journal of Psychiatry* 204, no. 2 (2014): 93–95.

Crary, David. "Across Much of US, a Serious Shortage of Psychiatrists." *Chicago Tribune*, September 7, 2015.

Criminal Justice. "Intelligence and Crime: V. IQ Differences Between Criminal and Noncriminal Groups." http://criminal-justice.iresearchnet.com/crime/intelligence-and-crime/3/. Accessed July 19, 2016.

Cuellar, Alison Evans, Sara Markowitz, and Anne M. Libby. "Mental Health and Substance Abuse Treatment and Juvenile Crime." *Journal of Mental Health Policy and Economics* (2004): 59–68.

Cullen, Francis. "Taking Rehabilitation Seriously." *Punishment and Society* 14, no. 1 (2012): 94–114.

Cunha, Paulo Jannuzzi, Sergio Nicastri, Arthur Guerra de Andrade, and Karen I. Bolla. "The Frontal Assessment Battery (FAB) Reveals Neurocognitive Dysfunction in Substance-Dependent Individuals in Distinct Executive Domains: Abstract Reasoning, Motor Programming, and Cognitive Flexibility." *Addictive Behaviors* 35, no. 10 (2010): 875–81.

Dahl, R. "Adolescent Brain Development: A Period of Vulnerabilities and Opportunities." *Annals New York Academy of Science* (2004).

Danese, A., and B. McEwen. "Adverse Childhood Experiences, Allostasis, Allostatic Load and Age-Related Disease." *Physiology and Behavior* 106, no. 1 (2012): 29–39.

De Bellis, MD. "The Psychobiology of Neglect." *Child Maltreatment* 10, no. 2 (2005): 150–72.

DePrince, Anne, Kristen Weinzierl, and Melody Combs. "Executive Function Performance and Trauma Exposure in a Community Sample of Children." *Child Abuse and Neglect* 33 (2009): 353–61.

Didden, Robert, Jeff Sigafoos, Russell Lang, Mark O'Reilly, Klaus Drieschner, and Giulio E. Lancioni. "Intellectual Disabilities." *Handbook of Evidence-Based Practice in Clinical Psychology* (2012).

Dolan, Sara L., Antoine Bechara, and Peter E. Nathan. "Executive Dysfunction as a Risk Marker for Substance Abuse: The Role of Impulsive Personality Traits." *Behavioral Sciences & the Law* 26, no. 6 (2008): 799–822.

Donley, S., L. Habib, T. Jonanovic, A. Kamkwalala, M. Evces, G. Egan, B. Bradley, and K. Ressler. "Civilian PTSD Symptoms and Risk for Involvement in the Criminal Justice System." *Journal of the American Academy of Psychiatry and the Law* 40, no. 4 (2012): 522–29.

Dowden, Craig, and S. L. Brown. "The Role of Substance Abuse Factors in Predicting Recidivism: A Meta-Analysis." *Psychology, Crime and Law* 8, no. 3 (2002): 243–64.

Drake, Robert E., Susan M. Essock, Andrew Shaner, Kate B. Carey, Kenneth Minkoff, Lenore Kola, David Lynde, Fred C. Osher, Robin E. Clark, and Lawrence Rickards. "Implementing Dual Diagnosis Services for Clients with Severe Mental Illness." *Psychiatric Services* (2001).

Dreyfuss, Michael, Kristina Caudle, Andrew T. Drysdale, Natalie E. Johnston, Alexandra O. Cohen, Leah H. Somerville, Adriana Galván, Nim Tottenham, Todd A. Hare, and B. J. Casey. "Teens Impulsively React Rather than Retreat from Threat." *Developmental Neuroscience* 36, no. 3–4 (2014): 220–27.

"Drug Use in America vs. Europe." *RecoveryBrands.com.* Accessed May 4, 2016.

Druss, B. G., and E. R. Walker. "Mental Disorders and Medical Comorbidity." *The Synthesis Project.* Research Synthesis Report 21 (2011): 1.

Duncan, J. R. "Current Perspectives on the Neurobiology of Drug Addiction: A Focus on Genetics and Factors Regulating Gene Expression." *ISRN Neurology* (2012).

Dykstra, Anne Schieber. "Ohio Leads the Way on Criminal Intent Reform: The Importance of a 'Guilty Mind' when Committing a Crime." December 24, 2014. http://www.michigancapitolconfidential.com/20850.

Effective Health Care Program. Comparative Effectiveness Review Number 121. "Interventions for Adult Offenders With Serious Mental Illness: Executive Summary." Agency for Healthcare Research Quality.

Einfield, S. L. Ellis, and E. Emerson. "Comorbidity of Intellectual Disability and Mental Disorder in Children and Adolescents: A Systematic Review." *Journal of Intellectual Development and Disability* 36, no. 2 (2011): 137–43.

Elbogen, E., and S. Johnson. "The Intricate Link Between Violence and Mental Disorder: Results from the National Epidemiologic Survey on Alcohol and Related Conditions." *Archives of General Psychiatry* 66, no. 2 (2009): 152–61.

Ellis, L., and A. Walsh. "Crime, Delinquency and Intelligence: A Review of the Worldwide Literature." In H. Nyborg (ed.), *The Scientific Study of General Intelligence: Tribute to Arthur R. Jensen*, 343–66. New York: Pergamon Press, 2003.

Elonis v. United States. 575 U.S. Argued 2014. Decided 2015.

"Enrolled House Bill No. 4713." State of Michigan 98th Leslature Regular Session of 2015. Introduced by Rep. McBroom.

Epperson, Matthew W., Nancy Wolff, Robert D. Morgan, William H. Fisher, B. Christopher Frueh, and Jessica Huening. "Envisioning the Next Generation of Behavioral Health and Criminal Justice Interventions." *International Journal of Law and Psychiatry* 37, no. 5 (2014): 427–38.

Epps, Garrett. "Too Vague to be Constitutional: Two Indecipherable Criminal Laws Passed in the 1980s Now Face Scrutiny at the Supreme Court." *Atlantic*. April 17, 2015. http://www.theatlantic.com/politics/archive/2015/04/too-vague-to-be-constitutional/390762/. Accessed April 20, 2015.

Ernest Paul McCarver v. State of North Carolina, Respondent. 2001. No. 00-8727.

Evan Miller v. State of Alabama. (Nos. 10-9646, 10-9647). "Brief for the American Medical Association and the American Academy of Child and Adolescent Psychiatry as Amici Curiae in Support of Neither Party." January 13, 2012.

Everington, C., and D. Keyes. "Diagnosing Mental Retardation in Criminal Proceedings: The Critical Importance of Documenting Adaptive Behavior." *Forensic Examiner* (July/August 1999): 31.

"Evidence-Based Practices." *DualDiagnosis.org*. 2016. http://www.dualdiagnosis.org/treatment-therapies-for-dual-diagnosis-patients/evidence-based-treatment-practices/.

"Evidence-Based Practice." *Social Work Policy Institute*. June 16, 2010. http://www.socialworkpolicy.org/research/evidence-based-practice-2.html.

Executive Office of the President of the United States. "Economic Perspectives on Incarceration and the Criminal Justice System." Washington, DC: White House, 2016.

Farah, Martha J., David M. Shera, Jessica H. Savage, Laura Betancourt, Joan M. Giannetta, Nancy L. Brodsky, Elsa K. Malmud, and Hallam Hurt. "Childhood Poverty: Specific Associations with Neurocognitive Development." *Brain Research* 1110, no. 1 (2006): 166–74.

Fazel, S., P. Lichtenstein, M. Grann, G. Goodwin, and N. Langstrom. "Bipolar Disorder and Violent Crime: New Evidence from Population-Based Longitudinal Studies and Systematic Review." *Archives of General Psychiatry* 67, no. 9 (2010): 931–38.

Fazel, S., N. Langstrom, and A. Hjern. "Schizophrenia, Substance Abuse and Violent Crime." *JAMA* 301, no. 19 (2009): 2016–23.

Federal Bureau of Investigation. "Uniform Crime Reports, 2008." Washington, DC: Federal Bureau of Investigation.

Fields, Gary, and Jennifer Corbett Dooren. "For the Mentally Ill, Finding Treatment Grows Harder: New Health-Care Law May Add to Crunch for Enough Treatment." 2014. http://www.wsj.com/articles/SB10001424052702304281004579218204163263142. Accessed July 21, 2016.

Fisher, Nicole. "4 Things to Understand About Youth, Mental Health & Juvenile Justice in the US." *Forbes*. January 2, 2015. http://www.forbes.com/sites/nicolefisher/2015/01/02/4-things-to-understand-about-youth-mental-health-juvenile-justice-in-the-us/#66fc053f551a.

Fontanarosa, Joann, Stacey Uhl, Olu Oyesanmi, and Karen M. Schoelles. "Interventions for Adult Offenders With Serious Mental Illness." Rockville, MD: Agency for Healthcare Research and Quality, 2013.

Ford, Julian D., John F. Chapman, Josephine Hawke, and David Albert. "Trauma Among Youth in the Juvenile Justice System: Critical Issues and New Directions." National Center for Mental Health and Juvenile Justice (2007): 1–8.

Fortney, John, Rebecca Sladek, Jurgen Unutzer, Patrick Kennedy, Henry Harbin, Bill, Emmet, Lauren Alfred, and Garry Carneal (The Kennedy Forum). "The Issue Brief: Fixing Behavioral Health Care in America: A National Call for Measurement-Based Care in the Delivery of Behavioral Health Services." 2015.

Fox, Maggie. "Being Poor Affects Kids' Brains, Study Finds." *NBC News*. March 30, 2015. http://www.nbcnews.com/health/kids-health/being-poor-affects-kids-brains-study-finds-n332661.

Fox, Michael, Patrick Kanary, Richard Shepler, Center for Innovation Practices at the Brain Center for Violence Prevention Research and Education, Joseph, Jack, and Morton Mandel School of Applied Social Sciences, and Case Western Reserve University. "Prevalence of Youth Drug Use, Mental Health and Co-Occurring Disorder." Technical Assistance Network for Children's Behavioral Health.

Friedman, Matthew A. "Post-Traumatic Stress Disorder." *Back to Psychopharmacology—The Fourth Generation of Progress* (2000). http://www.acnp.org/g4/GN401000111/CH109.html.

Frost, N., and C. Monteiro. "Administrative Segregation in U.S. Prisons." Washington, DC: National Institute of Justice, United States Department of Justice, 2016.

Frost, R., T. Farrer, M. Primosch, and D, Hedges. "Prevalence of Traumatic Brain Injury in the General Adult Population: A Meta-Analysis." *Neuroepidemiology* 40, no. 3 (2013).

Furman, Jason, and Douglas Holtz-Eakin. "Why Mass Incarceration Doesn't Pay." *New York Times*. April 21, 2016. http://www.nytimes.com/2016/04/21/opinion/why-mass-incarceration-doesnt-pay.html?_r=0.

Galvan, Adriana. "The Teenage Brain Sensitivity to Rewards." *Current Directions in Psychological Science* 22, no. 2 (2013): 88–93.

Gao, Yu, Andrea L. Glenn, Robert A. Schug, Yaling Yang, and Adrian Raine. "The Neurobiology of Psychopathy: A Neurodevelopmental Perspective." *Canadian Journal of Psychiatry* 54, no. 12 (2009): 813–23.

Gardner, Martin R. "Rethinking *Robinson v. California* in the Wake of *Jones v. Los Angeles*: Avoiding the 'Demise of the Criminal Law' by Attending to 'Punishment.'" *Journal of Criminal Law and Criminology* (2008): 429–87.

Ginther, Matthew R., Francis X. Shen, Richard J. Bonnie, Morris B. Hoffman, Owen D. Jones, Rene Marois, and Kenneth W. Simons. "The Language of Mens Rea." *Vanderbilt Law Review* 67, no. 5 (2014): 1327–72.

Glasner-Edwards, Suzette, and Richard Rawson. "Evidence-Based Practices in Addiction Treatment: Review and Recommendations for Public Policy." *Health Policy* 97, no. 2 (2010): 93–104.

Glenn, Andrea L., and Adrian Raine. "Neurocriminology: Implications for the Punishment, Prediction and Prevention of Criminal Behaviour." *Nature Reviews Neuroscience* 15, no. 1 (2014): 54–63.

Gold, Jenny. "Health Insurers Face Little Enforcement of Federal Mental Health Parity Law." NPR interview, June 29, 2015.

Goldstein, Rita Z., and Nora D. Volkow. "Dysfunction of the Prefrontal Cortex in Addiction: Neuroimaging Findings and Clinical Implications." *Nature Reviews Neuroscience* 12, no. 11 (2011): 652–69.

Gonzalez, Raul, Antoine Bechara, and Eileen M. Martin. "Executive Functions Among Individuals with Methamphetamine or Alcohol as Drugs of Choice: Preliminary Observations." *Journal of Clinical and Experimental Neuropsychology* 29, no. 2 (2007): 155–59.

Gould, Thomas J. "Addiction and Cognition." *Addiction Science & Clinical Practice* 5, no. 2 (2010).

Graham v. Florida, 560 U.S. 48 (2010).

Grant, Bridget. "Comorbidity Between DSM-IV Drug Use Disorders and Major Depression: Results of a National Survey of Adults." *Journal of Substance Abuse* 7, no. 4 (1995): 481–97.

Greene, Joshua, and Jonathan Cohen. "For the Law, Neuroscience Changes Nothing and Everything." *Philos Trans R Soc Lond B Biol Sci* 359, no. 1451 (2004): 1775–85.

Grohol, John M. "Why Getting Good Mental Health Treatment is Complicated." 2014. http://psychcentral.com/blog/archives/2014/02/25/why-getting-good-mental-health-treatment-is-complicated/. Accessed July 21 2016.

Hall, D., R. Miraglia, L. Lee, D. Chard-Wierschem, and D. Sawyer. "Predictors of General and Violent Recidivism Among SMI Prisoners Returning to Communities in New York State." *Journal of the American Academy of Psychiatry and the Law* 40, no. 2 (2012): 221–31.

Halligan, Peter W., and Derick T. Wade. *The Effectiveness of Rehabilitation for Cognitive Deficits.* New York: Oxford University Press, 2005.

Hampstead, Benjamin M., M. Meredith Gillis, and Anthony Y. Stringer. "Cognitive Rehabilitation of Memory for Mild Cognitive Impairment: A Methodological Review and Model for Future Research." *Journal of the International Neuropsychological Society* 20, no. 2 (2014): 135–51.

Hanson, Jamie, A. Chandra, B. Wolfe, and S. Pollak. "Association Between Income and the Hippocampus." *PLOS One* 6, no. 5 (2011).

Hanson, Jamie L., Nicole Hair, Dinggang G. Shen, Feng Shi, John H. Gilmore, Barbara L. Wolfe, and Seth D. Pollak. "Family Poverty Affects the Rate of Human Infant Brain Growth." *PloS one* 8, no. 12 (2013): e80954.

Harmon, Katherine. "Brain Injury Rate 7 Times Greater among U.S. Prisoners." *Scientific American.* February 4, 2012. https://www.scientificamerican.com/article/traumatic-brain-injury-prison/.

Harris, James C. "New Terminology for Mental Retardation in DSM-5 and ICD-11." *Curr Opin Psychiatry* 26, no. 3 (2013): 260–62. http://www.medscape.com/viewarticle/782769.

Hartz, S., C. Pato, H. Medeiros, P. Cavazos-Rehg, J. Sobell, J. Knoles, L. Bierut, and Michele Pato. "Comorbidity of Severe Psychotic Disorders with Measures of Substance Use." *JAMA Psychiatry* 71, no. 3 (2015): 248–54.

Harvey, David. *The Condition of Postmodernity: An Enquiry into the Conditions of Cultural Change.* Malden: Blackwell, 1990.

Hatch, Orrin G. "It's Time for Criminal Justice, Mens Rea Reform." Statement on the Senate Floor. September 21, 2015.

Hedden, Sarra L. "Behavioral Health Trends in the United States: Results from the 2014 National Survey on Drug Use and Health." Substance Abuse and Mental Health Services Administration, 2015.

Hernandez, Marc B. "Guilt without Mens Rea: How Florida's Elimination of Mens Rea for Drug Possession Is Constitutional." *Florida Law Review* 66 (2014): 1697. Available at http://scholarship.law.ufl.edu/flr/vol66/iss4/5.

Hester, Robert, and Hugh Garavan. "Executive Dysfunction in Cocaine Addiction: Evidence for Discordant Frontal, Cingulate, and Cerebellar Activity." *Journal of Neuroscience* 24, no. 49 (2004): 11017–22.

Hilt, L. M., J. L. Hanson, and S. D. Pollak. "Emotion Dysregulation." *Encyclopedia of Adolescence* 3 (2011): 160–69.

Holz, Nathalie E., Regina Boecker, Erika Hohm, Katrin Zohsel, Arlette F. Buchmann, Dorothea Blomeyer, Christine Jennen-Steinmetz, et al. "The Long-Term Impact of Early Life Poverty on Orbitofrontal Cortex Volume in Adulthood: Results from a Prospective Study over 25 Years." *Neuropsychopharmacology* 40, no. 4 (2015): 996–1004.

Hook, Cayce J., Gwendolyn M. Lawson, and Martha J. Farah. "Socioeconomic Status and the Development of Executive Function." *Encyclopedia on Early Childhood Development* (2013): 1–7.

Horvath, Tom A., Kaushik Misra, Amy K. Epner, and Galen Morgan Cooper. "The Diagnostic Criteria for Substance use disorders (Addiction)." http://www.amhc.org/1408-addictions/article/48502-the-diagnostic-criteria-for-substance-use-disorders-addiction.

Hosier, David. "Harmful Effects of Poverty on Early Brain Development." *Childhood Trauma Recovery* (2014). http://childhoodtraumarecovery.com/2014/04/16/harmful-effects-of-poverty-on-early-brain-development/.

Huffpost Politics. "The War on Drugs Has Failed, So Let's Shut It Down." June 3, 2013. http://www.huffingtonpost.com/richard-branson/the-war-on-drugs-has-fail_1_b_5439312.html.

Hughes, Nathan. "Neurodisability in the Youth Justice System Recognizing and Responding to the Criminalisation of Neurodevelopmental Impairment." Howard League *What Is Justice? Working Papers* 17 (2015): 1–21.

Human Rights Watch. "Callous and Cruel." 2015. Retrieved from https://www.hrw.org/report/2015/05/12/callous-and-cruel/use-force-against-inmates-mental-disabilities-us-jails-and.

Human Rights Watch. "Ill Equipped: U.S. Prisons and Offenders with Mental Illness." 2003. Retrieved from https://www.hrw.org/reports/2003/usa1003/usa1003.pdf.

Hwang, Kristen. "Rising Access to Substance Abuse Treatment Faces Shortage of Counselors." *Cronkite News*, April 21, 2015. http://cronkitenewsonline.com/2015/04/rising-access-to-substance-abuse-treatment-faces-shortage-of-counselors/.

Hyde, Pamela S. "Report to Congress on the Nation's Substance Abuse and Mental Health Workforce Issues." Substance Abuse and Mental Health Services Administration. 2013.

Hyman, S. "The Neurobiology of Addiction: Implications for Voluntary Control of Behavior." *American Journal of Bioethics* 7, no. 1 (2007): 8–11.

Illinois Models for Change Behavioral Health Assessment Team. "Report on the Behavioral Health Program for Youth Committed to Illinois Department of Juvenile Justice." *Systems Reform in Juvenile Justice*. July 2010.

Insel, Thomas. "Director's Blog: Transforming Diagnosis." *National Institute of Mental Health*. 2013. www.nimh.nih.gov/about/director/2013/transforming-diagnosis.shtml.

"Intellectual Disability." Wikipedia. Last Updated August 29, 2016. https://en.wikipedia.org/wiki/Intellectual_disability#Signs_and_symptoms.

International Society of Psychiatric Mental Health Nurses. "Meeting the Mental Health Needs of Youth in Juvenile Justice." 2008. http://www.ispn-psych.org/docs/JuvenileJustice.pdf.

Irigaray, Tatiana Quarti, Janaína Barbosa Pacheco, Rodrigo Grassi-Oliveira, Rochele Paz Fonseca, José Carlos de Carvalho Leite, and Christian Haag Kristensen. "Child Maltreatment and Later Cognitive Functioning: A Systematic Review." *Psicologia: Reflexão e Crítica* 26, no. 2 (2013): 376–87.

Jaffe, Adi, Jiang Du, David Huang, and Yih-Ing Hser. "Drug-abusing Offenders with Comorbid Mental Disorders: Problem Severity, Treatment Participation, and Recidivism." *Journal of Substance Abuse Treatment* 43, no. 2 (2012): 244–50.

James Parson v. State of Alaska, Department of Revenue, Alaska Housing Finance Corporation, 189 P.3d 1032 (S.C. AK 2008), LexisNexis.

James, Doris J., and Lauren E. Glaze. "Mental Health Problems of Prison and Jail Inmates." Bureau of Justice Statistics. *Special Report*. September 2006 (revised December 14, 2006).

Jarmolowicz, David, E. Terry Mueller, Mikhail N. Koffarnus, Anne E. Carter, Kirstin M. Gatchalian, and Warren K. Bickel. "Executive Dysfunction in Addiction." In J. MacKillop and Harriet de Wit (eds.), *The Wiley-Blackwell Handbook of Addiction Psychopharmacology* (2013).

Jednoróg, Katarzyna, Irene Altarelli, Karla Monzalvo, Joel Fluss, Jessica Dubois, Catherine Billard, Ghislaine Dehaene-Lambertz, and Franck Ramus. "The Influence of Socioeconomic Status on Children's Brain Structure." *PloS one* 7, no. 8 (2012): e42486.

Johnson, Eric A. "Rethinking the Presumption of Mens Rea." *Wake Forest Law Review* 47 (2012): 769.

Johnson, Eric A. "Rethinking the Presumption of Mens Rea." Working Paper 115. *University of Illinois Law and Economics Working Papers*. http://law.bepress.com/uiuclwps/art115.

Jones, Jessica. "Persons with Intellectual Disabilities in the Criminal Justice System: Review of Issues." *International Journal of Offender Therapy and Comparative Criminology* (2007).

Juth, Niklas, and Frank Lorentzon. "The Concept of Free Will and Forensic Psychiatry." *International Journal of Law and Psychiatry* 33, no. 1 (2010): 1–6.

Keller, Bill. "Criminal Justice Reform: An Obituary." The Marshall Project, September 29, 2016. Retrieved from https://www.themarshallproject.org/2016/09/29/criminal-justice-reform-an-obituary#.3KLtO7ZSY.

Kelly, Thomas M., and Dennis C. Daley. "Integrated Treatment of Substance Use and Psychiatric Disorders." *Social Work in Public Health* 28, no. 3–4 (2013): 388–406.

Kelly, William R. *Criminal Justice at the Crossroads: Transforming Crime and Punishment.* New York: Columbia University Press, 2015.

Kelly, William R. *The Future of Crime and Punishment: Smart Policies for Reducing Crime and Saving Money.* Lanham, MD: Rowman & Littlefield, 2016.

Kennedy Forum, The. "Fixing Behavioral Healthcare in America." Retrieved from https://www.thekennedyforum.org/issuebriefs.

Kennert, J., N. Vincent, and A. Snoek. "Drug Addiction and Criminal Responsibility." In N. Levy and J. Clausen (eds.), *Handbook on Neuroethics* (2013). Springer, The Netherlands.

Kessler, Ronald, Rosa Crum, and Lynn Warner. "Lifetime Co-occurrence of DSM-III-R Alcohol Abuse and Dependence with Other Psychiatric Disorders in the National Comorbidity Survey." *Archives of General Psychiatry* 54, no. 4 (1997): 313–21.

Kessler, Ronald, Wai Chiu, Olga Demier, and Ellen Walters. "Prevalence, Severity and Comorbidity of Twelve-Month DSM-IV Disorders in the National Comorbidity Survey Replication (NCS-R)." *Archives of General Psychiatry* 62, no. 6 (2010): 617–27.

Khazan, Olga. "Most Prisoners Are Mentally Ill: Can Mental-Health Courts, in Which People Are Sentenced to Therapy, Help?" *Atlantic.* April 7, 2015. www.theatlantic.com/health/archive/2015/04/more-than-half-of-prisoners-are-mentally-ill/389682/. Accessed July 6, 2016.

Kiehl, Kent A., and Morris B. Hoffman. "The Criminal Psychopath: History, Neuroscience, Treatment, and Economics." *Jurimetrics* 51 (2011): 355.

Kilmer, Beau, Susan S. Everingham, Jonathan P. Caulkins, Gregory Midgette, Rosalie Liccardo Pacula, Peter H. Reuter, Rachel M. Burns, Bing Han, and Russell Lundberg. *How Big Is the U.S. Market for Illegal Drugs?* Santa Monica: RAND Corporation, 2014. http://www.rand.org/pubs/research_briefs/RB9770.html.

Kim, KiDeuk, Miriam Becker-Cohen, and Maria Serakos. "The Processing and Treatment of Mentally Ill Persons in the Criminal Justice System." Research Report, Washington, DC: Urban Institute, 2015.

Kim, Pilyoung, Gary W. Evans, Michael Angstadt, S. Shaun Ho, Chandra S. Sripada, James E. Swain, Israel Liberzon, and K. Luan Phan. "Effects of Childhood Poverty and Chronic Stress on Emotion Regulatory Brain Function in Adulthood." *Proceedings of the National Academy of Sciences* 110, no. 46 (2013): 18442–47.

Kishiyama, M., W. Boyce, A. Jimenez, L. Perry, and R. Knight. "Socioeconomic Disparities Affect Frontal Function in Children" *Journal of Cognitive Neuroscience* 21, no. 6 (2009): 1106–15.

Klaming, Laura, and Bert-Jaap Koops. "Neuroscientific Evidence and Criminal Responsibility in the Netherlands." In *International Neurolaw*, 227–56. Berlin: Springer, 2012.

Koehler, Rebecca, Erin Wilhelm, and Ira Shoulson, eds. *Cognitive Rehabilitation Therapy for Traumatic Brain Injury: Evaluating the Evidence.* Washington, DC: National Academies Press, 2011.

Kozak, Michael J., and Bruce N. Cuthbert. "The NIMH Research Domain Criteria Initiative: Background, Issues, and Pragmatics." *Psychophysiology* 53, no. 3 (2016): 286–97.

Kozinski, Hon. Alex. "Criminal Law 2.0." *Georgetown Law Journal Annual Review of Criminal Procedure* 44 (2015): iii–1097.

Lamparello, Adam. "Neuroscience, Brain Damage, and the Criminal Defendant: Who Does It Help and Where in the Criminal Proceeding Is It Most Relevant?" *Rutgers Law Record* 39 (2012).

Lane, Scott D., Don R. Cherek, Cynthia J. Pietras, and Oleg V. Tcheremissine. "Alcohol Effects on Human Risk Taking." *Psychopharmacology* 172, no. 1 (2004): 68–77.

Larkin, Paul J. Jr., Jordan Richardson, and John-Michael Seibler. "The Supreme Court on Mens Rea: 2008–2015." Heritage Foundation. No. 171. 2016.

Latessa, Edward J., and Christopher Lowenkamp. "What Works in Reducing Recidivism." *U. St. Thomas LJ* 3 (2005): 521.

Lawrence, Alison. "Managing Corrections Costs." National Conference of State Legislatures. February 2014.

Lee, Timothy H. "Justice Reform Legislation: Prosecution Should Require Criminal Intent." Center for Individual Freedom. 2015. http://cfif.org/v/index.php/commentary/54-state-of-affairs/2890-justice-reform-legislation-prosecution-should-require-criminal-intent.

Legal Information Institute. 18 U.S. Code § 3582—Imposition of a Sentence of Imprisonment. https://www.law.cornell.edu/uscode/text/18/3582.

Liebowitz, Sarah, Peter J. Eliasberg, Ira A. Burnim, and Emily B. Read. "A Way Forward: Diverting People with Mental Illness from Inhumane and Expensive Jails into Community-Based Treatment that Works." ACLU and Bazelon Center for Mental Health Law, July 2014.

Loughan, Ashlee, and Robert Perna. "Neurocognitive Impacts for Children of Poverty and Neglect." American Psychological Association, July 2012. https://apa.org/pi/families/resources/newsletter/2012/07/neurocognitive-impacts.aspx.

Luby, Joan, Andy Belden, Kelly Botteron, Natasha Marrus, Michael P. Harms, Casey Babb, Tomoyuki Nishino, and Deanna Barch. "The Effects of Poverty on Childhood Brain Development: The Mediating Effect of Caregiving and Stressful Life Events." *JAMA Pediatrics* 167, no. 12 (2013): 1135–42.

Luna, Beatriz, David J. Paulsen, Aarthi Padmanabhan, and Charles Geier. "The Teenage Brain: Cognitive Control and Motivation." *Current Directions in Psychological Science* 22, no. 2 (2013): 94–100.

Lurigio, A. "People with Serious Mental Illness in the Criminal Justice System." *The Prison Journal* 91, no. 3 (2011): 665–85.

Lurigio, A., Y. Cho, J. Swartz, T. Johnson, I. Graf, and L. Pickup. "Standardized Assessment of Substance-Related, Other Psychiatric, and Comorbid Disorders among Probationers." *International Journal of Offender Therapy and Comparative Criminology* 47, no. 6 (2003): 630–82.

Lynch, Michael. "Consequences of Children's Exposure to Community Violence." *Clinical Child and Family Psychology Review* 6, no. 4 (2003): 265–74.

MacArthur Foundation Research Network on Adolescent Development and Juvenile Justice. *Less Guilty by Reason of Adolescence.* Issue Brief 3. Philadelphia: MacArthur Foundation, 2007.

Madoz-Gúrpide, Agustín, Hilario Blasco-Fontecilla, Enrique Baca-García, and Enriqueta Ochoa-Mangado. "Executive Dysfunction in Chronic Cocaine Users: An Exploratory Study." *Drug and Alcohol Dependence* 117, no. 1 (2011): 55–58.

Maguire, Eleanor A., Katherine Woollett, and Hugo J. Spiers. "London Taxi Drivers and Bus Drivers: A Structural MRI and Neuropsychological Analysis." *Hippocampus* 16, no. 12 (2006): 1091–1101.

Maisel, Albert Q. "Most US Mental Hospitals Are a Shame and a Disgrace." *PBS.org.* http://www.pbs.org/wgbh/americanexperience/features/primary-resources/lobotomist-bedlam-1946/. Accessed July 16, 2016.

Malcolm, John G. "The Pressing Need for Mens Rea Reform." Heritage Foundation. September 1, 2015.

Malcolm, John G. "Point/Counterpoint: Criminal Justice Reform and Mens Rea." The Federalist Society. November 17, 2015. http://www.fed-soc.org/blog/detail/pointcounterpoint-criminal-justice-reform-and-mens-rea-2.

Malia, Kit. "Summary of Evidence Base for Cognitive Rehabilitation as of May 2016." http://www.braintreetraining.co.uk/CRevidence.php. Accessed August 14, 2016.

Mallik-Kane, K., and C. Visher. "Health and Prisoner Reentry: How Physical, Mental and Substance Abuse Conditions Shape the Process of Reintegration." Washington, DC: Urban Institute, 2008.

Manchak, Sarah M., Jennifer L. Skeem, Patrick J. Kennealy, and Jennifer Eno Louden. "High-Fidelity Specialty Mental Health Probation Improves Officer Practices, Treatment Access, and Rule Compliance." *Law and Human Behavior* 38, no. 5 (2014): 450.

Marazziti, Donatella, Stefano Baroni, Paola Landi, Diana Ceresoli, and Liliana Dell'Osso. "The Neurobiology of Moral Sense: Facts or Hypotheses?" *Annals of General Psychiatry* 12, no. 1 (2013): 1.

Marceau, Roger, R. Meghani, and J. Reddon. "Neuropsychological Assessment of Adult Offenders." *Journal of Offender Rehabilitation* 47, no. 1–2 (2010): 41–73.

Marsh, Kevin, Chris Fox, and Carol Hedderman. "Do You Get What You Pay For? Assessing the Use of Prison from an Economic Perspective." *Howard Journal of Criminal Justice* 48, no. 2 (2009): 144–57.

Matthys, Walter, Louk JMJ Vanderschuren, Dennis JLG Schutter, and John E. Lochman. "Impaired Neurocognitive Functions Affect Social Learning Processes in Oppositional Defiant Disorder and Conduct Disorder: Implications for Interventions." *Clinical Child and Family Psychology Review* 15, no. 3 (2012): 234–46.

McCarver v. State of North Carolina, Amicus Brief, Supreme Court of the United States, No. 00-8727, American Psychiatric Association et al.

McCausland, Ruth. "People with Mental Health Disorders and Cognitive Impairment in the Criminal Justice System: Cost-Benefit Analysis of Early Support and Diversion." 2013.

McCrory, Eamon, Stephane A. De Brito, and Essi Viding. "The Impact of Childhood Maltreatment: A Review of Neurobiological and Genetic Factors." *Frontiers in Psychiatry* 2 (2011): 48.

McEwen, Bruce, and John Morrison. "The Brain on Stress: Vulnerability and Plasticity of the Prefrontal Cortex over the Life Course." *Neuron* (2013) Open Archive. http://www.cell.com/neuron/abstract/S0896-6273(13)00544-8.

McLaughlin, Katie. "How Can Trauma Affect the Brain?" *CBT+*. 2014.

McLaughlin, Michael, Carrie Pettus-Davis, Derek Brown, Chris Veeh, and Tanya Renn. "The Economic Burden of Incarceration in the US." July 2016. https://advancingjustice.wustl.edu/SiteCollectionDocuments/The%20Economic%20Burden%20of%20Incarceration%20in%20the%20US.pdf.

McNiel, Dale E., and Renee L. Binder. "Effectiveness of a Mental Health Court in Reducing Criminal Recidivism and Violence." *American Journal of Psychiatry* 164 (2007): 1395–1403.

McTeague, Lisa M. "Reconciling RDoC and DSM Approaches in Clinical Psychophysiology and Neuroscience." *Psychophysiology* 53, no. 3 (2016): 323–27.

McVay, Doug, Vincent Schiraldi, and Jason Ziedenberg. "Treatment or Incarceration?" Justice Policy Institute, 2004.

Mears, Daniel. "Mental Health Needs and Services in the Criminal Justice System." *Houston Journal of Health Law and Policy* 255 (2004).

"Meeting the Mental Health Needs of Youth in Juvenile Justice." *International Society of Psychiatric-Mental Health Nurses.* Approved February 6, 2008.

Meijers, Jesse, Joke Harte, Frank Jonker, and Gerben Meynen. "Prison Brain? Executive Dysfunction in Prisoners." *Frontiers in Psychology* 6 (2015).

Mendez, Mario F. "The Neurobiology of Moral Behavior: Review and Neuropsychiatric Implications." *CNS Spectrums* 14, no. 11 (2009): 608–20.

Mental Health America. "Parity or Disparity: The State of Mental Health in America." 2015. www.mentalhealthamerica.net/sites/default/files/Parity%20or%20Disparity%202015%20Report.pdf.

"Mental Illness Not Usually Linked to Crime, Research Finds." *American Psychological Association.* April 21, 2014. http://www.apa.org/news/press/releases/2014/04/mental-illness-crime.aspx.

Milbank, Dana. "The Problem with Obamacare's Mental-Health 'Parity' Measure." November 27, 2015. https://www.washingtonpost.com/opinions/the-problem-with-obamacares-mental-health-parity-measure/2015/11/27/f2c5fcfc-952b-11e5-a2d6-f57908580b1f_story.html?utm_term=.2ca06b3e7184. Accessed July 25, 2016.

Miller, William R., James L. Sorensen, Jeffrey A. Selzer, and Gregory S. Brigham. "Disseminating Evidence-Based Practices in Substance Abuse Treatment: A Review with Suggestions." *Journal of Substance Abuse Treatment* 31, no. 1 (2006): 25–39.

Miller v. Alabama, 132 S. Ct. 2455, 567 U.S., 183 L. Ed. 2d 407 (2012).

Miotto, Eliane Correa, Valéria Trunkl Serrao, Gláucia Benutte Guerra, M. C. S. Lúcia, and
    Milberto Scaff. "Cognitive Rehabilitation of Neuropsychological Deficits and Mild Cogni-
    tive Impairment." *Dementia and Neuropsychologia* 2, no. 2 (2008): 139–45.

M'Naghten Case, 1 C. & K. 130: 4 St. Tr. N.S. 947 (1843). Retrieved from http://www.
    casebriefs.com/blog/law/criminal-law/criminal-law-keyed-to-kadish/exculpation/mnaghtens
    -case/.

"Model Penal Code—Selected Provisions." http://www1.law.umkc.edu/suni/crimLaw/MPC_
    Provisions/model_penal_code_default_rules.htm.

Moffitt, Terrie, L. Arseneault, D. Belsky, N. Dickson, R. Hancox, H. Harrington, R. Houts, R.
    Poulton, B. Roberts, S. Ross, M. Sears, W. Thomson, and A. Caspi. "A Gradient of Child-
    hood Self-Control Predicts Health, Wealth and Public Safety." *Proceedings of the National
    Academy of Sciences* 108, no. 7 (1010): 2693–98.

Moffitt, Terrie E. "Life-Course-Persistent Versus Adolescence-Limited Antisocial Behavior."
    In *Developmental Psychopathology: Risk, Disorder, and Adaptation*, vol. 3, 2nd, edited by
    Dante Cicchetti and Donald Cohen, 570–98. Hoboken, NJ: John Wiley & Sons, 2006.

Moffitt, Terrie, A. Caspi, H. Harrington, and B. Milne. "Males on the Life-Course Persistent
    and Adolescent Limited Antisocial Pathways: Follow-up at Age 26 Years." *Developmental
    Psychopathology* 14, no. 1(2002): 179–207.

Monahan, Kathryn, Laurence Steinberg, and Alex R. Piquero. "Juvenile Justice Policy and
    Practice: A Developmental Perspective." *Crime & Justice* 44 (2015): 557.

Montgomery v. Louisiana, 577 U.S. (2016).

Morgan, R., D. Flora, D. Kroner, J. Mills, F. Varghese, and J. Steffan. "Treating Offenders with
    Mental Illness: A Research Synthesis." *Law and Human Behavior* 36, no. 1 (2013): 37–50.

Morissette v. United States, 342, U.S. 246 (72 S. Ct. 240, 96 L.Ed. 288).

Morrissey, Joseph P. "Forensic Assertive Community Treatment: Updating the
    Evidence." SAMHSA GAINS Center (2013).

Mumola, C., and J. C. Karberg. "Drug Use and Dependence, State and Federal Prisoners,
    2004." Washington, DC: U.S. Department of Justice, Office of Justice Programs, Bureau of
    Justice Statistics, 2007, available at www.bjs.gov/content/pub/pdf/dudsfp04.pdf.

Mumola, Christopher J., and Thomas P. Bonczar. "Substance Abuse and Treatment of Adults
    on Probation, 1995." Washington, DC: U.S. Department of Justice, Office of Justice Pro-
    grams, Bureau of Justice Statistics, 1998.

Murphey, David, Brigitte Vaughn, and Megan Berry. "Access to Mental Health Care." *Child
    Trends* (2013). http://www.childtrends.org/wp-content/uploads/2013/04/Child_Trends-
    2013_01_01_AHH_MHAccessl.pdf.

NADCP. "The Facts on Drugs and Crime in America." http://www.nadcp.org/sites/default/
    files/nadcp/Facts%20on%20Drug%20Courts%20.pdf.

NADD. "Information on Dual Diagnosis." http://thenadd.org/resources/information-on-dual-
    diagnosis-2/. Accessed September 25, 2016.

NAMI. "A Long Road Ahead: Achieving True Parity in Mental Health and Substance Use
    Care." 2015.

NAMI. "Jailing People with Mental Illness." 2015. http://www.nami.org/Learn-More/Public-
    Policy/Jailing-People-with-Mental-Illness.

NAMI. "State Mental Health Cuts: A National Crisis." 2011. Retrieved from https://www.
    nami.org/getattachment/About-NAMI/Publications/Reports/NAMIStateBudgetCrisis2011.
    pdf.

NAMI. "State Mental Health Legislation 2015: Trends, Themes and Effective Practices." 2015.

NAMI. "Numbers of Americans Affected by Mental Illness." *Mental Illness: Facts and Num-
    bers.* Reviewed by Ken Duckworth, MD, March 2013.

National Center on Addiction and Substance Abuse at Columbia University (CASA). "Addic-
    tion Medicine: Closing the Gap between Science and Practice." June 2012.

National Center on Addiction and Substance Abuse at Columbia University (CASA), and
    United States of America. "Criminal Neglect: Substance Abuse, Juvenile Justice and the
    Children Left Behind." 2004.

National Center for Children in Poverty. "No Easy Fixes: Disparities in How America Address-
    es Children's Mental Health Abound." New York, Columbia University.

National Commissions on Reform of the Federal Criminal Law, S. REP. NO. 605, Part 1, 95th Cong., 1st Sess. 55 (1977).

National Council for Behavioral Health. "The Business Case for Effective Mental Health Treatment." https://www.thenationalcouncil.org/wp-content/uploads/2015/01/14_Business-Case_Mental-Health.pdf.

National Institute of Mental Health. "Inmate Mental Health." http://www.nimh.nih.gov/health/statistics/prevalence/inmate-mental-health.shtml.

National Institute on Drug Abuse. "Principles of Drug Addiction Treatment: A Research-Based Guide" (3rd ed.). Last updated December 2012. http://www.drugabuse.gov/publications/principles-drug-addiction-treatment-research-based-guide-third-edition/acknowledgments.

National Institutes of Health. "Consensus Development Conference Statement on Rehabilitation of Persons with TBI." *JAMA* 282, no. 10 (1999): 974–83.

National Quality Forum. "Evidence-Based Treatment Practices for Substance Use Disorders." Washington, DC, 2005.

National Research Council (US). Committee on the Science of Adolescence. *The Science of Adolescent Risk-taking: Workshop Report*. Washington, DC: National Academies Press, 2011.

National Scientific Council on the Developing Child. "Excessive Stress Disrupts the Architecture of the Developing Brain: Working Paper No. 3" (2005). Updated 2014. Retrieved from http://www.developingchild.harvard.edu/.

NCADD New Jersey. "Access to Treatment." www.ncaddnj.org/page/access-to-treatment.aspx. Accessed August 15, 2016.

NCADD New Jersey. "The Addiction Treatment Gap: The Benefits of Expanding Treatment Resources." http://www.ncaddnj.org/file.axd?file=2010%2F3%2FTreatmentGapWeb.pdf.

Nevins-Saunders, Elizabeth. "Not Guilty as Charged: The Myth of Mens Rea for Defendants with Mental Retardation." *University of California at Davis Law Review* 45 (2012): 1419–86.

New Freedom Commission on Mental Health. "Subcommittee on Criminal Justice: Background Paper." White House, 2004.

Noble, Kimberly G., Suzanne M. Houston, Natalie H. Brito, Hauke Bartsch, Eric Kan, Joshua M. Kuperman, Natacha Akshoomoff, et al. "Family Income, Parental Education and Brain Structure in Children and Adolescents." *Nature Neuroscience* 18, no. 5 (2015): 773–78.

Noble, Kimberly G., Suzanne M. Houston, Eric Kan, and Elizabeth R. Sowell. "Neural Correlates of Socioeconomic Status in the Developing Human Brain." *Developmental Science* 15, no. 4 (2012): 516–27.

Noble, Kimberly, M. Norman, and M. Farah. "Neurocognitive Correlates of Socioeconomic Status in Kindergarten Children." *Developmental Sciences* 8, no. 1 (2005): 74–87.

Noël, Xavier, Antoine Bechara, Damien Brevers, Paul Verbanck, and Salvatore Campanella. "Alcoholism and the Loss of Willpower." *Journal of Psychophysiology* 24, no. 4 (2010).

Noël, Xavier, Damien Brevers, and Antoine Bechara. "A Triadic Neurocognitive Approach to Addiction for Clinical Interventions." *Frontiers in Psychiatry* 4 (2013): 179.

Nyberg, Fred. "Cognitive Impairments in Drug Addicts." *INTECH Open Access Publisher* (2012).

O'Dell, Matt, Dylan Casey, Mindy McGrath, Kevin Flintosh. "Fixing Mental Healthcare in the U.S." 2015. http://www.beckershospitalreview.com/hospital-management-administration/fixing-mental-healthcare-in-the-u-s.html.

Odgers, Candice L., Mandi L. Burnette, Preeti Chauhan, Marlene M. Moretti, and N. Dickon Reppucci. "Misdiagnosing the Problem: Mental Health Profiles of Incarcerated Juveniles." *Canadian Child and Adolescent Psychiatry Review* 14, no. 1 (2005): 26–29.

Office of the Surgeon General. "Youth Violence: A Report of the Surgeon General." Rockville, MD: Office of the Surgeon General, 2001.

Ogilvie, James, Anna Stewart, Raymond Chan, and David Shum. "Neuropsychological Measures of Executive Function and Antisocial Behavior: A Meta-Anaysis." http://www98.griffith.edu.au/dspace/bitstream/handle/10072/42010/74700_1.pdf?sequence=1.

Ollove, Michael. "Enforcement of Mental Health Care Coverage Lacking." *Stateline.* June 3, 2016. http://www.pewtrusts.org/en/research-and-analysis/blogs/stateline/2016/06/03/enforcement-of-mental-health-care-coverage-lacking.

Ornstein, Norm. "How to Fix a Broken Mental-Health System." *Atlantic.* June 8, 2016. www.theatlantic.com/politics/archive/2016/06/getting-mental-health-on-the-docket/485996/.

Osher, Fred C. "Integrating Mental Health/Substance Abuse Services for Justice-Involved Persons with Co-Occurring Disorders." Baltimore: National GAINS Center, 2006.

Ostermann, Michael, and Jason Matejkowski. "Exploring the Intersection of Mental Health and Release Status with Recidivism." *Justice Quarterly* 31, no. 4 (2014): 746–66.

Ostrow, Nicole. "Poverty, Neglect in Childhood Affect Brain Size." Bloomberg, October 28, 2013. http://www.bloomberg.com/news/articles/2013-10-28/poverty-neglect-in-childhood-affect-brain-size.

"Overcriminalization: An Explosion of Federal Criminal Law." Factsheet #86 on Overcriminalization. April 27, 2011. http://www.heritage.org/research/factsheets/2011/04/overcriminalization-an-explosion-of-federal-criminal-law.

Pan, Deanna. "MAP: Which States Have Cut Treatment for the Mentally Ill the Most?" *Mother Jones.* April 29, 2013. www.motherjones.com/mojo/2013/04/map-states-cut-treatment-for-mentally-ill.

Pascual-Leone, Alvaro, Amir Amedi, Felipe Fregni, and Lotfi B. Merabet. "The Plastic Human Brain Cortex." *Annual Review of Neuroscience* 28 (2005): 377–401.

Passetti, F., L. Clark, M. A. Mehta, E. Joyce, and M. King. "Neuropsychological Predictors of Clinical Outcome in Opiate Addiction." *Drug and Alcohol Dependence* 94, no. 1 (2008): 82–91.

Patel, Amit. "Mens Rea as an Element of Crime: Why the Supreme Court Got It Wrong in *Clark v. Arizona.*" *Quinnipiac Health Law Journal* 17 (2007–2008).

Patel, V., G. Belkin, A. Chockalingam, J. Cooper, S. Saxena, and J. Unutzer. "Grand Challenges: Integrating Mental Health Services into Priority Health Care Platforms." *PLOS Medicine.* Retrieved from http://journals.plos.org/plosmedicine/article?id=10.1371/journal.pmed.1001448.

Pau, Charles WH, Tatia MC Lee, and F. Chan Shui-Fun. "The Impact of Heroin on Frontal Executive Functions." *Archives of Clinical Neuropsychology* 17, no. 7 (2002): 663–70.

Pedrero-Perez, Eduardo J., Gloria Rojo-Mota, de Leon JM Ruiz-Sanchez, Marcos Llanero-Luque, and Carmen Puerta-Garcia. "Cognitive Remediation in Addictions Treatment." *Revista de neurologia* 52, no. 3 (2011): 163–72.

People v. Stark (1994) No. C013808. Third Dist. July 18, 1994. http://law.justia.com/cases/california/court-of-appeal/4th/26/1179.html.

Peters, R., H. Wexler, and A. Lurigio. "Co-Occurring Substance Abuse and Mental Disorders in the Criminal Justice System: A New Frontier of Clinical Practice and Research." *Psychiatric Rehabilitation Journal* 38, no. 1 (2015): 1–6.

Peterson, J., J. Skeem, P. Kennealy, B. Bray, and A. Zvonkovic. "How Often and How Consistently Do Symptoms Directly Precede Criminal Behavior Among Offenders With Mental Illness?" *Law and Human Behavior* 38, no. 5 (2014): 439–49.

Phillips, Susan D., Barbara J. Burns, Elizabeth R. Edgar, Kim T. Mueser, Karen W. Linkins, Robert A. Rosenheck, Robert E. Drake, and Elizabeth C. McDonel Herr. "Moving Assertive Community Treatment into Standard Practice." *Psychiatric Services* 52, no. 6 (2001): 771–79.

Piquero, Alex R., J. David Hawkins, Lila Kazemian, and David Petechuk. "Bulletin 2: Criminal Career Patterns (Study Group on the Transitions Between Juvenile Delinquency and Adult Crime)." 2013.

Polydorou, Soteri, Erik W. Gunderson, and Frances R. Levin. "Training Physicians to Treat Substance Use Disorders." *Current Psychiatry Reports* 10, no. 5 (2008): 399–404.

"Poverty Linked to Smaller Brains, Study Finds." *NBC News.* New York, October 28, 2013. http://www.nbcnews.com/health/poverty-linked-smaller-brains-study-finds-8C11484610.

Powell v. Texas (No. 405) 392 U.S. 514. 1968.

Prasher, V., and S. K. Routhu. "Epidemiology of Learning Disability and Comorbid Conditions." *Psychiatry* 2, no. 8 (2003).

President's New Freedom Commission on Mental Health. "Achieving the Promise: Transforming Mental Health Care in America." Washington, DC: White House, 2003.

"Prevalence." *Youth.gov.* http://youth.gov/youth-topics/youth-mental-health/prevalance-mental-health-disorders-among-youth. Accessed June 20, 2016.

Prins, S. "Prevalence of Mental Illness in U.S. State Prisons: A Systematic Review." *Psychiatric Services* 65, no. 7 (2014): 862–72.

Public Safety Performance Project. "Time Served: The High Cost, Low Return of Longer Prison Terms." PEW Center on the States. 2012.

Radochoński, Mieczysław, Adam Perenc, and Anna Radochońska. "Orbitofrontal Cortex Dysfunction and Risk for Antisocial Behavior: An Analytical Review." *Przegląd Medyczny Uniwersytetu Rzeszowskiego i Narodowego Instytutu Leków Warszawie* 1 (2015): 47–54.

Raine, Adrian. "The Biological Crime: Implications for Society and the Criminal Justice System." *Revista de Psiquiatria do Rio Grande do Sul* 30, no. 1 (2008): 5–8.

Raine, Adrian, and Yaling Yang. "Neural Foundations to Moral Reasoning and Antisocial Behavior." *Social Cognitive and Affective Neuroscience* 1, no. 3 (2006): 203–13.

Raine, Adrian, T. Moffit, A. Caspi, M. Stouthamer-Loeber, and D. Lynam. "Neurocognitive Impairments in Boys on the Life-Course Persistent Antisocial Path." *Journal of Abnormal Psychology* 114, no. 1 (2005): 38–49.

Reavis, J., J. Looman, K. Franco, and B. Rojas. "Adverse Childhood Experiences and Adult Criminality: How Long Must We Live Before We Possess Our Own Lives?" *The Permanente Journal* 17, no. 2 (2013): 44–48.

Redding, Richard E. "The Brain-Disordered Defendant: Neuroscience and Legal Insanity in the Twenty-First Century." *American University Law Review* 56 (2006): 51.

Regier, Darrel A., William E. Narrow, Diana E. Clarke, Helena C. Kraemer, S. Janet Kuramoto, Emily A. Kuhl, and David J. Kupfer. "DSM-5 Field Trials in the United States and Canada, Part II: Test-Retest Reliability of Selected Categorical Diagnoses." *American Journal of Psychiatry* (2013).

Rezapour, T., E. DeVito, M. Sofuoglu, and H. Ekhtiari. "Perspectives on Neurocognitive Rehabilitation as an Adjunct Treatment for Addictive Disorders: From Cognitive Improvement to Relapse Prevention." *Progress in Brain Research* (2016).

Rezapour, T., J. Hatami, A. Farhoudian, M. Sofuoglu, A. Noroozi, R. Daneshmand, A. Samiei, and H. Ekhtiari. "Neuro Cognitive Rehabilitation for Disease of Addiction (NECOREDA) Program: From Development to Trial." *Basic and Clinical Neuroscience* 5, no. 4 (2015): 291–98.

Robertson, Ian H., and Jaap MJ Murre. "Rehabilitation of Brain Damage: Brain Plasticity and Principles of Guided Recovery." *Psychological Bulletin* 125, no. 5 (1999): 544.

Robinson, Paul H. "Mens Rea." *Encyclopedia.com.* 2002. http://www.encyclopedia.com/doc/1G2-3403000173.html.

Robinson, Paul H., Markus Dirk Dubber, and Buffalo Criminal Law Center Director. "An Introduction to the Model Penal Code." *New Criminal Law Review* 10 (2007): 319–20.

Robinson v. California, 370 U.S. 660 (1962).

Rocque, Michael, Brandon C. Welsh, and Adrian Raine. "Biosocial Criminology and Modern Crime Prevention." *Journal of Criminal Justice* 40, no. 4 (2012): 306–12.

Roman, John. "Cost-Benefit Analysis of Criminal Justice Reforms." *NIJ Journal* (2013): 31–38.

Roper v. Simmons. (03-633) 543 U.S. 551 (2005) 112 S. W. 3d 397, affirmed. No. 03-633. Argued October 13, 2004–Decided March 1, 2005. www.law.cornell.edu/supct/html/03-633.ZS.html.

Rosenzweig, Paul, and Daniel J. Dew. "Guilty Until Proven Innocent: Undermining the Criminal Intent Requirement." Heritage Foundation. 2013. http://www.heritage.org/research/reports/2013/03/guilty-until-proven-innocent-undermining-the-criminal-intent-requirement.

Ross, Helen, Fredrick Glaser, and Teresa Germanson. "The Prevalence of Psychiatric Disorders in Patients with Alcohol and Other Drug Problems." *Archives of General Psychiatry* 45, no. 11 (1988): 1023–31.

Rowe, Genevieve and Laurie Sylla. "Evaluation of the Forensic Assertive Community Treatment Program." Department of Community and Human Services. 2012.

Ruiz v. Estelle, 503 F. Supp. 1265 (1980).

Salekin, Karen, J. Olley, and K. Hedge. "Offenders with Intellectual Disability: Characteristics, Prevalence and Issues in Forensic Assessment." *Journal of Mental Health Research in Intellectual Disabilities* 3 (2010): 97–116.

Salo, Ruth, Stefan Ursu, Michael H. Buonocore, Martin H. Leamon, and Cameron Carter. "Impaired Prefrontal Cortical Function and Disrupted Adaptive Cognitive Control in Methamphetamine Abusers: An fMRI Study." *Biological Psychiatry* 65, no. 8 (2009): 706–9.

Saltzburg, Stephen A. Testimony on behalf of the American Bar Association for the Hearing on the Adequacy of Criminal Intent Standards in Federal Prosecutions, before the Senate Judiciary Committee, January 20, 2016. Retrieved from https://www.judiciary.senate.gov/imo/media/doc/01-20-16%20Saltzburg%20Testimony.pdf.

SAMHSA. "Substance Use Disorders." Last updated October 27, 2015. http://www.samhsa.gov/disorders/substance-use.

SAMHSA. "Trends in Substance Use Disorders among Males Aged 18 to 49 on Probation or Parole." *The NSDUH Report.* 2014. http://www.samhsa.gov/data/sites/default/files/sr084-males-probation-parole/sr084-males-probation-parole/sr084-males-probation-parole.pdf.

Sapolsky, Robert. "The Frontal Cortex and the Criminal Justice System." *Philosophical Transactions of the Royal Society Biological Sciences* 359 (2004): 1787–96.

Sarteschi, Christine M. "Mentally Ill Offenders Involved with the U.S. Criminal Justice System." Sage Open , July 2013, 1–11. doi: 10.1177/2158244013497029.

Sayer, Francis. "Public Welfare Offenses." *Columbia Law Review* 33, no. 1 (1933): 55–88.

Scarpa, Angela. "The Effects of Child Maltreatment on the Hypothalamic-Pituitary-Adrenal Axis." *Trauma, Violence, & Abuse* 5, no. 4 (2004): 333–52.

Schilling, Elizabeth A., Robert H. Aseltine, and Susan Gore. "Adverse Childhood Experiences and Mental Health in Young Adults: A Longitudinal Survey." *BMC Public Health* 7, no. 1 (2007): 1.

Schnittker, Jason, Michael Massoglia, and Christopher Uggen. "Out and Down: Incarceration and Psychiatric Disorders." *Journal of Health and Social Behavior* 53, no. 4 (2012): 448–84.

Schubert, Carol, and Edward P. Mulvey. "Behavioral Health Problems, Treatment, and Outcomes in Serious Youthful Offenders." *Juvenile Justice Bulletin.* Washington, DC: Office of Juvenile Justice and Delinquency Prevention, 2014.

Schubert, Carol A., Edward P. Mulvey, and Cristie Glasheen. "Influence of Mental Health and Substance Use Problems and Criminogenic Risk on Outcomes in Serious Juvenile Offenders." *Journal of the American Academy of Child & Adolescent Psychiatry* 50, no. 9 (2011): 925–37.

Schubert, Carol, Edward Mulvey, and Amanda Alderfer. "Serious Juvenile Offenders: Do Mental Health Problems Elevate Risk?" *Reclaiming Futures.* 2011. Retrieved from http://reclaimingfutures.org/juvenile-justice-system-mental-health-criminogenic-risk-research-update.

Schwartz, A., R. Bradley, M. Sexton, A. Sherry, and K. Ressler. "Posttraumatic Stress Disorder among African-Americans in an Inner City Mental Health Clinic." *Psychiatric Services* 56, no. 2 (2005): 212–15.

"The Science of Drug Abuse and Addiction: The Basics." NIH. Last updated September 2014. http://www.drugabuse.gov/publications/media-guide/science-drug-abuse-addiction-basics.

Scott, Kelli, and Cara C. Lewis. "Using Measurement-Based Care to Enhance Any Treatment." *Cognitive and Behavioral Practice* 22, no. 1 (2015): 49–59.

Sederer, Lloyd. "Shoring Up Psychiatry's Supply." *US News.* September 22, 2015. http://www.usnews.com/opinion/blogs/policy-dose/2015/09/22/how-to-confront-psychiatrys-supply-problem.

Sederer, Lloyd. "Tinkering Can't Fix the Mental Health Care System." *US News.* March 20, 2015. http://www.usnews.com/opinion/blogs/opinion-blog/2015/03/20/fixing-the-mental-health-system-requires-disruptive-innovation.

Sederer, Lloyd, and S. Sharfstein. "Fixing the Troubled Mental Health System." *JAMA* 312, no. 12 (2014): 1195–96.

Shepherd, Joshua. "Scientific Challenges to Free Will and Moral Responsibility." *Philosophy Compass* 10, no. 3 (2015): 197–207.

Shim, Ruth. "How Committed Are We to Improving Our Nation's Mental Health?" *Philly.com.* January 12, 2016. http://www.philly.com/philly/blogs/public_health/How-committed-are-we-to-improving-our-nations-mental-health.html.

Shufelt, Jennie L., and Joseph J. Cocozza. *Youth with Mental Health Disorders in the Juvenile Justice System: Results From a Multi-State Prevalence Study.* Delmar, NY: National Center for Mental Health and Juvenile Justice, 2006.

Silverglate, Harvey. *Three Felonies a Day: How the Feds Target the Innocent.* New York: Encounter Books, 2009.

Sirotich, Frank. "Correlates of Crime and Violence among Persons with Mental Disorder: An Evidence-Based Review." *Brief Treatment and Crisis Intervention* 8, no. 2 (2008): 171–94.

Sirotich, Frank. "The Criminal Justice Outcomes of Jail Diversion Programs for Persons with Mental Illness: A Review of the Evidence." *Journal of the American Academy of Psychiatry and the Law Online* 37, no. 4 (2009): 461–72.

Skeem, Jennifer, Sarah Manchak, and Jillian Peterson. "Correctional Policy for Offenders with Mental Illness: Creating a New Paradigm for Recidivism Reduction." *Law and Human Behavior* 35 (2011): 110–26.

Skeem, Jennifer L., Eliza Winter, Patrick J. Kennealy, Jennifer Eno Louden, and Joseph R. Tatar II. "Offenders with Mental Illness Have Criminogenic Needs, Too: Toward Recidivism Reduction." *Law and Human Behavior* 38, no. 3 (2014): 212.

Skeem, Jennifer L., and Jennifer Eno Louden. "Toward Evidence-Based Practice for Probationers and Parolees Mandated to Mental Health Treatment." *Psychiatric Services* (2006).

Snyder, H. "Nothing Works, Something Works—But Still Few Proven Programs." *Corrections Today* 69 (2007): 6–28. http://connection.ebscohost.com/c/editorials/28144774/nothing-works-something-works-but-still-few-proven-programs.

Sofuoglu, Mehmet, Elise E. DeVito, Andrew J. Waters, and Kathleen M. Carroll. "Cognitive Enhancement as a Treatment for Drug Addictions." *Neuropharmacology* 64 (2013): 452–63.

Spohn, C., and D. Holleran. "The Effect of Imprisonment on Recidivism Rates of Felony Offenders: A Focus on Drug Offenders." *Criminology* 40, no. 2 (2002): 329–58.

Stagman, Shannon M., and Janice L. Cooper. "Children's Mental Health: What Every Policymaker Should Know." National Center for Children in Poverty (2010).

Steadman, Henry. "When Political Will Is Not Enough: Jails, Communities and Persons with Mental Health Disorders." White Paper 1. Delmar, NY: Policy Research Associates, 2014.

Steadman, Henry J., and Michelle Naples. "Assessing the Effectiveness of Jail Diversion Programs for Persons with Serious Mental Illness and Co-Occurring Substance Use Disorders." *Behavioral Sciences & the Law* 23, no. 2 (2005): 163–70.

Steadman, Henry J., Allison Redlich, Lisa Callahan, Pamela Clark Robbins, and Roumen Vesselinov. "Effect of Mental Health Courts on Arrests and Jail Days: A Multisite Study." *Arch Gen Psychiatry* 68, no. 2 (2011): 167–72. doi: 10.1001/archgenpsychiatry.2010.134.

Stein, Bradley D., Lisa H. Jaycox, Sheryl Kataoka, Hilary J. Rhodes, and Katherine D. Vestal. "Prevalence of Child and Adolescent Exposure to Community Violence." *Clinical Child and Family Psychology Review* 6, no. 4 (2003): 247–64.

Steinberg, Laurence. "A Social Neuroscience Perspective on Adolescent Risk-Taking." *Developmental Review* 28, no. 1 (2008): 78–106.

Stephens, Jaclyn A., Karen-Nicole C. Williamson, and Marian E. Berryhill. "Cognitive Rehabilitation After Traumatic Brain Injury: A Reference for Occupational Therapists." *OTJR: Occupation, Participation and Health* 35, no. 1 (2015): 5–22.

Sterbenz, Christina. "The Way We Diagnose Mental Illness Might Be a 'Mistake.'" *Business Insider* (2013). http://www.businessinsider.com/problems-with-the-dsm-2013-10.

Stevens, Laura, Antonio Verdejo-García, Anna E. Goudriaan, Herbert Roeyers, Geert Dom, and Wouter Vanderplasschen. "Impulsivity as a Vulnerability Factor for Poor Addiction Treatment Outcomes: A Review of Neurocognitive Findings Among Individuals with Substance Use Disorders." *Journal of Substance Abuse Treatment* 47, no. 1 (2014): 58–72.

Strong, Suzanne M., Ramona R. Rantala, and Tracey Kyckelhahn. "Census of Problem-Solving Courts, 2012." Bureau of Justice Statistics, 2016.

Stuart, Heather. "Violence and Mental Illness: An Overview." *World Psychiatry* 2, no. 2 (2003): 121–24.

"Study: Replacing Prison Terms with Drug Abuse Treatment Could Save Billions in Criminal Justice Costs." *RTI International News*. January 8, 2013. www.rti.org/news/study-replacing-prison-terms-drug-abuse-treatment-could-save-billions-criminal-justice-costs.

Stuntz, William. *The Collapse of American Criminal Justice*. Cambridge, MA: Harvard University Press, 2011.

Subramanian, Ram, and Alison Shames. "Sentencing and Prison Practices in Germany and the Netherlands: Implications for the United States." New York: Vera Institute of Justice, 2013.

Substance Abuse and Mental Health Services Administration. "Behavioral Health Equity." Rockville, MD: Substance Abuse and Mental Health Services Administration, www.samhsa.gov/behavioral-health-equity.

Substance Abuse and Mental Health Services Administration. "Mental and Substance Use Disorders." Rockville, MD: Substance Abuse and Mental Health Services Administration, 2014.

Substance Abuse and Mental Health Services Administration. "Results from the 2013 National Survey on Drug Use and Health: Summary of National Findings." NSDUH Series H-48, HHS Publication No. (SMA) 14-4863. Rockville, MD: Substance Abuse and Mental Health Services Administration, 2014.

Substance Abuse and Mental Health Services Administration. "Screening and Assessment of Co-occurring Disorders in the Justice System." Rockville, MD: Substance Abuse and Mental Health Services Administration, 2015.

Sullivan, Irene A. "Criminal Responsibility and the Drug Dependence Defense—A Need for Judicial Clarification." *Fordham Law Review* 42, no. 2 (1973): 361.

Swanson, Ana. "A Shocking Number of Mentally Ill Americans End Up in Prison Instead of Treatment." *Washington Post*. 2015. https://www.washingtonpost.com/news/wonk/wp/2015/04/30/a-shocking-number-of-mentally-ill-americans-end-up-in-prisons-instead-of-psychiatric-hospitals/.

Swanson, Ana. "These States Leave the Most Mentally Ill Adults Untreated. Guess What Else They Have in Common." *Washington Post*. 2015. www.washingtonpost.com/news/wonk/wp/2015/04/14/these-states-leave-the-most-mentally-ill-adults-untreated-guess-what-else-they-have-in-common/.

Swift, James. "Lack of Expertise, Inadequate Funding Plaguing Mental Health Delivery to Nation's Juvenile Justice System." *Juvenile Justice Information Exchange*. June 22, 2013. Retrieved from http://jjie.org/lack-of-expertise-inadequate-funding-plaguing-mental-health-delivery-to-nations-juvenile-justice-system/104933/.

Sykes v. United States, 131 S. Ct. 2267, 2288 (2011).

Teichner, Gordon, Michael D. Horner, John C. Roitzsch, Janice Herron, and Angelica Thevos. "Substance Abuse Treatment Outcomes for Cognitively Impaired and Intact Outpatients." *Addictive Behaviors* 27, no. 5 (2002): 751–63.

Teplin, Linda A., Karen M. Abram, Gary M. McClelland, and Mina K. Dulcan. "Comorbid Psychiatric Disorders in Youth in Juvenile Detention." *Archives of General Psychiatry* 60, no. 11 (2003): 1097.

Teplin, Linda A., Karen M. Abram, Gary M. McClelland, Mina K. Dulcan, and Amy A. Mericle. "Psychiatric Disorders in Youth in Juvenile Detention." *Archives of General Psychiatry* 59, no. 12 (2002): 1133–43.

Teplin, Linda A., Leah J. Welty, Karen M. Abram, Mina K. Dulcan, and Jason J. Washburn. "Prevalence and Persistence of Psychiatric Disorders in Youth after Detention: A Prospective Longitudinal Study." *Archives of General Psychiatry* 69, no. 10 (2012): 1031–43.

Texas Tribune. "Mentally Challenged Teen Faces 100 Years in Prison." August 26, 2010, https://www.texastribune.org/2010/08/26/mentally-challenged-teen-faces-100-years-in-prison/.

Tolin, David F. "Is Cognitive-Behavioral Therapy More Effective Than Other Therapies? A Meta-Analytic Review." *Clinical Psychology Review* 30, no. 6 (2010): 710–20.

Torrey, E. Fuller, Mary T. Zdanowicz, Aaron D. Kennard, H. Richard Lamb, Donald F. Eslinger, Michael C. Biasotti, and Doris A. Fuller. "The Treatment of Persons with Mental Illness in Prisons and Jails: A State Survey." Treatment Advocacy Center (2014).

Travis, Jeremy, Bruce Western, and Steve Redburn, eds. *The Growth of Incarceration in the United States*. Washington, DC: National Research Council of the National Academies, 2014.

Treatment Advocacy Center. "Consequences of Non-Treatment." 2016. Retrieved from http://www.treatmentadvocacycenter.org/key-issues/consequences-of-non-treatment.

Tuominen, T., T. Korhonen, H. Hamalainen, and H. Lauerma. "Neurocognitive Disorders in Sentenced Male Offenders: Implications for Rehabilitation." *Criminal Behavior and Mental Health* 24, no. 1 (2014).

Turner, Travis H., Steven LaRowe, Michael David Horner, Janice Herron, and Robert Malcolm. "Measures of Cognitive Functioning as Predictors of Treatment Outcome for Cocaine Dependence." *Journal of Substance Abuse Treatment* 37, no. 4 (2009): 328–34.

U.S. Department of Health and Human Services. "Examining Substance Use Disorder Treatment Demand and Provider Capacity in a Changing Health Care System." Washington, DC: USDHHS, 2015.

U.S. Department of Health and Human Services. "Medicaid and Permanent Supportive Housing for Chronically Homeless Individuals: Emerging Practices from the Field. 5.2. Who Qualifies for Medicaid Mental Health Services?" ASPE. August 20, 2014. https://aspe.hhs.gov/report/medicaid-and-permanent-supportive-housing-chronically-homeless-individuals-emerging-practices-field/52-who-qualifies-medicaid-mental-health-services.

U.S. Department of Health and Human Services. "Mental Health Myths and Facts." *MentalHealth.gov*. http://www.mentalhealth.gov/basics/myths-facts/. Accessed August 18, 2016.

U.S. Department of Health and Human Services. "Report of the Surgeon General's Conference on Children's Mental Health: A National Action Agenda." Washington, DC: USDHHS, Conference Summary, Background, 2002.

"Understanding the Effects of Maltreatment on Brain Development." *Child Welfare Information Gateway*. Issue Brief, April 2015. https://www.childwelfare.gov/pubs/issue-briefs/brain-development/.

Underwood, Lee, and Aryssa Washington. "Mental Illness and Juvenile Offenders." *International Journal of Environmental Research and Public Health* 13, no. 2 (2016).

United Nations Office on Drugs and Crime. *World Drug Report 2015*. United Nations publication. Sales No. E.15.XI.6.

United States v. Moore. 486 F.2d 1139,158 U.S. App. D.C. 375; 1973 U.S. App. www.casebriefs.com/blog/law/criminal-law/criminal-law-keyed-to-lafave/alcoholism-and-addiction-intoxication-immaturity/united-states-v-moore-2/. Accessed May 11, 2016.

University of Washington AIMS Center. "Evidence Base for Collaborative Care." 2016. http://aims.uw.edu/collaborative-care/evidence-base.

Unützer, Jürgen, Henry Harbin, and M. D. Druss. "The Collaborative Care Model: An Approach for Integrating Physical and Mental Health Care in Medicaid Health Homes." Center for Health Care Strategies and Mathematica Policy Research (2013).

Vallas, Rebecca. "Disabled Behind Bars: The Mass Incarceration of People with Disabilties in America's Jails and Prisons." Center for American Progress. July 18, 2016. www.americanprogress.org/issues/criminal-justice/report/2016/07/18/141447/disabled-behind-bars/.

van der Plas, Ellen AA, Eveline A. Crone, Wery PM van den Wildenberg, Daniel Tranel, and Antoine Bechara. "Executive Control Deficits in Substance-Dependent Individuals: A Comparison of Alcohol, Cocaine, and Methamphetamine and of Men and Women." *Journal of Clinical and Experimental Neuropsychology* 31, no. 6 (2009): 706–19.

Vanderplasschen, W., K. Colpaert, M. Autrique, R. Rapp, S. Pearce, E. Broekaert, and S. Vendevelde. "Therapeutic Communities for Addictions: A Review of Their Effectiveness from a Recovery-Oriented Perspective." *The Scientific World Journal* (2013).

Van Voorhees, E., and A. Scarpa. "The Effects of Child Maltreatment on the Hypothalamic-Pituitary-Adrenal Axis." *Trauma, Violence and Abuse* 5, no. 4 (2004): 333–52.

Vars, Fredrick E. "When God Spikes Your Drink: Guilty Without Mens Rea." *The Circuit.* Paper 27. 2013. http://scholarship.law.berkeley.edu/clrcircuit/27.

Villasenor, John. "Over-Criminalization and Mens Rea Reform: A Primer." *Brookings.* December 22, 2015. https://www.brookings.edu/blog/fixgov/2015/12/22/over-criminalization-and-mens-rea-reform-a-primer/.

Volkow, Nora. "A Major Step Forward for Addiction Medicine." *Huffington Post.* March 31, 2016. http://www.huffingtonpost.com/nora-volkow/a-major-step-forward-for_b_9583070.html.

Volkow, Nora. "Neurobiologic Advances from the Brain Disease Model of Addiction." *New England Journal of Medicine* 374 (2016): 363–71.

Volkow, Nora, and Joanna S. Fowler. "Addiction, a Disease of Compulsion and Drive: Involvement of the Orbitofrontal Cortex." *Cerebral Cortex* 10, no. 3 (2000): 318–25.

Waller, Mark S., Shannon M. Carey, Erin Farley, and Michael Rempel. "Testing the Cost Savings of Judicial Diversion." New York: Center for Court Innovation, 2013.

Walsh, Anthony, and Jonathan Bolen. *The Neurobiology of Criminal Behavior: Gene-Brain-Culture Interaction.* New York: Rutledge, 2016.

Walsh, Brian W., and Tiffany M. Joslyn. "Without Intent: How Congress Is Eroding the Criminal Intent Requirement in Federal Law." Heritage Foundation. May 10, 2010.

Walton, Alice G. "Why More Americans Suffer From Mental Disorders Than Anyone Else." *Atlantic.* October 4, 2011. http://www.theatlantic.com/health/archive/2011/10/why-more-americans-suffer-from-mental-disorders-than-anyone-else/246035/.

Wang, P., M. Lane, M. Olfson, H. Pincus, K. Wells, and R. Kessler. "Twelve-Month Use of Mental Health Services in the United States: Results from the National Comorbidity Survey Replication." *Archives of General Psychiatry* 62, no. 6 (2005): 629–40.

Wartna, B. S., N. Tollenaar, M. Blom, S. M. Alma, I. M. Bregman, A. A. M. Essers, and E. K. Van Straalen. "Recidivism Report 2002–2008. Trends in the Reconviction Rate of Dutch Offenders." The Hague, The Netherlands: Research and Documentation Centre of Ministry of Security and Justice (2011).

Washington State Institute for Public Policy. "Diversion, No Services (vs. Traditional Juvenile Court Processing)." *Benefit-Cost Results* (Benefit-cost methods last updated June 2016). http://www.wsipp.wa.gov/BenefitCost/ProgramPdf/549/Diversion-no-services-vs-tradition al-juvenile-court-processing.

Washington State Institute for Public Policy. "Diversion with Services (vs. Traditional Juvenile Court Processing)." *Benefit-Cost Results.* (Benefit-cost methods last updated June 2016).

Washington State Institute for Public Policy. "Drug Courts." *Benefit-Cost Results.* Updated August 2014. (Benefit-cost methods last updated June 2016). http://www.wsipp.wa.gov/BenefitCost/ProgramPdf/14/Drug-courts.

Washington State Institute for Public Policy. "Jail Diversion Programs for Offenders with Mental Illness (Post-Arrest Programs)." *Benefit-Cost Results* (Benefit-cost methods last updated June 2016). http://www.wsipp.wa.gov/BenefitCost/ProgramPdf/547/Diversion-with-services-vs-traditional-juvenile-court-processing.

Washington State Institute for Public Policy. "Mental Health Courts." *Benefit-Cost Results* (Benefit-cost methods last updated June 2016). http://www.wsipp.wa.gov/BenefitCost/Program/52.

Washington State Institute for Public Policy. "Swift and Certain Sanctions for Offenders on Community Supervision." *Benefit-Cost Results* (Benefit-cost methods last updated June 2016). www.wsipp.wa.gov/BenefitCost/ProgramPdf/559/Swift-and-Certain-sanctions-for-offenders-on-community-supervision.

Wegner, Daniel M. "The Mind's Best Trick: How We Experience Conscious Will." *Trends in Cognitive Sciences* 7, no. 2 (2003): 65–69.

Weiss, Elisabeth M. "Neuroimaging and Neurocognitive Correlates of Aggression and Violence in Schizophrenia." *Scientifica* (2012).

Welsh, Brandon C., David P. Farrington, and B. Raffan Gowar. "Benefit-Cost Analysis of Crime Prevention Programs." *Crime & Justice* 44 (2015): 447–557.

Will, George F. "When Everything Is a Crime." *Washington Post.* April 8, 2015. https://www.washingtonpost.com/opinions/when-everything-is-a-crime/2015/04/08/1929ab88-dd43-11e4-be40-566e2653afe5_story.html?utm_term=.b1bfcda45f9d.

Williams, Geoff. "Shortage of Child Psychiatrists Plagues the US." *Aljazeera America.* June 25, 2015. http://america.aljazeera.com/articles/2015/6/25/shortage-of-child-psychiatrists-in-us.html.

Williams, Val. "Evidence-Based Practice: Psychological Therapies for Adults with Intellectual Disabilities." *Disability & Society* 30, no. 4 (2015): 662–67.

Wilson, David. "Wishful Thinking?" *American Scientist.* 2002. http://www.americanscientist.org/bookshelf/pub/wishful-thinking.

Wilson, Holly A., and Robert D. Hoge. "The Effect of Youth Diversion Programs on Recidivism: A Meta-Analytic Review." *Criminal Justice and Behavior* 40, no. 5 (2013): 497–518.

Winkelman, Tyler NA, Edith C. Kieffer, Susan D. Goold, Jeffrey D. Morenoff, Kristen Cross, and John Z. Ayanian. "Health Insurance Trends and Access to Behavioral Healthcare Among Justice-Involved Individuals—United States, 2008–2014." *Journal of General Internal Medicine* (2016): 1–7.

Witt, Howard. "Mentally Retarded Texas Teen Serving 100-Year Prison Term for Sex Assault of Boy." *Chicago Tribune.* April 6, 2009. http://www.chicagotribune.com/news/nationworld/chi-paris_for_monapr06-story.html.

World Health Organization. "Mental Health Atlas 2014." Geneva 2015.

World Prison Brief. "Highest to Lowest Prison Population Total." Institute for Criminal Policy Research. Retrieved from www.prisonstudies.org/highest-to-lowest/prison-population-total.

Wortzel, Hal S., and David B. Arciniegas. "A Forensic Neuropsychiatric Approach to Traumatic Brain Injury, Aggression, and Suicide." *Journal of the American Academy of Psychiatry and the Law Online* 41, no. 2 (2013): 274–86.

Yaffe, Gideon. "A Republican Crime Proposal That Democrats Should Back." *New York Times.* February 12, 2016. http://www.nytimes.com/2016/02/12/opinion/a-republican-crime-proposal-that-democrats-should-back.html?_r=0.

Yaffe, Gideon. "Neurologic Disorder and Criminal Responsibility." *Handbook of Clinical Neurology* 118 (2013): 345–56.

Zarkin, Gary A., Alexander J. Cowell, Katherine A. Hicks, Michael J. Mills, Steven Belenko, Laura J. Dunlap, and Vincent Keyes. "Lifetime Benefits and Costs of Diverting Substance-Abusing Offenders from State Prison." *Crime & Delinquency* 61, no. 6 (2015): 829–50.

INDEX

intellectual disability treatment: as inadequate, 5–6; recommendations for, 112–113

international comparisons: incarceration rate, 10; juvenile justice, 142; mental illness prevalence, 97; punishment, 18–19; substance abuse, 32, 105

Jackson, Kuntrell, 72
Jackson v. Hobb, 72–73
Jones, William, 27
judgment, severe impairments in, 154
Justice, William Wayne, 85
Justice Center, Council on State Governments, 178
justice reinvestment initiative (JRI), 172–173
juvenile brain, 59–82; and criminal intent, 120; and comorbidity, 75–81; and legal responsibility, 69–75
juvenile courts, capacity issues, 165
juvenile offenders: cost-benefit and, 167–168; diversion model and, 142–145; persistence of psychiatric disorders in, 80; punishments for, 70–73, 144

Kaiser Permanente, 67
Keller, Bill, 176

Ladd, Robert, 29
law and order. *See* tough-on-crime stance
lead exposure, 50
least restrictive environment, 138
life course persistent offenders, 74
life without parole, juveniles and, 71–73, 144
limbic system, 44, 61
local level: and funding, 172; and mental illness treatment, 52; and reform, 178–179

Madrid v. Gomez, 94
mandatory sentencing, 14
measurement-based care, 103
Medicaid, 97; expansion of, 174–175
mens rea. *See* criminal intent
Mental Health America, 174

Mental Health Parity and Addictions Equity Act, 98–99
mental illness, 51–57; comorbidity and, 53, 111–112; diversion programs for, cost-benefit of, 167; in juveniles, 75–81; prevalence of, 52–53, 96; prison and, 84; in prison population, 10, 16, 52, 54; and recidivism, 130–131; and violence, 129–130
mental illness treatment: capacity issues, 97–98, 100; for criminal offenders, current status of, 84–91; current status of, 96–105; eligibility criteria for, 98; funding for, 100, 173–175; history of, 94–95; as inadequate, 5–6, 53, 93–96; international comparisons, 19; for juveniles, 76–77; obstacles to, 97–100, 137; in prison, 55; recommendations for, 101–105; reform efforts, 5–6; as right, 84–86
mental retardation (MR), 28. *See also* intellectual disability
Methylin, 114
Miller v. Alabama, 72, 73
M'Naghten rule, 119
Model Penal Code (American Law Institute), 119–120
Montgomery v. Louisiana, 73
moral issues: prefrontal cortex and, 47; substance abuse and, 34–38
Morissette v. United States, 118–119, 121
motivational interviewing, 109
MR. *See* mental retardation
myelination, 62
Mynors-Wallis, Laurence, 151

National Alliance on Mental Illness, 53, 99
National Association of Counties, 178
National Center for Children in Poverty, 77
National Institute on Drug Abuse, 110
National Institutes of Health, 5, 115
neglect, and juvenile brain, 65
Nesbitt, Eric, 27
neurocognitive development, 60–63
neurocognitive impairments, 43–51; and addiction, 108; and criminal justice involvement, 89–90; in juveniles, 63–69; in prison population, 11

war on drugs, 32; and crime control
    policies, 15
Washington University in St. Louis, 163

willpower, substance abuse and, 34–35, 37,
    40
Wilson, Marvin, 29